Sport and Politics in Canada

Sport and Politics in Canada

Federal Government Involvement since 1961

DONALD MACINTOSH
WITH
TOM BEDECKI
AND
C.E.S. FRANKS

McGill-Queen's University Press
Kingston and Montreal

© McGill-Queen's University Press 1987
ISBN 0-7735-0609-8 (cloth)
ISBN 0-7735-0665-9 (paper)

Legal deposit second quarter 1987
Bibliothèque nationale du Québec

Reprinted 1988
First paperback edition 1988

∞

Printed in Canada on acid free paper

This book has been published with the help of a
grant from the Social Science Federation of Canada,
using funds provided by the Social Sciences and
Humanities Research Council of Canada.

Canadian Cataloguing in Publication Data

Macintosh, Donald
  Sport and politics in Canada
  Includes bibliographical references and index.
  ISBN 0-7735-0609-8
  1. Sports and state – Canada. 2. Sports –
  Social aspects – Canada. I. Bedecki, Thomas.
  II. Franks, C. E. S. III. Title.
  GV585.M25 1987   796'.0971   C87-093265-9

Some of the material in this book appears in
another form in the forthcoming book *Sociology
of Sport in Canada*, edited by Jean Harvey and
Hart Cantelon (University of Ottawa Press), and has
appeared in part in *Sport and Politics*, the 1984
Olympic Scientific Congress Proceedings, vol. 7
(Human Kinetics Publishers, Inc.); in the
CAHPER Journal 17 (Sept.–Oct. 1985); and in the
History of Sport in Canada (Stipes Publishing
Company 1985), by M. and R. Howell. Reprinted
by permission.

Contents

Preface

This book has its origins in the early 1970s when Tom Bedecki and I saw the need to document federal government involvement in sport since the passage of Bill C-131 in 1961. Fortuitously perhaps, this concept never got off the ground, partly because neither of us had the time necessary to carry out the considerable document research needed for such a project. But the idea stayed alive and, in 1980, the two of us teamed up at Queen's University with Ned Franks, a political scientist, and Rick Gruneau, a sport sociologist. This group put together a much more comprehensive proposal to study federal government involvement in sport than was originally conceived. This proposal was supported by the Social Sciences and Humanities Research Council of Canada over two grant periods: April 1981 to September 1982; and April 1983 to September 1984. We gratefully acknowledge this generous support. We also wish to acknowledge the financial support given by the Faculty of Arts and Science and the School of Graduate Studies and Research at Queen's University to assist in the final preparation of the manuscript.

Despite our considerable efforts, this book provides only a broad framework for more detailed study of the many facets of recent federal government involvement in sport. Our major purpose is to explain why the federal government changed its focus from the original intent of the act, which was to encourage participation in amateur sport and fitness, to concentrate on the development of a corps of elite "state" athletes. In order to do this, we first determine what actually happened. Then, in order to understand why, we place this development in the wider political and social changes that occurred in Canada during this period. Finally, we examine some of the outcomes and consequences of this federal government involvement and the issues arising from it. We describe our approach and the analytical framework used in our work in chapter 2.

In pursuing these objectives, the focus of the book necessarily narrows to correspond with the focus of the federal government; thus, the matter of mass sport and fitness programs and recreation receives less attention as our story evolves. Our work also focuses on what used to be known as "amateur" sport, and therefore does not cover in any detail relationships between professional sport and the federal government in Canada. The term "amateur" athlete was replaced in the 1960s by "elite" athletes. By the late 1970s, "high performance" athletes became the buzz word in Ottawa. Since the distinction between professionalism and amateurism in sport has now all but disappeared, perhaps the best term to describe the persons who represent Canada in major international sport events is "state" athletes. It is our hope that the book accomplishes its major purposes and, at the same time, provides a framework from which others may go forward to more detailed analyses of the many events and issues that are raised in our work.

As would be expected in a project of this size, the efforts and co-operation of many people need to be acknowledged. Three full-time research assistants worked successively on the project – Donna Greenhorn, Bob Hollands, and Aniko Varpalotai. They all contributed diligently and effectively, making personal commitments to the project. Ms Greenhorn returned to the project in the final stages to put the manuscript into final form for McGill-Queen's University Press. Mrs Betty Schieck and Ms Carol Boyle performed miracles throughout the project, making sense out of our scribblings in transcribing the work onto the word processor. Our gratitude goes to all of these people.

Many others were generous of their time in providing information and personal perspectives. All these people cannot be acknowledged here, but our thanks are also extended to them. A few such people made particularly significant contributions: Lou Lefaive, a former director of Sport Canada, Bill Hallett, the author of a doctoral dissertation on this topic that we have used extensively in our work, and Bruce Kidd, the sport sociologist and historian at the University of Toronto, all participated in a formal review of the first stage of our work (up to 1969). Lefaive and Kidd also were most generous of their time through the second stage of the project, providing information and ideas and reviewing drafts of our work. The final product depends to a considerable extent on these contributions.

The contribution of Rick Gruneau needs particular acknowledgment. He was a member of our original group, but his untimely move to the University of British Columbia half-way through the SSHRC project precluded any further formal participation. He continued, however, to be a valuable resource in interpreting our findings and placing them in the wider perspective of sport and leisure in Canadian society. In particular, Rick served as a constant source of knowledge and inspiration to the principal author and took considerable time and effort to review the entire penultimate draft of the manuscript. Whatever insights we have about sport in the larger socio-cultural context can be attributed to him.

Finally, I acknowledge the work of the co-authors, Tom Bedecki and Ned Franks. They have worked on the project from its onset in 1981 until the completion of this book. They both contributed to the conceptual framework and to the development of the main themes and ideas. In addition, they reviewed drafts, discussed the implications of our findings, and prodded me to become more analytical and thoughtful. In particular, Ned laid out the analytical framework and put his considerable knowledge of the political scene in Canada to good use in our work. Tom's intimate knowledge of what had happened in Ottawa was invaluable in maintaining the credibility of our study. His extensive knowledge of sport and government and his contacts in Ottawa are central to any insights we have as to "how it happened."

Donald Macintosh
October 1986

Sport and Politics in Canada

CHAPTER ONE

Introduction

SETTING THE STAGE

Canada's international sport triumphs in 1984 were unparalleled in her post-World War II history. Gaetan Boucher delighted Canadians by winning two gold and one bronze medals at the 1984 Winter Olympics in Sarajevo, Yugoslavia. Canada's finest hour in Olympic history, however, was to be at the Summer Games in Los Angeles some months later. There Canada won forty-four medals, surpassing its best-ever previous performance in the 1932 Los Angeles Games and placing fourth in the unofficial medal standings. Despite the absence of the Soviet Union, East Germany, and other eastern European communist countries, Canada's performance placed her clearly ahead of such perennial rivals as Great Britain, Italy, Japan, France, Australia, and the Scandinavian countries.

Canada's victory in the Canada Cup Hockey series, only weeks after the Summer Olympic performances, provided a third highlight in 1984. The Canadian team comprised a core of Edmonton Oilers, winners of the 1984 Stanley Cup, emblematic of North American professional hockey supremacy. Bolstered by star performers from other National Hockey League teams, the Canadians managed to finish only fourth in the preliminary round-robin tournament. But Team Canada scored a stunning upset in the sudden-death semifinals. It defeated the favourites and preliminary tournament winners, the Soviet Union, 3-2 in overtime and went on to beat Sweden in two straight games in the finals of the Cup.

These Canadian sport triumphs were watched on television with pride and satisfaction by millions of Canadians. Sport apparently had fulfilled Prime Minister Trudeau's vision in 1969 as a symbol that could unite Canadians despite regional and cultural differences, and vindicated the federal government's sport policies in the 1970s and early 1980s. But many Canadians were unaware of the extent to which these sport "successes" were a function of government involvement.

Active federal government involvement in sport is a fairly recent occurrence. For most of Canadian history, federal government participation has been far more passive and indirect and its efforts primarily oriented towards fitness and mass participation. Even after the passage of the Fitness and Amateur Sport Act in 1961, the federal government's activity was limited. It made small grants to national sport governing bodies and entered into cost-sharing agreements with the provinces, leaving the program content and direction largely to these respective bodies. Key members of government held the naive belief that promoting mass fitness and sport programs would produce improved Canadian performances on the international scene. Autonomy of sport governing bodies also was valued highly. But the failure of these measures to produce any improvement in Canada's stature in international sports and the increased importance and significance of sport as a form of television entertainment caused the government to change its posture at the end of the 1960s. Sport gradually became an instrument that could be used to promote national unity. The federal government established arm's-length agencies to bolster the national sport organizations and began to give direct support to elite athletes. The government, however, still gave residual support for mass sport and fitness programs. There also was a growing realization in government circles of the importance of exercise to the health of Canadians.

The high visibility of international sport events, the prominent role that Canada played in hosting the 1976 Summer Olympics and the 1978 Commonwealth Games, combined with the assertion by provincial governments of their responsibilities for mass fitness and sports programs, led the federal government to concentrate on elite international sport. The federal government poured increasing funds into the development of sport, the support of athletes, and the construction of facilities and established itself as a major force in policy making and direction of sport in the 1980s.

What are the consequences of such government intervention in sport? In the first place, it has contributed to a dramatic change in the nature of the dominant form of sport in Canada. "Elite" amateur sport, or what is now known as "high performance" sport, has a high profile in Canada and as such has become highly rationalized. An extensive bureaucracy has evolved to support and direct sport. A large corps of public servants, executive and technical directors, and coaches not only operate at the national level in Ottawa, but have also become entrenched in most Canadian provinces. The focus of the new dominant form of sport has been on objective measures of performance and record; increasingly efficient athletes are essential if sport is to fulfil its role as a national unity symbol and to legitimize the government of the day. At the same time, professional sport has contributed greatly to the reshaping of sport. In its efforts to increase sport's attractiveness for television audiences, promoters have created a sport myth that focuses on virtuosity and super-human performances by star athletes and teams. This provides the stuff with which viewers can live out their own sport fantasies. These two forces have pushed to the background those traditional values of sport that previously held sway in Canada. Sport is less often seen as a form of play and social interaction and as a source of individual self-fulfilment and self-realization and more often as an instrument that has value as a political tool, as a way to attain health and beauty, and as a path to fame and fortune.

These changes are of interest and concern for those who undertake serious study of the place of sport in society. While it is too much to say that new government policies have been solely responsible for such changes, there can be no doubt about their significance for the development of sport as we know it in Canada today. Yet, what forces and events caused the federal government to embark on this course of action? What were the central issues and critical turning points in this saga? Who were the key actors in the play? Were there viable alternatives along the way? What are the consequences of these actions? Are there any viable alternatives today? If so, what steps can be taken to change the present stance of government?

There are no simple answers to these questions. They are imbedded in the complex social and political forces and events in Canadian society over the past few decades. It is our purpose to trace these events, and identify the critical forces, turning points, and central actors in this drama, and to assess the consequences of federal government involvement in sport. Finally, we wish to examine the broader implications of these consequences for sport in Canadian society, and to make suggestions as to what changes are desirable and possible at this time.

BACKGROUND TO THE STUDY

Attention to the federal government's role in sport by social scientists, politicians, and government officials has taken place primarily at two different levels of analysis. In the first instance, a number of comprehensive manuscripts have been written that trace the federal government's involvement in sport and physical fitness since Bill C-131 was enacted in 1961 (see, for instance, Broom & Baka 1978; Hallett 1981; West 1973; and Westland 1979). These studies have concentrated on the events and facts in regard to federal sport policies and have interpreted these in light of interpersonal relations and of interaction among actors, groups, and organizations that were central to this process. Most of this research has included a great deal of historical detail and has adopted the style of descriptive narrative. This approach treats federal government sport policy in isolation, thereby neglecting to take into account the larger social structural and cultural milieu in which sport functions in Canada. It offers little material that can be used to elaborate upon the complex interrelationships that exist between government policy in sport and broader forces and pressures associated with overall Canadian social development.

A counter-tradition in the literature has focused more directly upon the relationships between sport and broader forces in Canadian society. A few social scientists have speculated about the appropriate role of sport in our culture, what forces are instrumental in determining the nature and direction of sport in society, and the ways in which sport itself influences and changes certain aspects of Canadian life (see, for instance, Gruneau 1982 and 1983; and Kidd 1981 and 1982). In general, these social scientists have undertaken sweeping analyses, often at very high levels of abstraction and ranging over large spans of time. However much this work has contributed to our overall understanding of Canadian sport, and to alternative ways of studying the relationships between sport and society, it does not as yet include any detailed, systematic research on federal government involvement in Canadian sport. Observations and arguments about government and sport in this literature tend to have been limited to only a few specific events and occurrences. Furthermore, the high level of abstraction has tended to direct attention away from the detailed analysis of intra-organizational and personal factors actually involved in the policy-making process.

It is our contention that changes in the scope and direction of federal government policy making in sport can only be understood adequately in the context of an examination of broader social changes in sport and Canadian society. Consideration also needs to be given to the hitherto neglected study of the relationship between federal government sport initiatives and the government's larger political and social goals. Another dimension that has been overlooked in the existing literature is the extent to which the ensuing government-sponsored programs played a role in influencing future government policy decisions.

In so broadening the scope of this study, a number of underlying themes were fleshed out. First, the changing political and administrative structure that supports amateur sport has been particularly important in the shaping of sport policy in Canada. Here we are interested in the structure and growth of the federal government since World War II, the federal government's changing and stormy relationships with the provinces, and the growth of the sport bureaucracy in Canada. Second, the distribution and shift of power is also critical to any study of federal government sport policy making. Of particular interest is the shift of power from the sport governing bodies to the National Advisory Council, established in the 1961 Fitness and Amateur Sport Act, and subsequently, in the 1970s and 1980s, the consolidation of sport policy decision making at the federal ministerial and senior public-service levels. Such a concentration of decision making in sport policy within the government leads to the third theme, that of the role of sport in the wider goals of government. Here we are interested in the motives that originally caused the federal government to enact sport and fitness legislation in 1961, and the changing political and social events in Canada in the 1960s and 1970s that caused the federal government to use sport in a much more utilitarian manner. A fourth theme is the changes in the significance and meaning of sport in Canada. Here we are interested in the impact of the growing significance of international sport and of sports' affinity for television. These changes were significant factors in the federal government's change of stance towards the promotion of elite sport in the late 1960s. Significant also in this change was the growing commercialization and professionalization of sport in the 1970s and 1980s. These and other socio-economic factors constitute our fifth theme. Changes in socio-economic conditions in Canada after World War II also contributed to an increased significance and importance of sport. Consequently, professional and commercial sport enterprises became more prevalent and thus more influential factors in federal government sport policy making. It is our intention to enrich the story of federal government sport involvement over the last four decades with these themes, giving the narrative meaning and relevance.

ORGANIZATIONAL FRAMEWORK

The analytic themes that have been developed do not in themselves tell any kind of story. They are substantive, empirically oriented, and direct our attention to significant areas where one can identify clusters of causal processes that appear to have influenced the development of federal government policy in sport. Yet, any attempt to understand federal government policy making in sport in its broadest context, as a distinctive feature of Canadian social development, must try in some way to show how these themes might be organized into a coherent framework for analysing the particular policies that have been developed. Following is a brief description of the organizational framework developed for use in our work.

We have organized our analytic themes by dividing government activities into several dimensions for analysis. One such dimension distinguishes between a central core of actors and agencies whose behaviour is directed towards various individual, institutional, and social goals, and external forces and agencies with which the central core continuously interacts. It is assumed that government is not a monolith and that different agencies are quite likely to have different, and even competing, views of the role of government, the goals of government, and of the policies, tasks, and administrative procedures for a given program or agency. One of the important parts of the analysis is to identify competing and conflicting viewpoints and concepts of what a program is for, and how it should be carried out.

Conceptually, there are three levels of analyses in this study. First is the level of personalities and individuals in which significant individuals must be identified and both their contributions and the reasons for these contributions assessed. Second is the level of agencies and institutions, in which significant institutions, both inside and outside the central core, must be identified. Their interests as institutions, and the goals and purposes towards which they work, must be identified and examined. The structure and process of interaction between agencies is also part of the analysis. Third is the level of forces outside of institutions, such as changes in opinion, of ideology, and changed international circumstances. It is often easier to argue that these forces are significant than to prove it to be so, but they must be considered and evaluated. At times, we have separated these three levels; at others, they are combined. In the real world, they always interact, and they are easier to separate in theory than in practice.

Concurrent with this study of institutions and individuals, there must be an analysis of the reasoning and thinking that went into programs. One must always ask what different visions of the future are competing, and which ones triumph, and how and why. Further, these arguments and visions must be assessed against what they included and neglected, how accurate they turned out to be, and what their significance was.

A further analysis concerns whether the phenomena being studied fit into a more general theory of society and government, such as "political modernization" or "nation building." The literature dealing with sport and society might introduce some of these themes, but to a large extent, they must be uncovered in the analysis. For this sort of study, the processes of government can be divided into three stages. The first is the policy-making stage. How and why policies emerge must be examined. Second is the policy-implementation and adminis-tration stage. Often what actually gets done in a program bears little resemblance to what was intended. Finally, programs and policies are periodically reviewed and reconsidered. How, when, and why assessment happened must be discovered.

It is likely that general patterns of influence and lines of conflict relating program to pressure groups and clientele will develop. These patterns of influence and conflict need to be identified for each period, and the influence of various actors evaluated. These patterns will be altered on occasion by important events, such as the appoint-ment of a dynamic new minister or a major international occurrence. These shift points need to be identified and rationalized.

Finally, there are two types of end products that should be examined: first, the outputs of government policy, which may be classified into regulations and regulatory activity, distribution of funds, and the provision of goods and services; and second, the outcomes of government activity, or the actual changes and results in the real world.

Obviously this organizational framework does not represent a rigorously defined conceptual model. Our preference has been for a more flexible set of organizing concepts and delimiting ideas. We hope that this leads to insights and connections that might be suppressed by an overly structured analytic framework. The organiz-ing framework that has been developed forces us to look further than has been the case in previous studies of federal government involve-ment in sport. Yet, it allows us to avoid the trap of static categoriza-tions. Emphasis on certain aspects of the framework in one time period may be changed appropriately to other aspects in a subsequent time period.

In dealing with the substance, consequences, and outcomes of federal government involvement in sport, we make some suggestions as to how these issues might be ameliorated to the betterment of sport in Canada.

CHAPTER TWO

Origins of Bill C-131

Bill C-131, An Act to Encourage Fitness and Amateur Sport, was passed in the House of Commons with unanimous consent in September 1961. The Act was an uncontentious, non-partisan issue with wide acceptance but, at the same time, of little importance to the government and the public at large. For most of the ensuing decade, this attitude was to persist, and the activities of the federal government were confined largely to entering into cost-sharing agreements with the provinces and making grants to national sport-governing bodies. But certain social and political events were at work in the 1960s that would change all this. These changes had their roots in the forces and events that were instrumental in the creation of the fitness and amateur sport act.

The specific events associated with the passage of Bill C-131 have been well documented elsewhere (see for instance Hallett 1981; West 1973; and Westland 1979) and are relatively well known by students of the history of federal government sport involvement in Canada. For this reason, a brief overview of the role of the advocates of sport and fitness legislation will suffice.

Advocacy for federal government action concerning the perceived low level of fitness of Canadians was spearheaded by Lloyd Percival, director of the Sport College in Toronto, by the Canadian Sports Advisory Council, the Ontario Physical Fitness Committee, and Doris Plewes, physical fitness consultant for the federal Ministry of Health and Welfare. The Duke of Edinburgh's speech to the Canadian

This chapter appeared in a similar form in the *Proceedings of the 5th Canadian Symposium of Sport and Physical Education* (Bruce Kidd, editor, Toronto, August 1982).

Medical Association in June 1959 has been seen by most analysts as the focal point for the physical fitness lobby. In this speech, Prince Philip had decried the state of fitness of Canadians and challenged the medical profession to take steps to rectify this deficiency.

There was a parallel concern about Canadian international athletic performances and in particular, the country's sagging reputation in Olympic and World Cup hockey. This concern was evident in newspapers across Canada and in the House of Commons, where a number of members of Parliament during the late 1950s urged the government to take action to provide support to Canada's elite athletes. One of these advocates, J.R. Taylor, played a further important role in convincing Prime Minister Diefenbaker, who subsequently became a strong advocate of federal government fitness and amateur sport legislation, to visit the Canadian team at the Pan-American Games in Chicago in the summer of 1959.

LARGER FORCES AND EVENTS

Post-War Internationalism in Sport

The advent of sport as a matter of international interest and concern in Western industrialized nations after World War II played a powerful role in creating a favourable climate for federal government intervention in sport in Canada. This growth of international sport can best be understood in the larger political context. The Cold War that developed following World War II between the Soviet-aligned states and the United States and its allies reached its peak politically during the 1948 to 1952 period. It was in this political climate that the Soviet Union's application for membership in the International Olympic Association was approved in 1951. The Soviets realized that sport made an excellent vehicle for propagating its political ideology and, accordingly, took steps to intensify the development of outstanding international competitors. For the first time since 1912, the Soviet Union competed in the 1952 Summer Olympics. In the unofficial u.s.-estimated point standing at these Games, the Americans placed first with 614 points, followed closely by the USSR with $553\frac{1}{2}$ points and eighty-one medals (Chester 1971:104). Canada placed about seventeenth with a total of three medals (Jokl 1956:65–6).

The continued development of elite athletes in the Soviet Union resulted in an even more amazing performance at the Melbourne Olympics in 1956 when the Soviet Union compiled a total of 622 unofficial points compared to 497 for the United States. Canada's total of six medals did not compare favourably with the eighty-five earned by the Soviet team (Chester 1971:127, 133). The British-Israeli-French invasion of Egypt in October 1956 and the Soviet invasion of Hungary in November 1956 precipitated a major political controversy surrounding the Melbourne Olympics. Some teams threatened to boycott the Games and East-West rivalry was heightened.

The Soviet Union participated in the 1956 Winter Olympics for the first time and placed first in the unofficial point standings. They defeated the favoured Canadian hockey team and took the gold medal, while Canada placed third behind the United States (Bass 1971:198). This was only the second time in eight Olympics that Canada had not won the gold medal. A premonition of this phenomenal rise in hockey prominence in the Soviet Union was the Soviet victory over Canada in the 1954 World Hockey Championship. Canada's performance in Summer Olympic competition declined even further in Rome in 1960, when only one medal was garnered.

International sport had become an important factor in the foreign policy of the USSR. Other Eastern European socialist countries soon modelled the Soviet Union plan. The manner in which elite athletes in the Soviet Union had become supported by the state in the pursuit of their training endeavours caused the prevailing Victorian concept of amateur athletes, training and competing on their own time and at their own expense, to undergo substantial further modification. As a result, other countries began to re-examine their attitude toward government support for amateur sport. The ramifications of post-war internationalism in sport could be seen in the correspondence and discussions of the International Olympic Committee in the late 1950s that, despite the defusing of the Cold War in the political sphere, were often related to political squabbles and differences of opinion of amateur status based on traditional Cold War political alignments.

The success of Soviet Union athletes and an all-time low in Canadian performances abroad did not go unnoticed by Canadians. It was also the time of the advent of television in Canada; the exploits of international athletes were often filmed, flown to Canada, and viewed in the living rooms of millions of Canadians. These events created a climate that was favourable for the government to change its attitude toward the support of amateur sport in Canada. But there were also a number of wider political, social, and economic developments that were to influence positively attitudes towards sport legislation. Television in Canada probably was the most directly related of these developments to have such an impact.

Impact of Television

Television in Canada in the early 1950s was to have a profound effect on sport and physical activity in the culture. In the first place, the increased amount of time that Canadians were to devote to watching television in subsequent years was certain to add to the impact of industrialization and urbanization in contributing to a more sedentary lifestyle. Second, television was to bring sport into the lives of millions of Canadians who had hitherto had little exposure or interest in these endeavours. This circumstance served to enhance the social and political significance of sport, and thus played an important role in the changes that have occurred in the last two decades in Canadian sport.

Regular Canadian television service was inaugurated by the Canadian Broadcasting Corporation (CBC) in September 1952. Approximately 146,000 television sets were in operation at that time in Canada; by the end of the next year, the number of television sets had grown to nearly 600,000. By July 1954, 60 percent of the population was covered by existing Canadian television stations. By 1960, the English television network consisted of 46 stations and 13 satellites, and the French television network consisted of 12 stations. In January 1961, 83 percent of Canadian households had television sets and 94 percent of the population was covered by the contours of Canadian television networks. The number of televisions in use had climbed to 3,650,000, representing an expenditure of over one billion dollars by Canadians in the purchase of sets since television's inception (CBC 1962:52–4, 63). Watching television had become a major time-consuming leisure activity.

Sport was a part of CBC programming at the inception of television and was estimated to comprise a minimum of three hours per week, or about 13 percent of the total coverage by the end of 1952 (UNESCO 1953:43). The televising of the British Empire Games in Vancouver in August 1954 was the most extensive coverage of a sporting event ever undertaken in Canada to that time. One of the first uses of the microwave facilities through the United States was to carry the "Miracle Mile" at these Games, featuring Roger Bannister and the then world record holder, John Landy. The Canadian defeat of the Soviet team in the 1955 World Hockey Championship in Germany was filmed by CBC and the film was flown back to Canada the day following the game.

Professional football and hockey received extensive coverage during this period. In November 1954, the largest TV audience to date tuned in the CBC coverage of the Grey Cup Game. Broadcast of Grey Cup Games from coast to coast was made possible in the mid-to-late 1950s by leasing microwave facilities in the United States. By 1957, it was estimated that some 4,500,000 to 5,000,000 people across Canada watched the Grey Cup Game (CBC 1962:61). A survey in 1960 revealed that the largest television audience in the history of the CBC viewed the Stanley Cup hockey finals. This documentation of sport on Canadian TV does not take into account a parallel rapid growth of sport coverage on American television. Millions of Canadians living along the border took advantage of TV transmitters in adjacent U.S. cities.

The relatively poor performance of Canadian amateur athletes in international events, discussed earlier, was, for the first time in history, observed by large numbers of Canadians. The result of television exposure of sport was an increased interest in sport and an increase in its importance in the minds of Canadians. This was paralleled by a corresponding concern about the state of amateur sport in Canada and was another contributing factor in creating a receptive atmosphere for the federal government during its deliberations in the late 1950s about providing financial support for amateur sport.

Urbanization and Industrialization

Major changes in urbanization and industrialization after World War II were factors in creating lifestyle changes for Canadians that related to their physical activity patterns and their attitudes and concepts about sport. The industrial capacity of Canada expanded greatly during World War II in order to produce the weapons and related materials necessary for the Allied victory. Canada was able, in part, to switch this new-found World War II industrial and technological capacity to electronics, plastics, and television industries. The concentration of these industries in or near the large cities of Canada and the accompanying employment opportunities meant that there was a migration of population from rural areas and small towns to these cities. This migration process was enhanced by improved transportation and communication systems in the country after the war. The urbanization process was accompanied by a marked increase in the birth rate in the mid and late 1940s (with the resulting post-war baby boom) and by a large increase in immigration to Canada in the period 1946–52, mainly from European countries.

Post-World War II industrialization and urbanization in Canada brought with them certain socio-economic changes. The period 1950 to 1956 was one of general economic prosperity and growth. One of the outcomes of an accompanying increased productivity in this period was an increase in spending power. Canadian families realized a 38 percent increase in real income between 1951 and 1961 (Gilbert 1975:121). This increased spending power expanded the consumers' scope for choice in using disposable income; as a result, families had more money to spend on homes, entertainment, sports, and the like. The growing sophistication of business executives and the rising expectations of the labour force were reflected in the propensity for civic planners and politicians to view cultural centres and other amenities as attractions for the needed expanded work force (Ostry 1978:74).

Socio-Economic Changes

Changes in industrialization and urbanization in the twentieth century were accompanied by broad socio-economic changes. Between 1901 and 1961, farm workers declined from 40.3 percent of the work force to 10.2 percent, while the percentage of menial labourers declined from 7.2 to 5.4 during the same period. This drop in proportion was reflected in the growth of the white-collar sector from 15.2 percent in 1901 to 38.6 percent in 1961 (Johnson 1974:249, 239). The result was a growing Canadian "middle class," composed primarily of white-collar wage earners (Forcese 1980:155).

This prominence of the middle class in Canadian society has created a tendency for Canadians to understand themselves as belonging to an essentially middle-class society (Porter 1965:3). Furthermore, political demands have tended to reflect middle-class interests. Ironically, high degrees of politicization have not occurred in groups that most need to use recognized political activity to upgrade their conditions (White, Wagenberg, & Nelson 1972:92). This was in spite of the efforts of the Co-operative Commonwealth Federation (CCF) party and the labour movement to organize farmers and other workers as a political force. In the government sphere, members of Parliament have tended to come from middle- and upper-class occupations (Forcese 1980:60), while administrators in the public service generally reflect middle-class values (Nigro & Nigro 1980:72) and follow the pattern of upper-middle class persons occupying important bureaucratic positions (Forcese 1980:61). Although the middle class has benefited the most from the increases in public-sector spending (Bird 1979:86), they have also improved the condition of the lower classes and made Canada a more egalitarian society.

The early and mid 1950s was a period of financial prosperity in Canada, and it was also a period when the power and prestige of the Canadian middle class was high. This combination of factors created a situation in which professional and upper-middle classes were prone to join forces with the government in trying to introduce new legislation for social and other causes, and a time when the influence of such people in moulding the opinions of the rest of the population was substantial (Regenstreif 1965:21–2). In some areas, such as health and labour legislation, the CCF and certain arms of organized labour were active in bringing items to the political agenda. There is a tendency in such circumstances to perceive a convergence of the interests and objectives of successful interest groups with the needs and interests of all people. This trend appears to have been the case with the individuals and interest groups who championed sport and fitness in the late 1950s. The majority of advocates of federal government involvement in sport were members of Parliament, executives of sport governing bodies, professors, professional physical educators, and others who belonged to the middle or upper-middle classes (Gruneau & Hollands 1979).

Implications for Sport and Leisure

Canadians who migrated from rural to urban centres during the 1940s and 1950s adopted a more sedentary lifestyle. Such persons typically changed from jobs entailing long hours of vigorous outdoor work to shorter hours of less physically demanding factory work. In addition, traditional outdoor rural physical recreation activities were much more difficult to pursue in urban areas. Urban centres, however, possessed the potential to provide competitive sport opportunities because of better transportation and greater population density. As well, an increased standard of living and shorter working hours in the post-war period afforded Canadians more time and money for leisure-time activities. But rather than participate in sport and recreational activities, these new urban dwellers for the most part adopted sedentary lifestyle patterns. It has been hypothesized that this inactive lifestyle – developed during this period – could largely be accounted for by a lack of facilities. But this explanation is too simple. The sport activities and facilities that were available in urban clubs and voluntary organizational settings were unfamiliar not only to the rural immigrants, but to the skilled and unskilled workers who immigrated from Europe to the large cities of Canada. In addition to existing cultural barriers, many sport activities and facilities were too costly to afford for most new immigrants to the cities.

A view of sport as a form of idle and useless play was also a strong factor in contributing to an eschewing of organized sport activities by many adult urban Canadians after World War II. Sport was something that one outgrew when adulthood was reached. It was time to move on to the more important matter of making one's way in life.

At the same time, the tremendous growth of TV watching in the 1950s contributed greatly to this sedentary lifestyle. Paradoxically, however, sport coverage on television meant that many rural and European immigrants in urban centres were exposed to highly organized, competitive North American sport activities for the first time in their lives. This exposure set the stage for a change of attitude towards sport on the part of the Canadian public that would not fully manifest itself clearly for another decade or so. It would be even longer before any substantial number of adult Canadians actually started to participate in sport and physical activity.

IMPACT OF GOVERNMENT

Growth of Government

An unprecedented growth in the size of the federal government also contributed to the advent of sport legislation. Taxation had increased substantially during World War II to support the war effort. At the close of the war, the federal government found itself with a greatly expanded source of discretionary funds. The war also left the federal government with a newly found interest in providing leadership and direction for national policies. The propensity to spend newly found tax revenue on health and social welfare programs was supported by the Keynesian theory of economic management, which attracted interest and advocates in many circles in Western industrialized countries after World War II (Rice 1979:115). Keynes advocated government spending as a stimulus to the economy and employment. Subsequent tax revenue from a healthier economy could then be used for further government projects. Thus, government social-welfare programs began to be seen not only in the light of their direct benefit to the citizens, but also as a method of controlling economic downturns and employment. This marriage of social welfare and economic function tended to reduce resistance from the business community to new health and social-welfare programs.

The continuing industrialization and urbanization process in Canada also had an impact on this propensity of the federal government to develop national health and social-welfare programs. Migration to the cities forced the extended family, which before had been the focal point of social control in Canada, to modify and shrink in size in order to adapt to the urban environment (Boyd & Mozersky 1975:435). The more impersonal urban society meant that individuals were released from the social controls of smaller communities; the responsibility for defining and carrying out legal and social responsibilities fell more and more on government. Growing concern about social problems, combined with the reluctance of the federal government to give up its newly found revenue sources, made the late 1940s and early 1950s ripe for federal government excursions into health and social-welfare programs. The harrowing experience of the pre-war depression was still on the minds of many Canadians and thus provided an additional impetus for such programs. It was not surprising, therefore, that the 1950s and 1960s were the halcyon days for federal/provincial cost-sharing agreements. The successful negotiation of these agreements was aided and abetted by skilled federal government bureaucrats (Hockin 1975:56).

The growth in the size and scope of federal government activities after World War II and the government's propensity to enter into cost-sharing agreements with the provinces meant that it was a propitious time for the government to bring forth proposals for its support for sport and physical fitness, even though the jurisdictional responsibilities of these matters were in question.

Factors Inhibiting Government Action

Juxtaposed to the efforts of individuals and interest groups and the related forces and developments in Canada in the 1950s that gave support to federal government action in regard to formal involvement in the support of amateur sport and fitness were a number of factors that mitigated against such action. The Protestant concept of sport as a frivolous and unimportant aspect of life was very much alive in Canada in the first half of the twentieth century and was reflected in the speeches of government leaders and parliamentarians as late as the 1950s. In his speech in the House of Commons in 1957, Douglas Fisher opened discussion on "the very touchy field of sport and international sport," acknowledging that many saw this as "a very frivolous thing on which to spend money" (HC Debates, 21 December 1957:2750). In 1958, MP McIntosh suggested that spectators in the public galleries "must wonder at the value of introducing into this house material obtained from the sports pages of the daily newspapers" (ibid., 27 May 1958:559). This attitude was in part responsible for the view held by some people that the federal government did not have a legitimate role to play in supporting and developing sport.

In 1936, Mackenzie King told the House of Commons that "it is doubtful that anyone participating in the Olympic Games is a representative of the Government of this country" when questioned about Canadian participation in the Nazi Olympics (ibid., 13 February 1936:159; cited by Kidd 1981:240). This attitude contrasts sharply with references in the House of Commons years later to athletes as "ambassadors of good will" (HC *Debates*, 27 May 1958:517–18). In 1937, the King government rejected a bill proposing the creation of a ministry of sport on the grounds that government should stay out of sport (Kidd 1981:240). This view prevailed in the subsequent St Laurent government. Paul Martin, the minister of national health and welfare throughout most of the National Physical Fitness Program, stated that jurisdiction in the sport field was a provincial and municipal responsibility (Broom & Baka 1978:3–4). The members of the health division of his department recognized the value of sport programs, but they did not believe that they played a useful role in organized health programs (West 1973:2.5). Although the Liberal government of Louis St Laurent did promote cultural development through the establishment of the Canada Council, it was not common at that time for cultural activities to be associated with sport and consequently, sport was neglected as a form of culture in these early days of the Canada Council.

There were also two issues of autonomy that were obstacles to federal government legislation in support of amateur sport. The post-World War II industrialization and urbanization process that caused federal government concern for national health and social-welfare programs also awakened the provincial governments to their responsibilities under the BNA Act for health and education, and for related social-welfare programs. These forces have been seen as changing the legal boundaries of federalism during this time and thus opening the way for a decentralization of government. During the 1950s and 1960s, Canada witnessed a weakening of federal power in favour of the provinces (Schwartz 1967:vii). Because sport was largely associated with school and community-centred programs, jurisdiction over it was seen to be primarily provincial and municipal. Thus, federal government support of such programs had previously been indirect and largely provided under the auspices of other related endeavours through federal/provincial cost-sharing agreements.

The autonomy of sport organizations and governing bodies was a second obstacle to federal government involvement in amateur sport. This autonomy had been a feature of sport organizations in their development during the late nineteenth century (Wise 1974:100). The outcry against government control of sport greeting the announcement in 1945 by the director of the National Physical Fitness Program that the National Physical Fitness Council would serve as a link between Canadian sport organizations and government was strong evidence that sport organizations were still jealous of their independence and autonomy (Broom & Baka 1978:3; Kidd 1981: 241). This position was supported by a residual liberal-pluralist belief that the state had no business regulating the voluntary activity of Canadians (Gruneau 1982:19).

Role of Central Agencies

The Conservative government, elected in 1957, brought with it a different view of the role of government in Canada. Prime Minister Diefenbaker believed in the need to provide social support to minority groups and in particular to ethnic, farm, and low-income groups (Regenstreif 1965:52). In addition, Diefenbaker's fierce nationalism became an important issue in Canada in the 1950s. Changes in attitudes of Canadians during the 1950s towards a flag issue reflects this growing concern over Canadian identity. Gallup polls taken in 1953, 1955, and 1958 indicate that 39, 64, and 79 percent of Canadians were in favour of a new national flag in these three years respectively (Schwartz 1967:107).

Although the adoption of a new flag held a high priority for Prime Minister Pearson, neither he nor his Liberal Cabinet appeared to have associated sport with the building of Canadian unity. There had been as well no commitment to the support of sport by previous Liberal governments. This attitude may have been coloured by the bitterness that developed between the Liberal government and the National Fitness Council in 1950 over the jurisdiction of the council. The federal government was not happy with the way in which the provinces were using government funds nor with the independent status of the Fitness Council. Although the council's independent position was upheld by the Department of Justice, the Liberal government soon disbanded the council by revoking the National Fitness Act in 1954. The outcome of this controversy left a bad taste with Liberal Cabinet members and senior public servants.

Diefenbaker believed that success in sport by Canadians would have a positive effect on national pride. His charismatic style of leadership ensured that his own personal interests played a role in the priorities set by the central agencies. Diefenbaker's belief in the ideological importance of sport was reflected in his statements in the House of Commons when referring to the Speech from the Throne late in 1960: "In the field of sports today there are tremendous dividends in national pride from some degree of success in athletics. The uncommitted countries of the world are now using these athletic contests as measurements of the evidence of the strength and power of the nations participating" (HC *Debates*, 21 November 1960:39–40). Speeches by other members of the House of Commons during the late 1950s and during the debate of Bill C-131 reflected this belief.

A factor that changed the attitude of the central agencies was the replacement of George Davidson, the deputy minister of welfare, by J.W. Willard in 1960. Waldo Monteith was minister of national health and welfare at this time. Davidson had considered sport jurisdiction to be a provincial and municipal responsibility, so had advised the ministers in power not to act on briefs submitted by the Canadian Sports Advisory Council (West 1973:2.6). Also, Davidson's personality conflicted with that of Doris Plewes, and he had greeted her efforts to promote the National Physical Fitness Program with an indifference that bordered on opposition (Kidd 1965:20–1). According to West, Willard had a much greater interest in sport jurisdiction and probably was more supportive of the efforts of Plewes in her promotion of fitness and amateur sport legislation (West 1973:2.14). Following Willard's appointment as deputy minister of welfare, a series of conversations had taken place between Plewes and Willard, Willard and Monteith, and among Monteith and others outside the department that focused on the idea that something should be done to assist amateur sport and fitness (letter from J.A. Macdonald to B. Kidd, 16 July 1965).

A final important point is that the central agencies did not face counter pressures and proposals from opposing interest groups. The proposals and briefs the federal government received from various interest groups were incrementally rather than radically different. In addition, there was no apparent public opinion that opposed federal government support of fitness and amateur sport. It was easier, therefore, for the federal government to move ahead on this issue along the lines proposed by the interest groups.

COALESCING OF ENVIRONMENT
AND GOVERNMENT

The underlying political, social, and economic developments which occurred in Canada in the 1950s did not in themselves bring about new legislation; rather they imposed boundaries and limits on what legislative activity was possible and acceptable, and within which individual actors were able to pursue their interests. It is our contention that the boundaries of generally acceptable government activity expanded considerably during the 1950s to a point where fitness and amateur sport legislation became possible; previously existing barriers to this type of involvement were reduced or eliminated. The urbanization of Canada and the accompanying breakdown of the extended rural family contributed to a popular post-war belief that government could and should solve critical social problems. This belief was strengthened by the experiences of the Great Depression. Social and moral issues previously seen to be familial and community responsibilities were shifted to the government. This shift coincided with an emerging view that the state had a responsibility to provide equal social-welfare and health opportunities for all Canadians, regardless of geographic and economic disparities. In this sense, the concept of government was much more interventionist than was that of Canada's neighbour to the south. At the same time, the federal government found itself with additional tax revenue in the expanding post-World War II economy. Supported by the popular Keynesian economic theory, the federal government took an expansionist economic posture. It is not surprising, therefore, that the 1950s were characterized by increasing involvement by the federal government in health and social-welfare programs, and that federal/provincial cost-sharing programs expanded greatly during this period. These expansionist policies carried over into the government's attitude towards culture. The Canada Council was established and funded and the CBC greatly expanded its activities and extended into the realm of television.

This expansionist federal government policy was paralleled by a changing attitude towards sport in other countries, particularly in the Soviet Union and certain European countries. There was a much greater emphasis on improved performance in international sport events by athletes from these countries. Central to this was the great success of the Soviet hockey team. The supremacy of Canada in its "national" sport was usurped. The consternation that was felt can clearly be seen in the preoccupation over hockey in the House of Commons and in the press. The rapid growth of television in the late 1950s contributed greatly to widening this concern; as well, it brought about for the first time a wide exposure in Canada to sport, particularly professional hockey and football.

All these events helped to strengthen certain attitudes towards sport on the part of Canadians. Sport more often came to be seen as a focus for national pride and a vehicle through which the Canadian image could be extended abroad, and less often as an activity that, although enjoyable, held little importance. At the same time, resistance to governmental intervention on the part of sport organizations waned. The financial problems these groups were facing in staging national championships and financing teams to international events and the lack of success by Canadian teams in these events contributed to a growing acceptance that the federal government did have a supportive role to play in sport.

CIRCUMSTANCES SURROUNDING ENACTMENT

Given these changing circumstances and growing acceptance of federal government support of sport, it was most likely that some type of legislation would have been forthcoming in the 1960s. The election of a Conservative government in 1957 was the catalyst for action; it brought forward a prime minister with a strong belief in nationalism and the conviction that sport had an important role to play in developing national unity and international prestige. It could be argued that the distasteful experience of the previous Liberal government with the National Physical Fitness Act in the early 1950s would have been an impediment to the possibility of that party bringing forth new sport and fitness legislation in the early 1960s. But the Liberal government had brought forth similar legislation in support of culture during its post-World War II stint of power. Both parties held a paternalistic view of government's role in Canadian society, one that was conducive to the provision of monies to agencies and organizations so that sport could be supported indirectly through existing and independent channels. This role of patron was a familiar and acceptable one in amateur sport circles.

Much has been made by sport historians of the important role played by physical fitness advocates to induce the federal government to produce legislation to support physical fitness programs. In our view, there is little evidence to support this position. The concern about physical fitness in Canada centred largely around a small group of dedicated professionals in the field of physical education, who had neither much influence nor public support. This lobby had been in existence throughout the post-World War II period. Despite the presence of this lobby, the National Physical Fitness Act had been repealed in 1954. The federal government took this step because it was not happy with the way in which the provinces were using the funds nor with the independent status of the Fitness Council. These actors came to the realization in the late 1950s that their efforts would not be successful politically if physical fitness was not tied to sport. At the same time, the advocates of sport legislation could see advantages in tying their cause to the residual support for physical fitness legislation. The claim of sport advocates that sport was the vehicle through which the physical fitness of Canadians would be improved certainly could not have withstood much scrutiny. The paucity of indoor sport facilities in Canada at that time and the relatively small number of adults in the country who were interested in participating in sport programs made this claim a very dubious one. The marriage of convenience between amateur sport and physical fitness, although at first glance a compatible one, was subsequently to prove to be illusive.

The first memorandum on the new Act, sent to Cabinet by the Department of National Health and Welfare, suggested that action be considered along the lines of the motion by J.R. Taylor to establish a Canada Sports Council with the object of fostering and encouraging amateur sport in Canada (HC *Debates*, 16 February 1959:1037). After longer deliberation of alternative suggestions, a second, more comprehensive proposal was produced by the department suggesting that establishment of a national advisory council was the preferred modus operandi (FASD Files, No. 1020-01, Vol. 1). Cabinet study of this second proposal resulted in instructions given to the Department of National Health and Welfare to present legislation for a $5 million program instead of its proposed $500,000 program (letter from J. Macdonald to B. Kidd, 16 July 1965). Consequently Monteith prepared a third Cabinet submission that briefly summarized the content of the preceding proposal but contained the recommended expenditure of $5 million per annum. This proposal to establish a national fitness and recreation program and to raise standards of health through encouragement of amateur athletics was submitted to Cabinet in June 1961 (FASD Files, No. 1020-01, Vol. 1).

On 16 August 1961, Cabinet announced its agreement in principle to the recommendations of the minister of national health and welfare as follows:

(a) that a national fitness, recreation, and amateur athletic program be established,
(b) that an Advisory Council be established,
(c) that provision be made through grants and training courses for training of personnel and for research and surveys,
(d) that federal assistance be given in the preparation of informational and educational material on fitness, recreation, and athletics,
(e) that $5 million be made available,
(f) that a cabinet committee be established to consider the manner of presentation of the national fitness program

(FASD Files, PAC, No. RG29, Vol. 1356, File 2)

Ten days later, Prime Minister Diefenbaker made an official announcement at the opening of the Hockey Hall of Fame in Toronto of the government's intention to bring forth this legislation.

Following Cabinet's request for a proposal for a $5 million program, John Macdonald, executive assistant to the deputy minister of welfare, instructed Doris Plewes to draw up the first draft of the Act, based on the submission to cabinet (FASD Files, No. 1020-01, Vol. 1). Throughout the next three months, she was assisted by J.W. Willard, R.E. Curran, and J.A. Macdonald in preparing this document for submission to the Department of Justice (ibid., No. 1020-01, Vol. 1). The end product of their efforts was the "Fitness, Recreation, and Amateur Sport Act."

In the Cabinet meeting that considered the bill, Prime Minister Diefenbaker was said to have changed the emphasis to physical fitness through amateur sport by deleting several recreation clauses (Kidd 1965:26). The amended bill became "An Act to Promote Physical Fitness through Amateur Sport." These changes in content of the Act drew protests from the Department of National Health and Welfare. In correspondence from Monteith to Diefenbaker during September 1961, serious difficulties were forecast in the proposed legislation in terms of its public acceptance and passage in the House. Monteith believed that the word "through" rendered the legislation even more restrictive than the National Physical Fitness Act; he feared criticism that twenty-two times more money was being made available for a much more restrictive program. Second, he wanted the word "physical" dropped from "physical fitness" as it limited the concept of all-round fitness, which had received acceptance in other countries. Third, Monteith argued for inclusion of the word "recreation" in the Act in order to gain the support of the provinces and the public. The success of the program, he maintained, depended upon the full co-operation of the provinces, which could not be expected if assistance was not given for extending this important part of their own programs. Furthermore, Monteith reasoned that inclusion of recreation was essential because of the lack of interest in amateur sport participation on the part of the general public (FASD Files, No. 1020-01, Vol. 1).

Monteith's first two concerns were resolved by amendments to the resolution before it could be debated in the House of Commons. On a motion from Monteith, the wording of the resolution was changed from a measure respecting the encouragement of "physical fitness through amateur sport" to "fitness and amateur sport" (HC *Debates*, 18 September 1961:8601). Although these changes were simply cosmetic ones that did not alter the provisions of the Act, they did serve to avert opposition in the House. During the debate following the first reading of the bill, Lester Pearson, the leader of the Opposition, pointed out that he would have opposed the bill if "through" had not been changed to "and." Monteith's premonition of resistance in the House, then, was justified.

Monteith's suggestion to Diefenbaker to reinsert "recreation" in the bill was not supported; thus the recreation provision did not appear in the legislation. West has suggested that the belief that recreation was primarily an area of provincial jurisdiction led to its exclusion (West 1973:2.15–2.16). Another possible reason for this exclusion may be related to the previous experience of the National Physical Fitness Program. Involvement in recreational and cultural programs had spread its efforts so thinly that the funds channelled towards the development of physical fitness were limited. At any rate, this omission emphasized the sport aspect of the legislation and helped it to become the focus of the federal government in the years ahead.

This process reflected more a passive acceptance of proposals than a rethinking, or even re-examination, of the role of government in encouraging sport and fitness. As a result, in many aspects, the Act reflected former and existing program elements and policies rather than innovative measures that anticipated future needs. This incremental procedure is quite normal. Nevertheless, the inclusion of sport in the Act was a major departure from previous legislation and was the source of the subsequent revolution in the government's role in sport.

Despite the changes in attitude, the time was not yet ripe for direct federal government involvement. Thus, the legislation was phrased in general terms; statements of intentions indicated that the government's role would be one of support to existing sport agencies and organizations and to the provinces. This fitted in with the low priority that the Department of National Health and Welfare gave to this measure and with the lack of professional staff in the ministry at that time.

In Parliament, the bill received the unanimous support of all speakers and parties (HC *Debates*, 25 September 1961:8837). The Liberal party consented probably because it realized that the laissez-faire attitude towards international sport competition simply was no longer working. Recent events illustrated that government support appeared to be necessary if Canada's teams were to fare better. This legislation was also supported by the CCF party. Certainly the presence in its ranks of Douglas Fisher, a strong supporter of federal assistance to sport, was an important factor in this support. Research conducted in the 1970s of the composition of elite athletes in Canada, both at the turn of the century (Metcalfe 1976; Wise 1974) and subsequent to this period (Boileau, Landy, & Trempe 1976; Gruneau 1976; Hall 1976) has shown that participants were over-represented by males, anglophones, the middle class, and urban dwellers. But equalizing opportunities in sport was a non-issue on the political agenda in the early 1960s; the CCF party could not have reasonably been expected to raise this point as an objection to providing funds for elite athletes.

None of the major political parties in Canada had any formal policy or position in regard to sport and physical fitness. The general enthusiasm for sport as an expression of national pride was supported by a belief that the expansion of international sport competitions was one of the ways in which the Cold War could be defused. All these factors combined to ensure the unanimous support of all MPs for this legislation.

There is no record of any labour-union reaction to the legislation. Some unions in Canada had been part of an international labour movement between the two World Wars to establish and support a workers' Olympics in opposition to existing "bourgeoise-supported" Olympics. But this movement died out after World War II. The labour movement in Canada had undergone a post-war purge of Communist party links and was still trying to dissociate itself from international communism. A stand against support for Canada's falling hockey image in the face of Soviet supremacy would not have been popular.

There is no evidence in the House debate that sport organizations and interested individuals made any great attempt to influence or change the Act. This may reflect the naivety and political immaturity of the sport and physical activity fraternity at that time, but certainly it was due as well to a wide acceptance by this group of the measures proposed. The Canadian Sports Advisory Council believed that it would become the body responsible for co-ordinating and directing government funds earmarked for sport. This proposal had been included in its brief to the federal government. In conclusion, it can be safely said that the Act was uncontentious, non-partisan, and widely supported but, at the same time, apparently of no great importance in certain government and other circles.

An examination of the Act is instructive in determining the government's intentions and the manner in which the legislation was expected to meet the visions and expectations of its supporters. It also allows us to anticipate some of its problems and unintended consequences, and to suggest alternative courses of action. There was little in the Act to provide direction as to how the federal government might support programs, particularly in the realm of fitness. It was envisaged that fitness would be improved by funds made available to the provinces through provision for federal/provincial agreements. This reflects the faith that the federal government placed at that time in cost-sharing agreements with the provinces for bringing about social change. This optimism flew in the face of warnings about lack of facilities, inadequate leadership, and the small amount of money that was to be injected into the program. The belief in indirect measures also was consistent with the view that the government's role was to be catalytic, stimulating existing sport governing bodies and agencies without interfering with their autonomy.

Diefenbaker and Monteith contended that the implementation of this "people's program" would rest at the grass roots, but a reading of the Act suggests strongly that its major thrust was improving amateur sport performances. What new provisions were included dealt largely with this concern. Performance and leadership capabilities were to be improved by making federal grants to sport governing bodies; these groups, in turn, would be responsible for implementing appropriate programs. These federal grants were much more directly related to target agencies and programs than were those earmarked for fitness. But the federal government still was distanced from sport clients by the sport governing bodies. This was to cause frustration, a lack of visibility of federal government contributions, and a problem of accountability.

The matter of inadequate sport facilities, which had been raised by external groups, the media, and by concerned politicians, was not dealt with directly in the Act. It was recognized that the budget allocated for the total program would not be adequate to meet the costs of any significant efforts to construct new recreational or sport facilities across the country. The Act, however, did provide blanket coverage for any other projects or programs, including the provision of facilities that would further the objectives of the Act. This provision was eventually used to advantage by the federal government in building sport facilities in conjunction with the Canada, Pan-American, Olympic, and Commonwealth Games that were staged in Canada over the next two decades. The matter of how the federal government could stimulate the construction of other sport facilities, however, was to prove to be a vexatious problem in the years to come.

The creation of the National Advisory Council was a compromise to pressures from interest groups and some politicians to create an independent agency similar in nature and function to the Canada Council. On the one hand, the federal government was not prepared to create such a council, given its recent experience with the Bank of

Canada, and in the light of public criticism of the Canada Council (West 1973:3.3–3.4). On the other hand, it was not willing to take direct responsibility for implementing the provisions of the Act by establishing a regular division and bureaucracy within a federal government department. The federal government argued that it should not take this step because of its sensitivity to the autonomous nature of sport in Canada and because of the prevailing practice at that time to appoint an advisory committee with departmental administration for programs involving federal/provincial agreements. But the evidence suggests that the federal government was not willing to take any significant responsibility for developing policy and carrying out programs in these areas. In establishing a National Advisory Council, the federal government created a buffer group that would protect it from criticism and, at the same time, would provide advice from various regions and from different program biases.

The provisions of the Act were expressed in broad, general terms, in part because of an uncertainty about how to accomplish the outcomes that had been expressed in briefs to the government and debate in Parliament, and in part to accommodate changes and expansion of programs in future years. At first glance, the generality may be regarded as a deficiency because there was little in the Act to give direction and guidance for accomplishing its objectives. But the fact remains that the flexibility in the Act has allowed it to serve as a basis for federal government activities for over twenty-five years, accommodating many changes of direction and expansion of programs and professional staff.

The passage of the Fitness and Amateur Sport Act was accompanied by a great deal of optimism in the House of Commons and by the expression of high expectations and a good deal of idealism. The broadness of the Act also contributed to a great scope for individual interpretation. Expectations ranged from reducing juvenile delinquency to increasing Canada's international prestige. Such ambiguous legislation, according to Hockin (1975), often leads to a conflict between what the government said and what the people thought it would do. This ambiguity of purpose, combined with a lack of commitment by the federal government, provided the ingredients for future disappointments. It also meant that many decisions still had to be made about the implementation of the Act; specific directions had to be determined in its subsequent implementation. The passage of the Fitness and Amateur Sport Act, however, was of major significance because it officially committed the federal government, for the first time, to the promotion and development of amateur sport.

CHAPTER THREE

Impact of Early Programs on Future Policy

Bill C-131 officially committed the federal government "to encourage, promote, and develop fitness and amateur sport in Canada" (Canada 1961: Chapter 59, Section 3). According to speeches by Prime Minister Diefenbaker and Minister of National Health and Welfare Waldo Monteith, the Act was intended to encourage mass participation as well as improve international sport performances. Sport leaders and physical educators hoped for improvements in physical fitness levels of Canadians and an increase in the number of sport participants (West 1973:2.4–2.5). The media, supported by a substantial portion of the public, however, looked for increased success of Canadian amateur athletes (Paraschak 1978:46).

The Act was couched in broad, general terms, in part because few people had any clear, concise ideas of how to accomplish its goals, and in part, to accommodate change and expansion in future years. As a result, there was a great deal of scope left for the development of policies and programs. It was also necessary to develop policies quickly in order to get the program off the ground. It should be remembered that the implementation of social programs usually follows a pattern of grand pretensions, faulty execution, and puny results (Elmore 1978:186). What gets done often bears little resemblance to what was intended. The Fitness and Amateur Sport Act was no exception; the broad scope of its execution meant that expectations were often distanced considerably from the reality of implementation.

In the first few years following the enactment of Bill C-131, federal government involvement in the program was indirect and consisted mainly of distributing funds to sport governing bodies and to the provinces in the form of federal/provincial cost-sharing agreements. The government assumed a passive role and reacted to suggestions that were forthcoming from the National Advisory Council, a body established by the Act to advise the minister of national health and welfare on the implementation of the program. But there were a number of key agents and events associated with the fitness and amateur-sport program that played a role in changing the direction and nature of federal government involvement in sport. These included the administrative structure and personnel, federal/provincial cost-sharing agreements, grants to sport governing bodies, the Canada Games, and scholarships and research awards.

ADMINISTRATIVE STRUCTURE AND PERSONNEL

The Act provided little direction about an appropriate organizational structure or how responsibilities should be distributed for carrying out its provisions. The minister of national health and welfare was charged with the responsibility for carrying out the objectives of the Act. One such duty involved the establishment of federal/provincial cost-sharing agreements; the implications of this provision are examined below. The Act provided for the establishment of a national advisory council to advise the minister on matters referred to it, or on any other matters relating to the objects of the Act. The Advisory Council was given the authority to make rules for regulating the proceedings and the performance of its own functions, but it was not given any executive power, program funds, or an independent secretariat. Finally, the Act provided for the appointment of whatever public servants were necessary for its administration. The relationship between the public service and the Advisory Council, however, was not set down in the Act.

The tasks assumed by these groups and individuals bore only a weak resemblance to the responsibilities outlined in the Act. The federal government initially was content to let the Advisory Council take over the role of policy development and assume an executive function. An exception was the federal/provincial cost-sharing agreements; in this domain, policies and directions were determined by the minister. In the other major areas of the program, the minister made it clear that he was relying upon the advice of the Advisory Council in the formulation of policies (FASD Files, PAC, RG29, Vol. 1353). The federal government did not want to be seen to be interfering with the autonomy of national sport and related governing bodies and agencies (ibid., File 10). But it was quite apparent that the government was not very interested in this area of legislation and wished to establish a buffer group between itself and the anticipated flood of supplicants and petitions for support (West 1973:3.10). Another factor in this reluctance of the government to become involved in policy making was the absence of a qualified public service. The government paid little attention initially to putting a bureaucracy in place. Despite the enabling provision of the Act, only one professional public servant, Doris Plewes, was on hand at the onset of the program. It was not until mid 1962, some nine months after the selection of the members of the Advisory Council, that the first director, Gordon Wright, was appointed. It was the government's view that the directorate staff should be kept small because Ottawa did not want to appear to be taking over sport (FASD Files, PAC, RG29, Vol. 1353, File 10). Monteith stated that it was the government's plan to put in place a relatively small, highly trained nucleus to carry out federal policy and to help ensure co-ordination of efforts across the country (Dinning 1974:61).

This delegation of policy-making authority worked reasonably well for the first few years, until the scope and complexity of the tasks the Advisory Council had assumed became unmanageable, and members began to complain of being bogged down with excessive paperwork (NAC *Appendix 7 to the Minutes of the 19th Meeting*, 25 and 26 November 1968). Because of the broad mandate of the Act, the Advisory Council membership reflected diverse backgrounds and widely different views on key issues. As a result, the council's decisions were often based on bargain and compromise rather than agreement on policies and directions. As the directorate staff grew in size and maturity, it became increasingly opposed to this style of policy making. As a result, the minister was confronted often with two different sets of recommendations – one from the Advisory Council and a second from the directorate staff through Deputy Minister Joseph Willard. As was customary in the established programs under his jurisdiction, the minister began more often to listen to this second source of advice. The Advisory Council, in turn, resented the attempts of the public servants to become more actively involved in advising the minister on policy (Westland 1979:40–1). This disagreement came to a head in 1968. The resulting conflict and its resolution were critical to the development of sport policy and are examined later in this chapter.

FEDERAL/PROVINCIAL
COST-SHARING AGREEMENTS

Grants to the provinces were initiated in the 1962–3 fiscal year. Planning and organizational non-matching grants of $15,000 were made available to each province and territory and an additional amount on a per capita basis to a maximum total of $250,000 for all the provinces. Another grant of $250,000 was made available on the same basis for initiating new programs (NAC *Minutes of the Third Meeting*, 15 and 16 November 1962). In addition, the federal government agreed to meet all the costs of undergraduate physical education and recreation scholarships at Canadian universities. Order in Council stipulated that the money for the organizational grants had to be spent to conduct studies or surveys to indicate the present levels of activity in the fields of fitness and amateur sport, and to set priorities in achieving extensions in the programs. The balance of the allocation could be spent on administrative organization necessary to implement these plans. In 1963–4, each province and territory was awarded $35,000, with the remainder of the available $1 million divided on a per capita basis. These latter funds were provided on a 60–40 cost-sharing basis, with the federal government picking up the larger share. Funds available under this agreement were earmarked for extending and increasing provincial programs in existence in the base year, established as 1961–2. Two subsequent three-year cost-sharing agreements were signed with the provinces in 1964 and 1967 respectively. A $1 million ceiling was established in 1963–4 and remained in effect until the termination of the agreements in 1970 (Broom & Baka 1978:12). In addition to the monies spent on scholarships and bursaries, these funds were expended largely on provincial staff salaries, grants to communities, recreation leadership courses, sport clinics, books, and films.

Discrepancies between provincial allocations and actual expenditures were considerable. Part of this discrepancy resulted from Quebec's refusal to participate in these cost-sharing agreements until the last year of the program. This was consistent with Quebec's refusal to participate in any of the federal/provincial cost-sharing agreements because they were seen to be an intrusion by the federal government into jurisdictions where the province considered itself to have constitutional power and autonomy. Another reason for the marked differences in allocation and expenditures was that some of the poorer provinces were unable to provide the provincial share of the federal allocation. The wealthier provinces that had well-established programs during the base year were hard pressed to find the extra funds needed to extend these programs in order to be eligible for financial assistance (FASD Files, PAC, RG29, Vol. 1353, File 10).

It became evident during the 1960s that these federal/provincial cost-sharing agreements were ineffective in fostering mass sport and physical fitness programs. The dilution of the minimal levels of monies set aside for these programs across the entire country meant that mass sport and fitness funding represented only a drop in a very large bucket. The growing desire of the provinces to assert their constitutional authority vis-à-vis the federal government made it more difficult for the federal government to determine the direction and scope of the joint programs, and to garner political credit for expenditures in this area. Similar problems were encountered in other cost-sharing agreements in this period. By the late 1960s, the federal government had come to the realization that it must either seek other avenues to have any impact on mass sport participation or relegate this responsibility to the provinces and municipalities.

GRANTS TO SPORT GOVERNING BODIES

The National Advisory Council established a detailed set of criteria for making grants to national associations (NAC *Summary of Policy Statements and Decisions*, 1967b:6.1–6.6). The types of organizations considered eligible for financial assistance were national sport governing bodies, non-competitive sport organizations, national program operating agencies that conducted or co-ordinated fitness and amateur sport programs, and national co-ordinating bodies of multiple international competitive events, such as the Canadian Olympic Association. Grants were made only for extending and strengthening existing services. They were restricted to a percentage of the costs so that the principle of self-help would be maintained. Monies were also awarded for assistance to travel to national trials or competitions, to international sport events, and for leadership training and special projects related to the promotion and development of fitness and amateur sport. Initially, grants were not made for the construction of sport facilities (NAC *Appendix G to the Minutes of the 13th Meeting*, 28 and 29 October 1966).

Although some progress was made in the development of elite athletes, the period 1961–8 was more notable for laying bare the substantial barriers to further improvement. The sport governing bodies, for the most part, did not have the organizational skills or leadership necessary for this task. The National Advisory Council became convinced that full-time professional staff was needed to streamline administrative and organizational capacities and urged the minister to make administrative grants to sport governing bodies. This recommendation was finally accepted in 1966. Amateur sport officials and federal sport bureaucrats also perceived that the sporadic and uncoordinated offering of clinics was not effective in developing coaches of elite athletes. More continuity and planning would be necessary in the future. Poor levels of officiating in most sports and the almost complete lack of a sports medicine component to Canadian amateur sport also were identified as barriers to further progress. It also became clear to all concerned that elite Canadian athletes would need to spend a much greater percentage of their time in training and competing in top-level events if dramatic improvements in international performances were to be attained. In order to accomplish these ends, a growing number of sport officials, sport writers and reporters, and politicians advocated direct financial assistance for elite athletes.

Inquiries and addresses in the House of Commons during the 1961–8 period reflected concerns about elite sport. Specific mention of the Fitness and Amateur Sport Program usually entailed questions about finances, with occasional criticism about the lack of facilities, coaches, and fitness programs. Requests for financial support for the Olympics, Canada Games, and Pan-American Games were very common, as were requests for increased television coverage of sport. Canadian representation in international sport, particularly hockey, was of continuing concern. In 1965, John Diefenbaker expressed concern over Canada's loss of national prestige because of poor showings in hockey. He suggested that a parliamentary committee be established to work with the National Advisory Council to "assure hereafter that Canada's representation in the field of international competition, particularly in amateur sport, shall be of the very best" (HC *Debates*, 15 March 1965:12336). Diefenbaker's comments reflected the belief that success in hockey was an important aspect of Canada's international prestige. Father Bauer's National Hockey Team previously had been praised for the esteem that it brought to Canada through its unique display of sportsmanship. But this reputation was overshadowed by the fact that the team had finished out of the medals in 1964 for the first time in the history of Canadian Olympic Hockey (Hallett 1981:553–4).

Some members of Parliament believed that Canada's poor representation in international hockey was due to the control that the National Hockey League (NHL) exerted over all hockey. Prime Minister Pearson pointed out that "every good player in Canada under the age of 10 is on the negotiating list, at least, of some professional club" (HC *Debates*, 15 March 1965:12336). There were increasing requests by members of Parliament for federal legislation to protect young hockey players from being signed by the Canadian Amateur Hockey Association and then sold to the NHL (ibid., 31 January 1967:12457). Another concern was the failure of Quebec and Vancouver to obtain NHL franchises. The procedures and rights for obtaining these franchises came under increasing scrutiny. In

1966, Ronald Basford from Vancouver introduced a private member's bill "to bring the operation of all professional sporting leagues within the purview of the Combines Investigation Act" (ibid., 13 June 1966:6364). Although this amendment to the Combines Act was defeated, members of Parliament were in favour of an investigation into the relationship between amateur and professional sport. It was only a few weeks later that the Hockey Committee of the National Advisory Council announced its study of amateur hockey in Canada. This report formed the basis of the recommendations contained in the 1969 Task Force Report, which is examined in greater detail in the next chapter.

The monies that were distributed to national sport governing bodies did allow for greater numbers to participate in national and international sport competitions (FASD Files, PAC, RG29, Vol. 1331). Modest improvements at the international level were accomplished in many sports (FASD Annual Report, 1965–6:1–2). But these did not meet the expectations that had been raised. It became apparent in the late 1960s that two avenues for rectifying these shortcomings were open to the federal government. First, it could increase greatly its financial support to sport governing bodies, depending upon them to upgrade coaching and stimulate elite sport. Second, it could opt for the development of its own agencies and bodies and deal more directly with athletes and coaches. In its new policy statement in 1970, the government opted largely for the second course of action. This critical decision was influenced greatly by larger political issues that the federal government faced at this time, i.e., national unity, relations with the provinces, and self-determination in Quebec. These issues are discussed in the next chapter.

Anticipated opposition to federal government sport involvement by the sport organizations and agencies in the early 1960s did not materialize. On the contrary, demands for federal support in the form of submissions for financial assistance escalated (FASD Files, PAC, RG29, Vol. 1331). As a consequence, any inhibitions that the federal government held about accusations of unwarranted interference had abated by the middle 1960s. The introduction of administrative grants to sport governing bodies and allied agencies was one of the first manifestations of this changing attitude. Initially, the government had hesitated to give administrative grants because it did not want to appear to be controlling amateur sport (NAC Minutes of the 12th Meeting, 22 and 23 April 1966). With the introduction of administrative grants in 1966, sport organizations became accountable to the government for the use of these funds. This precedent proved to be the forerunner of the establishment of the administrative centre for sport and recreation in 1970 (West 1973:5.13–5.14). These growing influences of the federal government on the national sport governing bodies also helped to shape future sport direction in Canada.

Although the federal government supported the 1967 Canada Games as part of its program to assist national sport organizations, these first games warrant separate treatment because of their significance in the development of Canadian amateur sport. The idea of a Canada Games Festival had been promoted since the 1920s (McLaughlin & McDonald 1978:2), but it was not until the early years of the Fitness and Amateur Sport Program that the idea was transformed into reality. The Canada Games brought together athletes from across the country in a highly visible event that generated considerable interest and enthusiasm in Canadian amateur sport. The concept has rightly been called one of the most exciting milestones in Canadian sport history (FASD Annual Report, 1966–7:2).

The national unity crisis in Canada, which is discussed in some detail in the next chapter, was becoming of greater concern to the federal government during the time that the first Canada Games were being organized. It was in this atmosphere that federal government leaders saw the value of sport as a political tool for counteracting these divisive forces. Sport possessed elements of commonality and universality that could combat the divisive forces in the country. As the Games approached, their focus changed from one of a sport celebration to that of the promotion of national unity. The adoption of the motto "Unity through Sport" for these first Canada Games demonstrated their political attractiveness in promoting national unity. Significantly, these first Games were held in Quebec City at the time of the Quiet Revolution.

The Canada Games had other more direct and profound effects on sport. First, each province was to select athletes for the competition. This forced provincial departments responsible for recreation and culture to develop a sport arm, and to devote personnel and money to the purpose of organizing, bringing together, and selecting athletes for the Canada Games in collaboration with provincial sport governing bodies. This contributed greatly to the subsequent development of sport bureaucracies in the public service of most provinces; in the case of the "have" provinces and Quebec, these were to grow to substantial proportions in the 1970s. Second, the commitment of the federal government to share the capital costs of sport facilities for the

Quebec Games and for subsequent winter and summer games, assured that provinces and municipalities became financially involved in the provision of sport facilities for elite sport. At the same time, there was a growing propensity for the federal government to commit itself to support bids to host international sport events in Canada. These developments represented a substantial commitment of taxpayers' dollars to building elaborate sport facilities. These facilities, in many cases, were to become financial liabilities for municipal and provincial governments and often were not well suited to use by many sport participants. This issue receives further attention in chapter 10.

SCHOLARSHIP AND RESEARCH PROGRAMS

Two main avenues of funding were established for the support of higher education in the fields of physical education and recreation. Undergraduate scholarships and bursaries were provided by the federal/provincial agreements and administered by the provinces. Awards came out of the funds allocated to each province, and were restricted to Canadian universities. Graduate, post-doctoral, and special fellowships were funded and administered directly by the federal government because of the scarcity of post-graduate programs in these fields in Canadian universities (FASD Annual Report, 1963– 4:5).

Research in sport, physical fitness, and recreation was supported in two ways. Grants were made to individual university researchers after a review process conducted by a standing committee of the National Advisory Council. Although this program was intended to support a variety of projects, such as surveys of facilities, equipment evaluation, personnel evaluation, and methods of operation, its major focus proved to be centred on training for physical fitness and elite sport competition. The other main thrust of the program was the establishment of three research institutes, located at the University of Alberta, the University of Toronto, and the Université de Montréal respectively. Difficulties in getting these programs off the ground and controversy over the focus and value of the institutions meant that support for this project was not continued when the initial five-year agreement expired in 1969 (NAC Minutes of the 16th Meeting, 28 and 29 October 1967).

The scholarship, bursary, and research-assistance programs provided a stimulus that contributed substantially to the great growth of professional programs in physical education and recreation in

Canadian universities in the late 1960s and early 1970s (Broom & Baka 1978:25). Early recipients of the post-graduate bursaries and scholarships played prominent roles in the changes that have taken place in these burgeoning programs as they moved from a practical and professional to a scientific and academic orientation. The federal research-support program gave an additional impetus to this movement. The graduates of these new scientifically and academically oriented programs became the federal and provincial sport bureaucrats of the 1970s; they helped change the concept of sport from an emphasis on competition and struggle between individuals to focus on objective measures of performance and preoccupation with standards and records. This new emphasis fitted in nicely with an increasing propensity for government to use sport as an instrument in promoting its objects of national unity and pride and as a reflection of the accomplishments of the politicians and government.

TRANSFORMATION OF FEDERAL GOVERNMENT SPORT POLICY

Early efforts in federal government sport involvement were small and insignificant relative to other more important issues in Canada. But by 1968, conflicting views of the federal government's role in the promotion of sport and physical fitness had become crystallized. The marriage between mass programs and the development of elite athletes made in the original Act in 1961 was becoming increasingly hard to hold together. On the one hand, the federal government was having little success in promoting and developing mass fitness and sport programs. At the same time, provincial directors of recreation saw increased funding of their "grass roots" programs as being of highest priority. On the other hand, federal government efforts in the development of elite sport were not effective. Spurred on by the press and the Canadian public, sport governing bodies clamoured for more money to improve international performance.

At a broader level, the federal government was meeting more and more resistance to its efforts to influence and change the social and educational fabric of Canadian society through federal/provincial cost-sharing agreements. To add to these frustrations was the realization that the federal government was getting very little political mileage from these joint programs. National unity had become an issue that the federal government felt could be parlayed to its advantage. This theme might help offset the nationalism that had grown up in Quebec in the 1960s as well as the growing demand for more autonomy from the provinces. The national-unity theme tied in with a wave of economic nationalism that had sprung up in English-speaking Canada. The growing American domination of Canadian culture and commerce had sparked these sentiments.

In this environment, a "palace revolt" was staged by the National Advisory Council in 1968 that forced the federal government's hand in defining its role in sport. Because of its growing resentment at being relegated to the advisory role intended by the Act, the Advisory Council put forward an elaborate proposal that it become the policy-making and executive branch of the Fitness and Amateur Sport Program (NAC *Appendix 7 to the Minutes of the 19th Meeting*, 25 and 26 November 1968). (This episode is developed more fully in chapter 5.) Given the political climate and the mood of the federal government, this proposal was bound to be rejected. The federal government was in a position to take a more direct role in sport development. It now had a professional staff in place from which it could receive sound advice on policy matters. The government also perceived that the initial resistance to interference in amateur sport had been overcome. This perception was borne out by the fact that there was little support for the Advisory Council's proposal from the sport community at large. These specific factors coincided with the federal government's realization that sport could be an effective vehicle in attaining some of its political goals concerning unity and nationalism.

It may be that the minister considered abolishing the Advisory Council entirely in favour of a regular branch within his jurisdiction. This, however, would have required an amendment to the Fitness and Amateur Sport Act, and would have drawn public attention to the matter. It was easier to relegate the council to a purely advisory role and to the development of long-range plans. By this time the federal government also had come to the realization that the federal/provincial cost-sharing agreements were not accomplishing their goals of stimulating mass participation in sport and fitness programs. Other approaches would have to be developed. A structure whereby the Advisory Council could still be used as a sounding board for proposals initiated by the directorate staff appeared to suit the minister.

The Advisory Council's proposal to establish itself as an executive sport council was squelched by the minister without protest from the amateur sport community and without attracting debate from politicians or the public. The relegation of the council to its original role as an advisory body suited the objectives that the minister and the director wished to pursue; it remained to act as a sounding board for proposals developed by the directorate staff (FASD Files, PAC, RG29,

Vol. 1357, File 9). These developments receive more attention in chapter 5.

The programs and events coming out of the early years of the fitness and amateur sport legislation identified in this chapter helped to shape the future direction of government involvement in sport. The impotency of the federal/provincial fitness and sport cost-sharing agreements, the administrative and leadership inadequacies of sport governing bodies, a federal sport bureaucracy that had grown in size and competency, the dispute between the government and the National Advisory Council on Fitness and Amateur Sport over policy jurisdiction, and the success of the "Unity through Sport" theme of the first Canada Games in Quebec City all influenced the course of these new directions. These issues interacted with broader forces and events in Canada to cause the government to move to more direct involvement in elite sport.

CHAPTER FOUR

Forces that Shaped Government Sport Directions in the 1970s

A *Proposed Sports Policy for Canadians*, announced in 1970 by John Munro, minister of national health and welfare, was the most significant event in the history of federal government involvement in sport. It asserted for the first time that the federal government had a legitimate role in the pursuit of "excellence" in elite sport. This document also legitimatized what was already a fait accompli; the federal government had established a number of new organizations that allowed it to exert more direct influence on the development of elite athletes. But these initiatives did not occur within the context of sport itself. Our analysis in the previous chapter suggested that certain sport programs and events were important in determining the specific direction of new federal government sport initiatives in the 1970s. But larger social and political events occurred in the 1960s that pushed the federal government towards these new sport initiatives. Sport's affinity with television caused it to become an attractive commodity in post-war patterns of consumption. As such, it took on a new meaning and importance in Canadian society. As a result, sport became an instrument that could be used to counteract the prevailing divisive political program of the day – the national-unity crisis.

THE NATIONAL-UNITY CRISIS

Since Confederation there have always been tensions between the two levels of government in Canada. At some times the federal has been the dominant force, at others the provincial. The Second World War and the decade and a half that followed was a period in which the federal level dominated in a way it has neither before nor since. Not only had the war given enormous impetus to the industrialization of Canada, it had also given government new functions in managing the economy and ensuring the provision of essential services to all Canadians. The federal government had the dominant role and responsibility in these new program areas. The post-war Liberal government under Prime Minister William Lyon Mackenzie King was among the first in the world to adopt Keynesian fiscal and monetary policies to ensure continued economic growth. The successes of these policies were reinforced by the development of a web of welfare programs, including universal hospital insurance, old-age pension, and unemployment insurance, which attempted to ensure standards of equity across Canada. The Liberal government also strongly supported business in an effort to build a national, and advanced, economy.

Despite this growth of the importance and power of the federal level, provincial governments still retained constitutional responsibilities for education, culture, natural resources, health and welfare, and many other fields. These were growing centres of government activity as the peacetime state evolved. Some of the tension between the two levels in Canada has arisen simply because the dividing line between federal and provincial responsibilities is inevitably blurred and overlapping. The various governments claim as much authority as possible and use the other level as the scapegoat for failures and problems. But these inevitable complications of a federal state have been exacerbated in Canada by regional cultural diversity in this huge country, which is dispersed and spread out across half a continent. In particular, the French fact – and the uniqueness of Quebec – are realities with which every political generation must come to terms in one way or another.

The halcyon days of a powerful central federal government began to wane in the late 1950s and early 1960s. The economic prosperity and growth that had been experienced in the Western industrialized nations after World War II came to an end in the late 1950s. The impact of the ensuing increase in unemployment in Canada was magnified by regional disparities and placed a severe strain on Canadian federalism. The inability of the Diefenbaker government to develop coherent policies to solve the economic issues and its ineptitude in many aspects of public policy, including federal/provincial relations, contributed substantially to the declining influence of the federal government (Smiley 1967:50).

The portion of total public expenditures made by the provincial and local governments began to expand. The provinces recruited greater numbers of public servants; these new and competent administrators were less inclined to acquiesce to federal government dominance in matters of major importance. These factors all contributed to a growing tension between the federal and provincial governments and gave rise to a demand for a more formalized approach to federal/provincial negotiations.

This demand led to a breakdown of the horizontal relations that had existed during the post-war period between ministers or officials with similar interests at both levels of government (Simeon 1972:37). The relationship was replaced by a form of "executive federalism," whereby negotiations were carried out between both elected and appointed officials from the two levels of government. The advent of executive federalism and the attenuation of federal dominance meant that the machinery for intergovernment collaboration was increasingly institutionalized at senior political levels. Federal/provincial relations became much more important to all levels of government and, consequently, a vast and complex network of federal/provincial organizations was established to deal with more specific matters (Smiley 1972:56–60).

The force that caused the greatest changes in federal/provincial relations, however, was the Quiet Revolution in Quebec. In the late 1950s, this large and predominantly French-speaking province began a process of rapid social, political, and economic change that is still under way. This force has transformed Quebec and also transformed Canadian politics. The repressive and reactionary regime of the Union Nationale under Maurice Duplessis began to dissolve with his death in 1958. A new, well-educated and ambitious French-Canadian elite began to demand a greater role for itself, particularly in the Quebec civil service, which was the one major power structure controlled by French Canadians. At the same time, this elite pushed for greater participation by francophones, and greater use of the French language, not only within Quebec, but also in Canada as a whole. The Jean Lesage Liberal government, elected in 1960, began to modernize the economy and government. Language and culture were asserted by the new Quebec elite. Confrontation began with the dominant English-speaking minority that controlled finance and business in Quebec, and with the English-speaking majority, which dominated all aspects of Canadian political and national life. Smiley maintains that "the rise of nationalist interventionism in Quebec after the death of Duplessis has contributed more to changes in Canadian federalism than any other single factor" (Smiley 1967:54).

Under Lesage, French-speaking Quebec began to move from a traditional to a modern society. These sweeping changes created heavy demands on the federal government for greater provincial autonomy. These demands, for the most part, were met, and during the Pearson administration in the mid 1960s, there was extensive decentralization to the provinces (Smiley 1972:149–50). There were also demands for more formalized procedures for intergovernment collaboration. This was the era of co-operative federalism. Nevertheless, these upheavals in federal/provincial relations and the Quiet Revolution caused severe strains on the federal system in the 1960s. The legitimacy and authority of the federal government were questioned. The provinces became more powerful. The Quiet Revolution became, in part, a much less quiet demand for Quebec separation. Concern grew that many important but piecemeal changes in federal/provincial relations had been made without adequate consideration of their cumulative effect on the federal system (ibid., 42).

By the time the Lesage government left office in 1966, Quebec had attained considerable elements of special status in the Canadian federal system. Initial sympathy and support that had been expressed for Quebec gave way to scepticism as the possibility of separation was raised. Anglophone opposition to separatism was expressed through the Canadian Committee and other similar groups (Resnick 1977: 119–20). The Quebec general election of 1966 again brought to power the Union Nationale, which was committed to reform of the Constitution on bi-national lines; it shifted the focus of conflict between Quebec and Ottawa from specific demands for provincial autonomy to broader and more symbolic matters of constitutional reform and the role of the province in international affairs. This mutual isolation of Ottawa and Quebec posed further challenges to national unity.

Anglophone nationalism – sparked by the growing threat of separatism – was fanned by another perceived threat to national unity, that is, the domination of the Canadian economy and culture by the United States. Economic growth in Canada in the 1950s had accelerated, facilitated by American direct investment in the Canadian economy (Cook 1971:47). By the middle 1950s, American control of Canadian industry approached the 50 percent level, and doubts were expressed as to whether Canadians still held the reins of their own economy (Bliss 1966:370). Although most Canadians accepted the reality of some measure of this continentalism, there were different interpretations of just what degree of American investment control or ownership was desirable; concern was more strongly articulated in specific areas such as culture (Resnick 1977:43). The 1957 Walter Gordon Report on economic prospects clearly described the dominance of Canadian economy, industry, and commerce by the United States and made suggestions for increased Canadian influence in the use and development of her resources. These warnings were largely ignored, and by the mid 1960s, there had been no significant reduction in the growth of American control (Bliss 1966: 370). George Grant articulated the concerns of many Canadians in 1965, in *Lament for a Nation*. Canada had developed into a northern extension of the continental economy. Grant described the Canadian role as that of "a branch-plant of American capitalism" and he maintained that the ruling class looked across the border for its final authority in both politics and culture (Grant 1965:8–9).

The national crisis debates of the mid 1960s caused the federal government to adopt a firmer stance on federal/provincial relations (Simeon 1972:209–10). But it was not until the landslide Liberal victory in 1968, which Prime Minister Trudeau won on a strongly federalist platform, and which resulted in French-Canadian representation at the highest policy-making levels (ibid.,211), that this resolve could be translated into action. Trudeau's views of federalism were based on a belief in a Canada united under a strong federal government. He was not sympathetic to French-Canadian or any other kind of nationalism. Special status for Quebec was unacceptable, but federal authorities must respect provincial jurisdictions. Most important, Trudeau saw liberal and nationalist values to be diametrically opposed; strong nationalistic views were not compatible with Canadian federalism.

Trudeau took a much more aggressive strategy in reasserting federal identity than had Pearson, and accepted a personal mandate to undertake a major restructuring of the central decision making in government (French 1980:20). This restructuring was to include a formalization of the system of standing committees of Cabinet, an encouragement of consultation or collegiality among ministers, a reassertion of the political responsibility of ministers relative to the bureaucracy, and an emphasis upon rational decision making and planning in policy formulation. Central to the organizational structure of Trudeau's Cabinet committees was the Priorities and Planning Committee. It was to set the direction of government policy by choosing priorities, initiating major policy reviews, assigning certain responsibilities to other Cabinet committees, and considering the most pressing and politically important issues. Trudeau's reforms stemmed partly from his determination to avoid the government-by-crisis pattern that had characterized the Diefenbaker and Pearson administrations. They also reflected pressures for increased planning exerted on all Western governments by the arrival of the pervasive state, and by an explosion of activity in the social sciences. Trudeau was intellectually and culturally sympathetic to the rationalism of the planning movement, and its formality helped him compensate for the lack of an extensive network of personal acquaintances and breadth of experience on which Lester Pearson had relied (ibid.,20–1).

Prime Minister Trudeau, who at least as much as Jean Lesage or René Lévesque, was a member of the new French-Canadian elite, differed from many of these contemporaries in his strong belief in a united Canada and the importance of Quebec's membership in the federal state. Many other influential French Canadians, including Gérard Pelletier, who had been editor of a leading newspaper, *Le Devoir*, and Jean Marchand, a labour leader, joined him in his efforts to assure a greater place for francophones at the national level, and to counteract the threat of Quebec separatism.

The efforts of the Trudeau government to ensure that Canada survived and became a more truly bilingual nation demanded a greater role for French Canadians in the federal government. The Official Languages Act, which was passed in 1969, began a process of changing the federal public service from an almost exclusively English-speaking organization to a bilingual one. French Canadians were recruited to both politics and administration. A Department of Regional Economic Expansion was established to give the federal government a presence in support of business and industry. Under the leadership of Jean Marchand, it spent large sums in efforts to equalize economic opportunities across Canada. The national parks system was expanded. One notable addition was Forillon, the first national park in Quebec. More active and dynamic policy making, a stronger role for the federal government, bilingualism and bicul-turalism as national goals and as the practice in national institutions and the federal government were all parts of the changes introduced by the Trudeau government. Trudeau also resisted demands from the provinces for greater power and autonomy. Federal/provincial relations became less co-operative and more confrontational. In particular, Trudeau was hostile to special status for Quebec.

Another area that Trudeau turned to in his national unity efforts was culture. His new government helped to expand the arts, broad-casting, television programming, book and magazine publishing, movie production, and the recording industry in Canada. Sport found its place in these thrusts towards a stronger federal presence and greater national unity. This is the focus of the final section in this chapter.

SPORT TRANSFORMATION

The political issues in Canada in the 1960s that together constituted the national unity crisis and helped shape the direction of federal government sport policy in the 1970s cannot, in themselves, account for the change in direction in this sport policy. Sport itself had undergone changes in order for Prime Minister Trudeau to mention it in the context of culture and national unity and to state that the federal government had to do more for sport.

Central to this transformation was the powerful and unique affinity between television and sport. It has been aptly described: "On a continuing basis, with the added advantage of its escapist values, there was nothing better suited to television than sport. Football, because it was an action game, an acting out of war, with form – violent, competitive, full of strategy, marked with surprise, was the consummate television show" (Brown 1971:303). Improved television technology enhanced this relationship even more. "Slow motion" and "instant replay" were ideally suited to sport broadcasting; by 1964, the instant replay had become standard fare, particularly in football. One camera showed an overview of the live action while other cameras focused on individual key players in close-up. All were linked to videotape machines with the result that within seconds, key aspects of the developed play could be shown in close-up and in slow motion. Barnouw describes this process as resulting in "incredible transformations: brutal collisions become ballets and end runs and forward passes become miracles of human coordination" (Barnouw 1975:347).

The inauguration of TV in the early 1950s coincided with a period when both the disposable income and leisure time of most Canadians was increasing. Television was both part of, and contributed to, an expanding post-war consumer society. By 1962, 89 percent of Canadian households had television sets. The number of television stations in Canada had grown from two in 1953 to sixty-one a decade later (Shea 1980:31, 110). In addition, the vast majority of Canadians lived close enough to the United States border to have access to American channels. By 1972, it was estimated that Canadians spent an average of four hours a day watching television, and that up to two-thirds of this time was devoted to American programs (Green 1972:43).

Because sport made up a significant part of television programming, it was brought into the living rooms of millions of Canadians, many of whom had very little previous exposure or knowledge of competitive sport. By 1961–2, a comprehensive 52-week package of television sport programs was carried over both English and French networks in the series "World of Sports," which covered Canadian international sporting events. Representative sport programming had increased from six to sixteen features: some of the new additions were Wimbledon Tennis, Pro-Am Golf, and Inter-Collegiate Football (CBC *Annual Report*, 1961–2:34, 41). In the 52 weeks from 15 October 1961 to 15 October 1962, the total number of hours of sport broadcasts carried on the English and French radio and television networks of the CBC was approximately 814 hours. Of this total, 333 hours were devoted to American sport and 481 hours to Canadian sport events. The appeal of hockey to Canadian audiences was reflected in the fact that CBC devoted 252 of these hours to hockey coverage (HC *Debates*, 21 January 1963:2919). The 1964 Olympics in Japan were given exclusive daily coverage by CBC. In addition to satellite pictures, videotapes of the athletic events were flown by jet airliner for telecast the day following each event. By 1964, the estimated programming time devoted to sports was 12 percent for the English CBC network and 6 percent for the French CBC network (CBC *Annual Report*, 1964–5:36, 38). The advent of colour television in 1966–7 enhanced even further sport broadcasts, most notably hockey and outdoor events. New sport programming included the Canadian Winter Games ceremonies, Scotch Cup curling, and the Clay-Folley fight.

Given the strong attraction that hockey held for Canadians, it is not surprising that National Hockey League (NHL) play was the dominant sport aired in Canada in the 1960s. In the mid 1960s, the Nielsen TV ratings consistently showed that the Saturday night hockey telecasts were the most popular programs in Canada (HC *Debates*, 28 June 1965:2915). The CBC 1969–70 *Annual Report* cited the coverage of NHL hockey games as the most popular Canadian television show. In 1969, 6.2 million Canadians watched the Stanley Cup finals between Boston and Montreal (CBC *Annual Report* 1970–1). Kidd and Macfarlane, writing about the centrality of hockey in the lives of Canadians, claimed that more Canadians watched hockey than engaged in any other single public activity. "Hockey Night in Canada really *is* hockey night in Canada. We schedule our lives around it" (Kidd and Macfarlane 1972:8). During elections, Canadian political parties told their canvassers not to knock on doors during hockey games so as not to lose votes. At play-off time, Canadian churches held their services early to accommodate game times, and students evacuated university libraries, "even scholarly discipline having its limits" (ibid.). Sport pages confirmed the centrality of hockey. A survey of the *Edmonton Journal* in the early 1970s revealed that 46 percent of the sport pages were devoted to hockey (ibid., 157).

With the financial incentives provided by lucrative television contracts, sport became increasingly professionalized. Encouragement and enticements to young athletes to pursue sport as a career became much more prevalent, and sport became more an occupational category of work and less a leisure-time activity and pastime (Heinila 1973:353). Athletes became increasingly committed to organizations and to contractual relationships comparable to those in industry and commerce. Financial incentives, controls, and limits on athletes' actions and behaviour were features of these contractual relationships. Intensified training regimens and the increasing complexity of modern sport meant that practices and games came more to resemble work and less to resemble play (ibid., 353–4). This transformation applied not only to professional sport, but increasingly became part of what was known as amateur sport.

The strong ties between sport and television and the increasing professionalization of sport meant that sport not only became associated with commercial products, but also became a commodity itself, increasingly packaged for easy consumption (Gruneau 1983: 122). The sport "package" was shaped to be attractive to viewers to ensure its continued success and commercial backing. All forms of sport on television, whether professional or amateur, were motivated to adopt the logic of "professional presentation" and were viewed as legitimate entertainment rather than game forms.

The extent to which the modern Olympic Games became infused with commercial interests probably best exemplifies the impact of changes in sport in the 1960s and 1970s on government attitudes towards sport policies. As if to match step with professional sport, Olympic competitions became vast economic enterprises (Gruneau & Cantelon 1986). A sizable proportion of the funds that were poured into the Games came from the sale of television rights. Without the television dollars, the lavish Olympic spectaculars of recent years would have been only threadbare facsimiles (Johnson 1973:460).

The rapid escalation of broadcast revenues for televising the Olympic Games in the 1960s can be seen in the following statistics. In 1956, television corporations had refused to broadcast the Olympic Games, arguing that the rights should be free because the Games, as a news event, were a matter of public interest (Espy 1979:73). But for the 1960 Rome Olympics, the total television rights were sold for approximately $1.2 million. The CBS bought the United States rights for $550,000 (Snyder & Spreitzer 1978:151). In 1968, ABC paid $2 million for the competition at Grenoble (Johnson 1973:460). The television rights for the 1972 Munich Olympics cost ABC $13.5 million, and NBC $6.4 million (Snyder & Spreitzer 1978:151). Although not of direct relevance to our argument in this chapter, these figures continued to escalate rapidly. In 1976, the rights to the Summer Games at Montreal went to ABC for $25 million. The NBC paid $85 million for the rights to the 1980 Moscow Olympics (ibid.).

The United States television rights to the 1984 Summer Olympics in Los Angeles sold to ABC for $225 million. International rights garnered another approximate $80 million (Whannel 1984:33).

As the price of broadcasting rights to televise the Olympic Games increased to astronomical heights, so too did the expenditures of the host countries in staging the Games. As hosts for the 1964 Olympics, Japan was reported to have spent more than $56 million for sport facilities, $16.8 million for operating expenses, and $280 million on new roads. In Mexico in 1968, $153.2 million was spent on installation, organization, and administration of the Olympic Games (Miller & Russell 1971:156). The estimated cost of the 1972 Munich Olympics started off at $150 million. By the time it was over, the most conservative estimate of total cost was $600 million. When calculated on a per-Olympic-minute basis, the Germans ended up having to pay almost $30,000 a minute for the privilege of hosting the two-week spectacle (McMurtry 1976:53).

It was clear by the completion of the 1968 Winter Games in Grenoble that commercialization and professionalism had firmly established themselves as permanent features of the Olympic movement. There were two aspects of this commercialization of the Olympics: first, the money made "around" the Games (i.e., commercial sponsors, television rights, advertising, facilities, and tourism); and second, the money paid directly to athletes for testing and promoting certain brands of sports equipment. At Grenoble, with the backing of the French government, the organizing committee took as one of its prime tasks the promotion of regional development, based on tourism and winter sports in the Alps. The French government, representing the huge interests tied up in the winter-sport industry – including hotel trade, sports equipment manufacturers, ski instructors, ski lift firms, etc. – was aiming to capture a large part of the world ski tourist market. In explaining his intentions, French Prime Minister Pompidou said that the Games provided a unique opportunity to develop facilities and give unprecedented publicity to the resorts. This factor, as much as the Games themselves, was what justified the exceptional financial effort (Brohm 1978:123).

The struggle among ski-equipment manufacturers for domination of the winter-sport market was the second commercial feature at Grenoble. The ski manufacturers hoped to use the staging of the Olympics as a springboard to a lion's share of the ski market. The manufacturers exploited the commercial and advertising possibilities opened up by Jean-Claude Killy's spectacular success in international downhill skiing. Killy was an ideal model for the selling of goods. Another reflection of the sharp competition among the manufacturers was the matter of the wearing of brand names by competitors. In return for buying exclusive rights to supply equipment to well-known competitors, the ski manufacturers hoped to profit from the publicity given to the sport. Ski champions were progressively turned into sandwich-board men – the accredited representatives of brands of skis or socks – turning sport contests into confrontations among manufacturers fighting each other for domination of the market (ibid., 123–4).

Nancy Greene, who won a skiing gold medal for Canada at Grenoble, pointed out that with this kind of money at stake, it was necessary to appeal to a gigantic audience to pay for it all. In her autobiography, she stated that "the result inevitably is that the Olympic Games descend to the level of spectacle and begin to resemble some kind of circus" (Hoch 1976:44). We raise the issue of earnings in the 1980s of such star Canadian "amateur" athletes as skier Steve Podborski in another context in chapter 8.

During the 71st session of the International Olympic Committee, the president, Avery Brundage, declared that he was determined to prevent athletes who blatantly represented sport manufacturers from taking part. If this rule had been applied at Grenoble, 90 percent of the athletes would have been disqualified (Brohm 1978: 126).

The organization of the 1972 Sapporo Winter Olympics was another demonstration of the increasing contradiction between official Olympic ideology concerning amateurism and the reality of the struggle among the winter-sport manufacturers. Despite numerous declarations of intent on amateurism, it was generally accepted that an amateur member of the French ski team, for example, earned an average of $40,000 a year. This sort of "shamateurism" showed that competing in the Olympics had become a profession (Brohm 1978:127).

We relate these dramatic changes in the nature of the Olympic Games not to raise the amateur/professional issue. Brundage's concept of the amateur athlete has long since disappeared. Rather we focus on this commercialization and professionalization to point out why sport became so much more important to government and the private sector, as well as to the general public. These changes were central to the federal government's newly found interest in sport in the late 1960s.

SPORT AND NATIONAL UNITY

Of what relevance to our story are these discussions of the national-unity crisis and the transformation of sport that took place in the 1950s and 1960s? We return to our contention in the introduction to this chapter that these two seemingly unrelated developments combined to influence greatly the course of action that the federal government took in sport in the 1970s and 1980s. In 1968, Trudeau was searching for ways out of the crisis of unity and identity, and these issues were an important part of his campaign speeches. Trudeau's 1968 campaign promise that, if re-elected, he would establish a task force to investigate amateur sport in Canada, must be seen in this light. This promise was delivered in a campaign speech in Selkirk, British Columbia, in the context of remarks about the contribution of culture to national unity. Trudeau viewed sport as a part of Canadian culture and connected it with the theme of national unity, one with which he was preoccupied in that campaign.

Like every other important issue in Canadian politics, sport policy was affected by the context of federal/provincial relations. A focus on elite athletes was attractive to the federal government; it left room for a provincial role in mass recreation and sports participation. This could assuage the provincial hunger for a share of this appealing field, and the federal government was free to assert its pre-eminence in the areas that could generate support for national unity and identity. The logic of these arguments for rethinking and redirecting federal government sport policies found their justification and force in the changes that, at the time, were transforming sport itself.

The greatly increased prominence and importance of sport gave it a particular attractiveness as an instrument for achieving a symbolic goal like national unity. It did not cost government a great deal; it had mass audiences and citizen appeal and support; there was no serious opposition to it; and athletic achievement appeared to be independent of language, culture, or regional origin. Canada had not been successful in international sports. Particularly galling was the demise of the country's international hockey reputation and declining performances in other prestigious sport competitions. The dramatic changes that took place in the Olympics in the 1960s meant that international sport events received much greater attention and held much more importance to Canadians than previously. The development of elite athletes and success in international competition were an obvious and easy road to accolades for the federal government. Sport also appealed, though this was seldom mentioned, to intensely nationalistic and jingoistic emotions.

Some of the programs that the Trudeau government introduced in its national-unity campaign were outlined earlier in this chapter. It is easy to see the threads of national unity in the important sport documents that appeared in the late 1960s and early 1970s. The *Report of the Task Force on Sport for Canadians* decried "how scant the previous involvement of the government [has been] in encouraging the development of so potentially influential a psychological nation-builder [i.e., sport]" (Task Force 1969:13). The Task Force also referred to the Canada Games as an "excellent unifying force." The *Proposed Sports Policy for Canadians*, which set the directions for government involvement in sport in the 1970s, contained a whole section on national unity. The federal government document *Sport Canada/Recreation Canada* referred to the Canada Games as "an exercise in Canadianism" (Munro 1971:3) and pointed to the potential of these Games for promoting co-operation among the provinces and between the respective provinces and the federal government.

CHAPTER FIVE

Federal Government Sport Policy, 1970

The new federal government sport policy was announced by John Munro, minister of national health and welfare, in March 1970 in a statement entitled, *A Proposed Sports Policy for Canadians*. A central part of this document was the confirmation of a number of specific steps that the federal government had already taken to improve elite sport performance in Canada. The most significant of these new measures was the establishment of new organizations that allowed the federal government to exert a more direct influence on elite athletes. These new initiatives emanated largely from the federal government *Report of the Task Force on Sports for Canadians*, which was tabled in the House of Commons in 1969. Part of the new 1970 sport policy statement was devoted to reasserting the federal government's commitment to mass sport and fitness programs. But unlike the elite sport initiatives, there were few concrete program commitments to accomplish these goals. These residual views for a focus on mass sport and fitness programs were championed by the National Advisory Council and reflected in the 1969 P.S. Ross Report, entitled *A Report on Physical Recreation, Fitness and Amateur Sport in Canada*. The P.S. Ross Report had been commissioned by the ministry at the request of the National Advisory Council because of the council's concern that the Task Force Report focused almost entirely on elite sport, and in particular, on hockey.

DEVELOPMENT OF THE NEW POLICY STATEMENT

The minister of national health and welfare, John Munro, described his new policy statement as the culmination of recommendations that had been made during the previous two years. In addition to the internal contribution of his ministry, credit for the policy statement was given to the Task Force Report, the P.S. Ross Report, the Montmorency Conference on Leisure, and the recommendations of the National Advisory Council (NAC *Minutes of the 23rd Meeting*, 20 March 1970). An evaluation of the impact of the first three of these often competing and conflicting inputs contributes to a better understanding of the role that the federal government was to play and the forms of its sport involvement. The influence of the National Advisory Council is examined in the third section of this chapter.

Central Agencies and Actors

The emphasis placed on priorities and planning and on a rational comprehensive approach to policy making by the Trudeau government played an important role in the approach taken by government in the late 1960s to the problems faced by sport. It is not coincidental that in 1968, Munro identified the prime needs of sport as being "priorities and planning" (Munro 1968:7). The establishment of the Task Force on Sport to come to grips with these problems was the first step in this rational comprehensive approach. The subsequent P.S. Ross Report provided a broader and more comprehensive study of sport, recreation, and physical fitness. Time was then taken to consider these studies and other recommendations before the *Proposed Sports Policy for Canadians* was finalized. In the words of Munro, this period of deliberation was essential "in order to ensure that we had a good grasp of the overall direction in which we wanted to head. We also wanted to be able to move in a comprehensive and coordinated manner in order to ensure that we were effecting some fundamental change, rather than just another slap-assortment of temporary band-aid partial solutions" (Munro 1970:5). Although crude and miniscule in relation to the development of policy in other more important areas of federal government jurisdiction, policy making in sport was, for the first time, subjected to a rational, comprehensive approach.

Changes in personnel at the top echelons of sport decision making in the late 1960s were important in shaping the new sport initiatives. John Munro was appointed minister of national health and welfare in June 1968, shortly after Trudeau's promise of a task force on sport. Munro's appointment also coincided with Trudeau's attempts to reassert the political responsibility of ministers relative to the bureaucracy. According to Bill Hallett (1981:600), close associates of Munro felt that he had a much greater interest in sport than had his predecessors. Munro also seemed to realize the "publicity potential of this relatively small responsibility in his huge portfolio" (Hallett 1981:599).

The increased responsibility assigned to Cabinet ministers, and the vehicle that the Task Force provided for political action, gave John Munro substantially more scope for personal intervention into sport policy than had previously been the case. These factors combined with his personality and interest in sport to elevate the position and importance of sport within the Department of National Health and Welfare.

Coincidentally, Lou Lefaive was appointed as director of the Fitness and Amateur Sport Directorate in 1968. Lefaive was a public-service bureaucrat with considerable technical experience and expertise, but was not professionally trained in physical education or recreation. At the same time, John Macdonald, the director general of special programs, who had previously acted at times as a block between the director and the minister, was transferred from the Department of National Health and Welfare to a position at the United Nations (Hallett 1981:590). Lefaive was able to establish a close working and social relationship with John Munro; this provided the directorate with much more face-to-face contact with the minister than had been the case previously (ibid., 599). As a result, Lefaive had considerable scope and capacity to influence the direction of federal government sport policy. His own personal philosophy of sport, which is discussed later, helped to shape the new directions that the federal government was to take.

Task Force Report

It will be recalled that Trudeau had promised, during the election campaign of 1968, to investigate amateur sport in Canada. His promise had been made in the context of remarks about the contribution of culture to national unity, and he placed sport, as well, in this context: "There are a certain number of symptoms which worry me – the fact that hockey is our national sport and yet in the world championship we have not been able, as amateurs, to perform as well as we know we can" (cited in Broom & Baka 1978:27). He was also concerned that Canadian cities, particularly Vancouver, were having difficulty in obtaining National Hockey League franchises.

Trudeau won a majority in 1968, the first prime minister to do so in the four elections of the decade, and flush with enthusiasm, his new government set about making reforms and implementing campaign promises. A task force to investigate amateur sport in Canada was created in August of 1968. The Task Force included Harold Rea, a

Toronto business consultant, as chairman; Dr Paul Wintle Des Ruisseaux, a sports-medicine specialist from Quebec City who had served on the National Advisory Council; and Nancy Greene, a world championship skier and national sport hero. Christopher Lang, a banker, was appointed as the director of administration for the Task Force. Political considerations were paramount in making these appointments. The fact that none of the members possessed any background or knowledge about the total field of amateur sport, recreation, and physical education was a factor that certainly limited the scope and breadth of the Task Force Report. The mandate given to the Task Force was quite general:

1 to report on prevailing concepts and definitions of both amateur and professional sport in Canada and the effect of professional sport on amateur sport;
2 to assess the role of the federal government in relation to non-governmental, national and international organizations and agencies in promoting and developing Canadian participation in sport; and
3 to explore ways in which the Government could improve further, the extent and quality of Canadian participation in both sport at home and abroad.

(Task Force 1969:Preface)

The concern about hockey and success in international sport has already been noted. But there were other factors that made a comprehensive review desirable. The federal Fitness and Amateur Sport Program had reached a plateau after seven years of operation. The need for facilities at the local level and problems relating to the administration of amateur sport in Canada were increasingly obvious. The Fitness and Amateur Sport Directorate itself felt that the federal government should re-evaluate its role in amateur sport (FASD *Annual Report*, 1968–9:2). It is significant to note that the Task Force was commissioned to determine how (not if) the federal government should become more involved in sport in Canada (Helmes 1981: 213–4).

In fulfilling these terms, the members of the Task Force travelled throughout the country meeting with interested groups and individuals. They also received assistance from Douglas Maxwell Limited, a Toronto consulting firm, which prepared a questionnaire on the problems faced by Canadian sport (West 1973:6.5). This survey was sent to sport governing bodies, Olympic and Pan-American athletes, and people who were closely involved with competitive sport.

The final report of the Task Force was written by Christopher Lang, the director of administration for the Task Force, Douglas Fisher, a journalist and former MP (and an influential personal advisor to Munro), and Sydney Wise, a professor of history at Carleton University. The report was presented to Munro in February 1969, but not tabled in the House of Commons until May 1969 (West 1973:6.5). Some have attributed the recommendations in the Task Force Report largely to Lefaive, Lang, Fisher, and Wise, but a close examination reveals that almost all had been made prior to 1969 (Hallett 1981:604–5).

Despite its mandate, and despite the more general concerns which had led to its creation, the Task Force devoted more than half its report to professional sport, particularly hockey. It reported that problems in hockey had serious international consequences: "Officials of the Department of External Affairs have assured us that this deterioration in the overall image of Canada abroad, and especially in Europe, because of our recent failures in hockey, is of much concern to them" (Task Force 1969:30). The Task Force worked in haste. Its report was submitted to Parliament in May 1969, and this short time frame meant that it could not perform or commission thorough original research in its areas of concern.

In its main focus, the Task Force fulfilled Trudeau's election promise to look into the control and effect of professional hockey on the lives of young Canadians. The report was extremely critical. It held up hockey as an example of how a professional sport organization could destroy the talent basis of an international sport. A second and related problem was the difficulty Vancouver was having obtaining a National Hockey League (NHL) franchise over its American rivals. The Task Force considered the Canadian Football League (CFL) to be a good model of professional/amateur relationships. The fact that the CFL was a uniquely Canadian league was lauded.

To resolve these problems, the Task Force recommended the establishment of Hockey Canada. This was to be a non-profit corporation with a mandate to manage and finance Canada's national hockey teams. This recommendation was actually pre-empted by the announcement of the formation of Hockey Canada eight days before the Task Force Report was submitted to the minister of national health and welfare, John Munro.

In the remainder of its report, the Task Force looked at more general issues. It concluded that the prime orientation of members of the National Advisory Council on Fitness and Amateur Sport was towards physical fitness and recreation. Because of the broad scope of its concerns, the council was not effective in other areas. The Task

Force recommended that its name be changed to "The National Advisory Council on Fitness and Recreation." A new, non-profit organization, to be called "Sport Canada" would provide the focus for the administrative support and growth of elite competitive sport.

The Task Force also suggested that the private and public sectors should work together in creating a sport structure extending from mass participation to national team athletes. There should be a high degree of co-operation among municipal, provincial, and federal agencies in the public sector; among club, provincial, and national organizations in the private sector; and finally, between the public and private sectors at each level.

Although it contained overstatements and omissions, the report can be excused in the light of its historical impact and forthrightness. What the Task Force did was to legitimate federal involvement in amateur sport. It asserted that there was no longer any reason to be embarrassed about promoting amateur sport. As a result, the focus of policy turned to special problems and structural weaknesses concerned with the development of amateur sport in Canada, and in particular with national and international athletics.

The government took action on many of the Task Force recommendations even before the report was made public, another indication that most of them had been in the wings for some time. Seven months after the report had been delivered to Munro, action had been taken on about 80 percent of the recommendations, and about half that number had been completed (West 1973:6.13–6.14).

The Task Force Report served to draw attention to many proposals that had lain dormant during the 1960s. It was used as the launching pad for many of the new federal government sport policy initiatives in the 1970s; most of these initiatives were taken before the official enunciation of new directions by Munro in 1970. In this way, it served to spark public awareness and interest and to attract extensive press coverage that went beyond the sport pages.

P.S. Ross Report

After the Task Force Report was made public, some individuals and organizations and, in particular, the National Advisory Council reacted adversely to its narrow focus on sport. Consequently, the chairman of the council, Phillipe de Gaspé Beaubien, requested that a broader, more encompassing study of sport, recreation, and physical fitness in Canadian society be undertaken (NAC Minutes of the 22nd Meeting, 17–18 December 1969).

The government responded by appointing the management consulting firm of P.S. Ross and Partners to carry out such a study. As the Task Force had just recently completed its report, P.S. Ross and Partners put most of its efforts into the study of fitness and recreation, focusing largely on recreation and the encouragement of physical activity as a constructive leisure-time activity (P.S. Ross & Partners 1969:iii). The official objectives of the study were twofold:

1 To describe and assess the total system and the population it serves in Canada today – to include as much information as could be assembled on organization, programs, facilities, population characteristics, attitudes, problems, gaps and needs.
2 To recommend a set of national objectives, the role of the Federal government and, more specifically, programs and organization for the Directorate of Fitness and Amateur Sport.

(P.S. Ross Report, cited by Hallett 1981:613)

The final report, entitled *A Report on Physical Recreation, Fitness and Amateur Sport in Canada*, was submitted to the minister in November 1969. The P.S. Ross Report was never tabled in the House of Commons, nor did it receive the publicity that the Task Force Report did. As Hallett notes (1981:614), it was considered an in-house, confidential report to the government.

The basic recommendations of the P.S. Ross Report were for increased federal government involvement in recreation. It made only one recommendation on fitness, a general statement that every Canadian should develop a level of fitness sufficient to contribute positively to physical and mental health. Reference to amateur sport was expressed by the support of two points from the Task Force Report: first, Canada should develop a level of performance in national and international competition that would contribute to national unity and international prestige; and second, the directorate should take initiative in organizing Sport Canada. The rest of the report – and national objectives, which were defined – dealt with the importance of recreation for Canadians and the need to provide adequate education, opportunities, and services to meet this need.

The report provided a good overview of the fitness, recreation, and amateur-sport system in Canada, but as Broom and Baka have argued (1978:28), it failed to come to grips with data that would verify the demand and use of this system by Canadians. It also failed to tackle the delicate matter of amateur versus professional sport in Canada (Anderson 1974:94). Despite these weaknesses, the influence of the P.S. Ross Report could be seen in the federal government's new 1970 sport policy statement and subsequently, on the fitness and amateur sport program and structure.

The basic P.S. Ross recommendation for increased federal government involvement in recreation was never acted upon. Recreation had for years been a touchy matter because of the issue of federal/ provincial jurisdiction, and it would continue to be a controversial area throughout the 1970s. The P.S. Ross Report was to languish for some time and then drop into obscurity.

Montmorency Conference on Leisure

During the time that the P.S. Ross Report was being completed, the Department of National Health and Welfare sponsored a five-day conference on leisure in Canada at Montmorency, Quebec. The aim of the conference was to provide an opportunity for participants from different disciplinary backgrounds and spheres of interest and experience to develop the framework for a philosophy of leisure that would be meaningful and relevant for Canadians (FASD *Proceedings of the Montmorency Conference on Leisure*, 1969:ix). The Fitness and Amateur Sport Directorate considered the conference to be very successful in motivating delegates to make a commitment to take action on the recommendations adopted (FASD *Annual Report*, 1969– 70:2–3). Similarities have been noted between the recommendations contained in the conference proceedings and some of those contained in Part 2 of the P.S. Ross Report (Hallett 1981:619).

Certain individuals and pressure groups also contributed to the final form of the *Proposed Sports Policy for Canadians*. In particular, a number of MPs at the time exerted pressure in the House of Commons for government action in the realm of fitness, recreation, and amateur sport. As noted in chapter 3, elements of the Fitness and Amateur Sport Program in the 1960s also influenced the new policy statement. These, along with the specific influence of the preceding central actors and groups on the new federal government sport policy, are analysed in the following section.

NEW SPORT POLICY

The government's synthesis of the above elements was presented to the House of Commons by John Munro in March 1970 as *A Proposed Sports Policy for Canadians*. The introduction to the white paper stated:

Our policy is about people – the greatest number of Canadians possible –

increasing their participation in sports and recreational activities, and improving the benefits they can enjoy from such participation. If, along the way, it also serves to upgrade the calibre of Canadian participation in the world sports arena – which we are completely confident it will – then we will be able to really take pride in ourselves for having achieved something that very few other nations have been able to develop – a successful yet well balanced total national sports program.

(Munro 1970:1)

This comment suggested that the focus was to be primarily on mass participation. But the programs proposed in the document were focused primarily on competitive, elite sport. Among the major suggested programs were administrative and financial support for national sport organizations; Canadian national competitions on an annual basis (between the Canada Games); the creation of a new sport Canada division within the directorate; a communications agency to work on publicity and promotion; and grants-in-aid to promising athletes. Only a few of the specific recommendations were directed towards the fitness and recreation elements.

The new policy statement iterated the reasons for greater government efforts in sport, fitness, and recreation. These were national unity; the quality of Canadian life, regardless of income or social position; the cultural significance of sport; and the need to place the pursuit of international excellence in proper perspective. The philosophy of the proposed policy was centred on three values attributed to physical activity: 1) improved physical fitness; 2) improved mental health; and 3) improved involvement in a range of societal issues. It expressed a strong concern for individual welfare and quality of life. John Munro stated that he wanted to increase the amount and forms of assistance to sport to develop programs that would encourage mass participation. The concept of a mutually reinforcing pyramid was espoused with a few elite athletes at the top and a broad base of participating people at the bottom (see West 1973:6.15–6.17).

The *Proposed Sports Policy for Canadians* established the basis for federal government involvement in sport in the 1970s. It was the source of the federal government's commitment towards direct administrative assistance to sport governing bodies and agencies (the Administrative Centre in Ottawa); the beginnings of in-house administrative reorganization (Sport Canada); increased subsidizations of travel grants for athletes and officials; and the formal creation of the Canada Games.

Like many government policy documents, the proposed sports

policy tried to please all people and to look in opposite directions at the same time. Elite and mass sport, it suggested, were uniform parts of an integrated structure. On this score, it had run contrary to the general emphasis of the Task Force Report. Elite sport, the new policy statement proposed, should not stand alone on its own. Phillipe de Gaspé Beaubien, chairman of the National Advisory Council, agreed with this notion. Sport could not be left alone to proceed in isolation. Somehow it had to play a role in recreation. Through the proposed integration, competitive sport could reap the benefits of a wider base, increased participation, quality athletes, and greater international success (NAC *Minutes of the 23rd Meeting*, 20 March 1970).

But there were also doubts. Des Ruisseaux, a member of the Task Force, put forth an opposing point of view. He recognized as distinct and separate the areas of fitness and recreation on the one hand, and international success in sport on the other. Excellence in sport was seen as the business of a small group, totally devoted to success in competition. Fitness and recreation, in contrast, were the business of municipal, provincial, and federal agencies, which already had structure and competence to act successfully in these arenas. Des Ruisseaux said that his group (the Task Force) was of the belief that any hope about getting professional sport, amateur sport, and recreational groups to work together towards participation of the masses for recreational purposes was futile indeed (ibid.).

There were others who supported an increased emphasis on elite athletes. Lou Lefaive, director of fitness and amateur sport at the time, felt that the Task Force Report brought about a change in attitude:

The Task Force identified very clearly that this kind of approach was not nearly as repugnant to sport people as some people on the Advisory Council and within the Directorate would have you believe when they kept saying that sport wouldn't let you do it. The Task Force helped to allay that fear – not only were they (the recommendations) acceptable to sport people, the sport people wanted it – it was an idea whose time had come. The Task Force was an expression of what was happening ... it was an evolution of knowledge and thinking ... the Task Force gave some direction and thinking and a time frame when things would happen which resulted in the *Proposed Sports Policy*.
(Lefaive 1977, cited by Hallett 1981:621–2)

Regardless of what happened to fitness and mass participation, the Proposed Sports Policy clearly signalled the government's intention to put more effort and resources into the improvement of Canadian performance in international competition and the development of elite athletes. Trudeau's musings on the campaign trail in 1968 were now bearing fruit in a substantial change in government policy that was to have great impact on sport in Canada.

CRITICAL ISSUES IN FEDERAL GOVERNMENT SPORT INVOLVEMENT

Two issues are central to any study of new federal government sport policy initiatives in the 1970s. The first is the question of the direction of federal government policies; the second is the matter of the role of the government in implementing these policies. It should be noted that although the direction of federal government sport policy initiatives was largely determined by the political environment and the changes in sport in Canada in the 1960s, certain groups and actors who held contrary views to the promotion of elite sport were able to influence the form in which the federal government's new initiatives evolved.

Scope and Direction

A number of conflicting views about the desirable scope and direction of federal government involvement crystallized during the formulation of the new sport initiatives in the late 1960s. One view advocated a narrow scope centred on competitive "excellence," where excellence is defined in terms of record setting and international success. Proponents of this view included the incumbent minister and the new director of the fitness and amateur sport directorate. John Munro's bias towards the prominence of excellence in sport in any new federal government sport initiatives has been alluded to already. In a speech delivered in November 1968, he stated that it was essential to build Canadian excellence in international amateur athletics in order to promote national unity, to give Canadians renewed national confidence, to boost Canadian international stature, to spark enthusiasm for the national sport program, and to inspire mass participation. For these reasons, he considered the promotion of excellence to be a worthy national objective. He added that "excellence must become a national goal in sport as well as in education, the arts, and all the other fields of human achievement ... and government has a moral duty to assist in the development of this excellence" (Munro 1968:6).

Lou Lefaive also became a champion of excellence and elite sport soon after he assumed his position as director of the Fitness and Amateur Sport Program. Hallett (1981:589–90) has argued that the philosophical and personality compatibility of Munro and Lefaive meant that the "elite" sport emphasis was pushed to the forefront of any discussion of new federal government sport initiatives in the directorate.

Given the composition of the Task Force and its preoccupation with sport and in particular hockey, it is not surprising that its recommendations centred primarily on elite sport concerns. The Task Force Report authors believed that sport warranted federal support through its own merit, and "should not be condemned to walk in the shadow of fitness as its retarded brother" (Task Force 1969:16). The Task Force served to legitimize involvement in sport for its own sake, maintaining that "Sport is too important, both objectively as a bringer of national benefits, and subjectively, in the minds of the Canadian people, to be smuggled into government politics as merely another phase of physical fitness" (Task Force 1969:47).

Certain shortcomings and inadequacies in the Fitness and Amateur Sport Program during the 1961–8 period (identified in chapter 3) also contributed towards this narrow focus on amateur sport. Most obvious in this regard was the federal government's impotence in developing mass sports and physical fitness programs. The federal/ provincial cost-sharing agreements had done little to foster such programs; the federal government announced that these cost-sharing agreements would be terminated in 1970. This removed any intervening mechanism that the federal government possessed for delivering fitness and recreation programs to the masses. In addition, barriers to further improvement in elite competition were identified during the 1961–8 period. The sport governing bodies, for the most part, did not have the organizational skills nor the leadership necessary for the development of elite athletes. It was evident that funds would have to be expended to hire professional full-time staff and to streamline administrative and organizational capacities. It also became apparent in these earlier years that sporadic and uncoordinated efforts to improve coaching were not effective. Poor levels of officiating in most sports and the almost complete lack of a sports-medicine component to Canadian amateur sport also presented obstacles to progress. It also was clear that elite Canadian athletes would need to spend a much greater percentage of their time in training and competing in top-level events if improvements in international performances were to be attained. In order to accomplish these ends, more and more people advocated financial support for elite athletes.

The instigation of the Canada Games in 1967 (see chapter 3) also contributed to the move towards more government involvement in elite sport. The provincial departments responsible for recreation and culture were forced to develop a sport arm in order to select athletes to compete in the Games. Furthermore, the commitment of the federal government to share the capital costs of sport facilities for the Games assured that provinces and municipalities became financially involved in the provision of sport facilities for elite competition.

Pressure for increased government involvement in support of elite athletes was exerted by certain MPs in the House of Commons during this period. In discussing the results of the 1968 Mexico Olympics, MP Forrestall said that "Many of us are disappointed that our athletes have not performed as well as might be hoped ... I wonder about the true depth of our participation as a nation in what led up to this tremendous event ... One of the reasons for our failure to do as well as we might have done is that as a nation we have neglected to do enough to help our athletes" (HC *Debates*, 18 October 1968:1554). This lack of success in the 1968 Olympics triggered criticism by other MPs that there had been insufficient funding of elite athletes by the federal government. These influences all served to reinforce the direction in which federal government involvement in sport was heading.

At the same time, there were residual pressures to broaden the scope of the program to encompass recreation, fitness, and sport for the masses. The P.S. Ross Report, discussed earlier, was one such force. The major impact of this report was that it helped to maintain a façade of a broad fitness and amateur sport orientation of the Fitness and Amateur Sport Program. Hallett (1981:616) contends that if the Task Force Report had been the only guide for the new program initiatives, then the organizational structure likely would have been narrowed to the elite competitive sport perspective that Lefaive preferred. As previously mentioned, another factor that had an influence on maintaining the broader scope of the program was the Montmorency Conference on Leisure.

In 1966, Cor Westland, a former YWCA director, was hired by the directorate to act as a recreation consultant. Prior to his appointment, the recreation field had been left to the provinces and municipalities. He was influential in convincing the directorate to sponsor a symposium on leisure in Montreal in June 1967. This conference aided in developing a leisure philosophy for government. The National Advisory Council also played a role in maintaining a broader scope for the program and in developing a rationale for the inclusion of recreation. After receiving the P.S. Ross Report, the National Advisory Council in 1969 urged that Sport Canada should concern itself not only with the achievement of excellence in sport, but also with the development of mass participation in sport at the recreational level (NAC *Minutes of the 22nd Meeting*, 17–18 December 1969).

During the 1960s, concern surfaced again in the House of Commons debates about opportunities for physical activity at the grass-roots level. Members of Parliament lamented the shortage of facilities and adequate coaching for such participation (HC *Debates*, 13 May 1964:3209). A group of supporters of fitness advocated more federal government involvement in promoting the fitness of Canadians. Individuals such as Lloyd Percival continued to preach the benefits of physical fitness for the health of everyone in society.

These residual pressures caused John Munro to ask the Advisory Council to advise him on a reorientation of the directorate program towards placing greater stress on physical recreation. He wanted the council's input on developing a particular theme that would enhance efforts to motivate and spark positive attitudes of Canadians towards sport and physical activity. Munro also asked for advice on what the federal government could do, within its constitutional mandate, to set the scene for recreation in Canada (NAC *Minutes of the 22nd Meeting*, 17–18 December 1969). The author of the *Proposed Sports Policy for Canadians*, Tony Pearson, who was a special assistant to John Munro, was particularly sensitive to these pressures for a broadened mandate and personally sought to give special emphasis to mass participation in physical activity (West 1973:6.20).

In coming to grips with these competing and conflicting viewpoints concerning the desirable scope and direction of federal government involvement, the *Proposed Sports Policy for Canadians* accommodated all viewpoints by advocating federal government involvement that extended from promotion of mass participation at the grass-roots level to the development of competitive excellence of elite athletes. On this continuum of involvement, emphasis was placed on promoting mass participation at the grass-roots level. The Fitness and Amateur Sport Directorate, in its Annual Report for that year, summarized this stance by stating that the policy was based essentially on two major aims:

1 to effectively involve the greatest possible number of Canadians in sport and recreation activities.
2 to upgrade the calibre of Canadian participation in international sports events.
                              (FASD *Annual Report*, 1969–70:3).

Munro stated, "Our purpose is people. We view sports and recreation as one means – and potentially, a crucial means – of helping Canadians get more out of life" (Munro 1970:7). In conclusion, Munro stated that "We have advocated the purpose and objective of mass participation and the inculcation of sports and recreation into the Canadian mass culture, toward the goal of improving the overall calibre of Canadian society and maximizing the personal potential of Canadians for a happier existence." Munro believed that fostering the objective of mass participation would in turn benefit the pursuit of Canadian excellence in international sports. The reason that stress was placed on the social benefits of sports and recreation was the belief that "Canadian sports bodies have tended to pay lip service to both goals, but in practice have devoted the lion's share of their talents and energies to the pursuit of excellence" (ibid., 22–3). While the new policy aimed primarily at reinforcing and increasing the administrative strength of Canadian sport, it sought to "change the focus of that administrative effort – chiefly by putting the pursuit of international excellence in its proper perspective – as a consequence and not as a goal of mass participation" (ibid., 23).

There are a number of significant points about this policy statement. The first is that while the Task Force had suggested that the government should be willing to support sport for its own sake, the Proposed Sports Policy considered sport to be a segment of recreation in its widest sense (Hallett 1981:623). At the National Advisory Council meeting at which Munro explained his policy statement, the minutes of the meeting stated that "the chairman reiterated the assumption that sport cannot be left alone to proceed in isolation. Somehow sport had to play a role in recreation" (NAC Minutes of the 23rd Meeting, 20 March 1970). This suggests that the residual views supporting mass participation had modified Munro's views and that it was clear in his mind that the time was not yet ripe for a clear commitment to support elite sport on its own merit. It was still necessary to tie such initiatives to mass sport and recreation rhetoric. It was significant, however, that the "pursuit of excellence" was adopted for the first time as part of stated federal government policy.

Given this ambivalence, the policy statement itself was bound to contain discrepancies and contradictions. The philosophical content placed a higher priority on mass participation than on competitive excellence; the program recommendations, however, leaned largely towards developing competitive excellence.

This emphasis on "elite" sport was obvious in Helmes's content analysis of the Task Force Report, the *Proposed Sports Policy for Canadians*, and other Canadian sport policy and media documents. Despite the rhetoric in the Proposed Sports Policy, Helmes found that over 28 percent of the coded entries in his analysis of these documents emphasized the significance of "skill" and "victory," while only 2 percent of the coded entries emphasized recreational "participation" (Helmes 1981:215).

Given the momentum generated by the introduction of the elite sport initiatives, which had already been implemented before the new sport policy statement, the chances of success of a policy stressing the promotion of mass participation but containing little in the way of program initiatives was jeopardized. Finally, the rhetoric supporting mass participation ran contrary to the political and social pressures discussed earlier that were sweeping the government in the opposite direction.

Role of the Federal Government

Conflicting views and suggestions about the desirable scope and direction of federal government sport involvement led naturally to a debate about the appropriate role that the federal government should play. On the one hand were advocates of an indirect supportive role; on the other were those who pressed for a direct, forceful role.

The major advocates of the indirect approach were members of the National Advisory Council. In 1968, just before Trudeau's announcement of the formation of the Task Force, the National Advisory Council had presented a report to the minister entitled *A Look at the Future in Fitness and Amateur Sport*. This report recommended that the Advisory Council become the policy-making and executive branch of the Fitness and Amateur Sport Program. Under this plan, there was to be a full-time executive from the council, consisting of a chairman and two vice-chairmen for terms of seven years each; the directorate was to be removed from the public service and established as the administrative and technical/professional arm of the council. The Advisory Council actually thought that a program to promote fitness and amateur sport would be most effective along the model of the quasi-independent Canada Council, but saw that the proposal was politically unpalatable. The Advisory Council put forward a compromise structure whereby an executive committee would direct and administer the program based on policies recommended by council and approved by the minister (NAC *Appendix 7 to the Minutes of the 19th Meeting*, 25–6 November 1968).

Neither Lefaive nor Munro supported this proposal. Lefaive believed that the directorate should be playing a more important role in policy making. He said: "When I arrived on the scene the National Advisory Council was the most influential body in existence in sport. The Fitness and Amateur Sport Directorate viewed itself and indeed was almost exclusively a secretariat for the Council. The Directorate was a reactionary group. It was not a decision-maker ... That was an insane position for the government to take. I would have resigned had the Directorate continued to act as a secretariat to the Council" (Lefaive as cited by Hallett 1981:514). Lefaive pressed for the relegation of the National Advisory Council to a purely advisory role, and a more assertive role for the directorate in the program. A strong and influential Advisory Council was seen by both Munro and Lefaive as being antithetical to such a development. In their eyes, the council was dominated by professional physical educators, whose home base was the university and whose bias was towards the development of mass sport and fitness programs.

The Task Force Report supported Munro's and Lefaive's desires to terminate the executive functions of the National Advisory Council. It recommended that the proper role of the council, as iterated in the Fitness and Amateur Sport Act, was advisory. The Task Force Report perceived that the council was unable to discharge its responsibilities with equal effectiveness in all areas because of the broad scope of concerns and limited meeting times. Thus, as noted earlier, the report recommended that the scope and title of the council be changed to "The National Advisory Council on Fitness and Recreation" (Task Force 1969:43–4, 48). This could either be interpreted as reducing the council's involvement in sport or as increasing the scope of its involvement by including recreation, which encompassed sport. The P.S. Ross Report concurred with the Task Force's assessment, and recommended that the National Advisory Council be disbanded and replaced by a Fitness and Recreation Council (P.S. Ross & Partners, Part II, 1969:132–5, cited by Anderson 1974:44–5).

Munro and Lefaive used the Task Force recommendations to relegate the National Advisory Council to its advisory role, one they viewed as subservient to the directorate (Hallett 1981:592). Because the council's recommendations to Munro had failed, William L'Heureux had little choice but to step aside as chairman. His successor, Phillipe de Gaspé Beaubien, acquiesced to the new advisory role of the council. The conflict over the relative roles of the National Advisory Council and the directorate therefore was resolved before the *Proposed Sports Policy for Canadians* was completed.

The Task Force, in recommending that immediate responsibility for policy formulation should rest with the Directorate of Fitness and Amateur Sport, saw staff shortages as a major obstacle to fulfilling this role. It was suggested that the directorate needed a corps of accomplished and qualified athletes and coaches to advise and guide the national sport associations, and to act as resource persons to sport groups across the country.

The Task Force also saw the need to elevate sport in the public

service hierarchy to a point commensurate with the national importance of physical fitness, recreation, and amateur sports (Task Force
1969:43, 45). It was recommended that the position of a director
general of sport be created within the Department of National Health
and Welfare. This director general would be given the responsibility
of making all recommendations concerning grants to the deputy
minister, and would be provided with increased funds to permit an
expansion of the professional staff of the directorate (Task Force
1969:48). Upon reviewing these recommendations of the Task Force,
the National Advisory Council agreed that the increased responsibilities of the directorate warranted expansion of the staff. However, the
council advised the minister that the reference to a director general of
sport should be omitted (NAC *Minutes of the 20th Meeting*, 20–22 June
1969).

There were other factors that supported a more prominent role for
the directorate. The P.S. Ross Report recommended that the
directorate be given the major responsibility of providing leadership
in the field of recreation and that the Fitness and Amateur Sport Act
be amended to this end. This report also suggested that the
directorate be elevated to the assistant deputy-minister level.

Developments within the directorate also helped the federal
government to move towards a more direct role vis-à-vis sport. The
experience and expertise of the directorate staff grew during the
1960s. Its increased involvement in the sport activities associated with
Canada's Centennial celebrations, and increased responsibilities
related to the rapid growth of grants to sport governing bodies,
meant that more and more the directorate became the repository of
the facts and knowledge that were necessary to make decisions about
policy matters. The directorate staff grew to resent the policy-making
role that the National Advisory Council had assumed, and became
anxious to advise the minister in policy and program matters. The
production of the new breed of sport scientists through the post-
graduate bursaries and scholarships programs also contributed to
this maturity of directorate staff. The public service gradually
recruited these persons, who in turn, wished to play a more
prominent role in the program.

Government fear of criticism about interfering with the autonomy
of sport organizations was not realized during the 1961–8 period. On
the contrary, demands for federal support in the form of submissions
for financial assistance escalated. As a consequence, the inhibitions
that the federal government had about accusations of unwarranted
interference had abated. The introduction of administrative grants in
1966 to sport governing bodies and allied agencies served as a clear

sign of this changing relationship. Initially, the government had hesitated to give administrative grants because it did not want to be in a position where it would be seen to be controlling amateur sport. Lefaive also has suggested that the absence of protests to the Task Force recommendations helped allay fears that this kind of federal involvement was repugnant to people connected with elite sport (Hallett 1981:621).

The federal government realized that expectations for improvement of Canadians at the international sport level had not been met during the 1961–8 period. In hockey, for example, there was a further deterioration in Canada's standing in international competitions. Efforts by the National Advisory Council and the directorate to rectify this were ineffective in the face of the Canadian Amateur Hockey Association, the National Hockey League, and the complexities of amateurism and professionalism in international hockey. It was obvious that the federal government would have to adopt a much more aggressive stance if it was to play a role in regaining Canada's former world hockey prominence.

The political setting in Canada also pointed toward a more direct role for the federal government. It was in the process of reasserting its identity vis-à-vis the provincial governments. It was a general goal of the federal government at this time to detach itself from program areas that fell within the jurisdiction of provincial authorities, and to place emphasis on national programs, rather than on programs dealing with individuals, municipalities, and provinces. The termination of the federal/provincial fitness and amateur sport cost-sharing agreement was consistent with this direction. This left the federal government without an intervening mechanism for reaching the grass roots of sports. With the growing desire of the provinces to assert their authority in sport and recreation, it had become increasingly difficult for the federal government to have its way in determining the direction and scope of the joint programs, and in getting any political credit for its expenditures in this area. Because of these frustrations, it was becoming more attractive to the federal government to pursue a course of action that would allow it a direct role in sport.

There was little in the way of specifics in the proposed new sport policy about the role of government in attaining the goals proposed. There was, however, a great deal of rhetoric that left much to the imagination. Emphasis was placed on a "national sports program." In explaining this concept to the National Advisory Council, John Munro said that for the first time there was a cogent policy on sport properly grounded on the needs of people and on the structure of the existing system. Only now was it realistic to anticipate leading the country in a total co-ordinated effort to enhance the role and significance of sport and recreation in Canadian culture. The role of the federal government was to help provide leadership in terms of fostering acceptance of national goals and acting through support programs. Provincial officers in charge of recreation and sport were advised on the reorientation towards national programs. The relationship between the council and the directorate was to be through the minister. The directorate was to remain as part of the bureaucracy to carry out the directives of the government, and the council's role was to review objectives of the program and make recommendations to the minister. In no sense was the council to be supervisory to the directorate (NAC *Minutes of the 23rd Meeting*, 20 March 1970).

We have argued that the 1970 statement of federal government intentions in sport can best be understood in the context of both changes in Canadian sport itself and in the larger political and social events of the 1960s. The political situation in Canada in the later 1960s created an opportunity for the federal government to change its stance on sport. The Liberal party's new leader, Pierre Trudeau, was searching for national-unity symbols to counteract divisive forces in the country. Jurisdictional disputes between the provinces and the federal government and the growing forces of separatism in Quebec were creating increased tension across the nation. Sport was one of the symbols that Trudeau grasped in the 1968 federal election campaign. The "Unity through Sport" theme of the first Canada Games in Quebec in 1967 had struck a harmonious chord.

The report of the Task Force on Sport – a study undertaken as a result of Trudeau's campaign promise – argued that sport was also an effective antidote to economic and cultural domination by the United States. The history of sport in Canada, according to the Task Force Report, had been characterized by a drive for national championships and by common community endeavours (Task Force 1969: 9–13). It was ironic that this claim was made at a time when Canadians were becoming increasingly aware that professional sport was purely a business enterprise and that most North American professional leagues, including the National Hockey League, were controlled by American entrepreneurs and business interests.

The growth in size and ambition of provincial governments in the 1960s made federal/provincial agreements less tenable and attractive to the federal government, which saw its hands tied with respect to cost-sharing programs dealing with mass sport and physical activity programs. It had little control over expenditures and received little political kudos for its efforts. Becoming directly involved in elite sport became an increasingly more attractive alternative.

Another aspect of the programs that the federal government had undertaken in the 1960s under the auspices of the 1961 Fitness and Amateur Sport Act also was instrumental in pointing to this new direction. Federal government grants to sport governing bodies had not been effective in improving Canada's sport performances. In fact, these grants served more to lay bare the administrative, coaching, and technical support weaknesses of most Canadian sport governing bodies. There were increasing demands that the federal government remedy these deficiencies by creating a central administrative sport centre, awarding grants-in-aid to athletes, and improving coaching. These demands made the federal government less fearful of traditional protests of government take-over of sport.

The dramatic change in the role and significance of sport in Canadian society (outlined in the previous chapter) allowed the federal government to assert, for the first time, that sport in itself was an important and significant endeavour and one which the government could support as a goal in itself. The affinity of sport for television had transformed sport into a highly visible aspect of popular entertainment. Sport had become part of the mass culture of the country, and as such, acceptable as a worthwhile endeavour.

The rhetoric about the federal government's continued commitment to mass sport and physical activity programs in the new proposed policy statement reflected residual support for these more traditional activities. Most significant was the National Advisory Council on Fitness and Amateur Sport. Its concern about the Task Force Report's emphasis on sport, and particularly hockey, led the council to petition the minister for a wider study of sport and physical fitness. Such a study was conducted and the resultant P.S. Ross Report reflected this concern for the physical well-being of all Canadians. The influence of this report was seen in the new sport policy statement. The creation of Recreation Canada as a parallel administrative unit to Sport Canada was one concrete outcome of this residual support for mass sport programs. But the impotence of the federal government in intruding in areas of provincial jurisdiction and the lack of political pay-off in mass programs spelled doom for Recreation Canada before it was even created.

The commitment of the minister, John Munro, and the newly appointed director of the Fitness and Amateur Sport Directorate, Lou Lefaive, to promoting elite sport was instrumental in ensuring that the specific initiatives contained in the new policy statement were directed towards improving Canada's sport performances. Indeed, their efforts were a major reason that most of these initiatives had already been taken by the time that Munro espoused the "new" policy statement in 1970.

It is interesting that the Task Force recommended that an independent body, along the lines of the Canada Council, be established to deal with elite sport development, and that the existing structure of the Advisory Council and directorate be left with the responsibilities for mass participation programs. The concept of a quasi-autonomous body to deal with sport in Canada had been raised in the House of Commons in the 1950s and by the Advisory Council itself in 1968. But the government's desire to gain more political credit for its endeavours, its growing interest in sport as a political instrument, and the personal ambitions of Munro and Lefaive were all factors that mitigated against an independent Sport Canada.

The new policy statement made it clear that the federal government saw sport as an instrument to achieve the goal of national unity. But embracing sport in this manner meant a commitment to success on the international sport scene. The poor performance of Canadian athletes in World Cup and Olympic hockey and the country's declining performance in other international sport events in the 1960s were not consistent with the political use of sport by the federal government. In allying itself with elite sport, the federal government was inextricably tied to improving Canada's future international sport fortunes.

The new sport policy proposals served to confirm a number of steps the federal government had already taken to improve elite sport performance in Canada. These initiatives emanated largely from the 1969 Task Force Report on Sport. They allowed the federal government to intervene directly with the development of elite athletes; hitherto it had been content to play a passive and indirect role in this process. This policy statement also was significant in that it proclaimed that excellence in sport was in itself an important goal and deserving of federal government support; previously the worth of sport had always been tied to mass participation and physical fitness. Although the policy statement was couched in rhetoric about commitments to mass sport participation and recreation, it heralded a new era of federal government involvement, and committed the government to improved international sport performances in the 1970s.

CHAPTER SIX

Policies and Programs in the 1970s

The *Proposed Sports Policy for Canadians*, issued by the national health and welfare minister John Munro in 1970, was a unique occasion in the history of the Fitness and Amateur Sport Act. After the passage of the Act in 1961, the government had been content to leave matters of policy and program to the National Advisory Council on Fitness and Amateur Sport and to allow the provinces to use federal funds allocated to federal/provincial cost-sharing agreements largely in the manner which the provinces saw fit. But the transformation of sport that took place in the 1960s (documented in chapter 4) made sport important enough to become useful to the federal government in its quest to promote national unity and identity in the country. For the first time, a document from the minister responsible for fitness and amateur sport outlined the government's philosophy and intent in these matters. The new sport policy contained a great deal of rhetoric about maintaining the federal government's commitment to mass sport and physical activity programs. But its real intent was made clear by the specific program proposals contained in the document; these proposals were related largely to establishing programs and agencies to improve the standards of top "amateur" athletes in Canada. Even more significant was the fact that most of these originated from the *Report of the Task Force on Sports for Canadians*, a document that focused almost exclusively on problems relating to hockey and amateur sport, and that these specific program proposals had largely been put in place by the time the minister announced the new sport policy document in March 1970. It should be noted that although Munro's new sport policy was tabled in the House of Commons, it was never formally debated or ratified. One reason for this may have been that most of the sport recommendations were already in the process of being implemented.

This chapter traces federal government policies and programs in fitness and amateur sport over the period 1970–8, most of which were contained in the Proposed Sports Policy. Because this study is concerned with the evolution of the federal government's sport policy, our analysis focuses mainly on those programs concerned with sport rather than the areas of fitness and recreation. However, later in this chapter, we do discuss the reasons for the federal government's change of emphasis during the 1970s from recreation to fitness.

DISTRIBUTION OF POWER AND CENTRAL ACTORS

The announcement of the *Proposed Sports Policy for Canadians* by John Munro in 1970 marked a turning point in the Fitness and Amateur Sport Act. The predominance of the National Advisory Council in establishing policies and programs during the 1960s had ended in 1968 when Munro rejected the council's proposal to become the formal policy-making and executive arm of the Fitness and Amateur Sport Directorate. At the same time, the professional staff of the Fitness and Amateur Sport Directorate had grown in size and competency and was now ready and anxious to assume a major role in developing policies and programs. The relationship between Lou Lefaive, the director of Fitness and Amateur Sport, and John Munro (discussed in chapter 5), meant that there was a strong force within the federal government for intervention in sport development. The announcement in 1971 that Montreal had been formally awarded the 1976 Summer Olympic Games gave additional impetus to this thrust. There was increased concern during the early 1970s about the possible impact of poor performance by Canadian athletes in the first Summer Olympics ever staged in Canada and this helped to build momentum for increased federal government funding and activity to ensure adequate preparation of the country's athletes for the 1976 Games. An "in-house" structural change in May 1971 to create separate Sport Canada and Recreation Canada units within the directorate also helped the former unit to focus more squarely on elite athletes. In April 1973, the Fitness and Amateur Sport Directorate was elevated in the federal government organizational structure to a Branch. All these factors contributed to create an environment favourable for the development of agencies and programs designed to improve elite athlete performance in Canada.

The Task Force Report had recommended that an independent organization to be known as Sport Canada be created to deal with the development of elite sport. The Fitness and Amateur Sport Directorate then could concentrate its efforts on the mandate to develop mass fitness and recreation programs (Task Force 1969:75, 86). Dan Pugliese, a physical education administrator from the University of Waterloo, was commissioned to look at alternatives to the present structure and he recommended that a private, non-profit corporation, outside of government, be established. Pugliese felt that such an independent agency had the best chance of spawning and encouraging the development of provincial sport associations, an essential step if elite sport performance was to improve across the whole of Canada (Pugliese 1970:2). National health and welfare minister John Munro rejected this proposal, claiming it was premature; he stated that the creation of arm's-length agencies such as the National Sports and Recreation Centre and the Coaching Association of Canada would pave the way for the creation of an independent Sport Canada some time in the future. Instead, Munro announced in 1971 that two separate directorates were to be created: Sport Canada and Recreation Canada. Sport Canada, according to Munro, was to provide Canadians with an opportunity to pursue excellence in competitive sport, and to improve the level of Canadian performances in international sport competitions. Recreation Canada, in contrast, was to provide all Canadians with opportunities to participate in physical recreation and to improve their fitness levels (Munro 1971:26).

During the next two years, the Fitness and Amateur Sport Directorate worked at reorganizing itself into two separate divisions. Cor Westland, an experienced recreation professional and strong and effective advocate of recreation opportunities for all Canadians, was appointed unofficially the director of Recreation Canada. Lou Lefaive focused his efforts on sport and became, in effect, the director of Sport Canada.

In the early 1970s there was considerable discussion about the desirability of moving the directorate from the welfare to the health side of the ministry. The appointment of Marc Lalonde (who held a strong interest in preventive health measures) as minister of health and welfare in 1972 gave impetus to this proposal. These developments also caused pressure to change Cor Westland's title from acting director of Recreation Canada to acting director of Fitness Canada. Westland not only feared that the move to health would narrow the scope of Recreation Canada considerably, but also objected strenuously to the proposal to change his title. Westland presented a brief to both the minister and deputy minister of health, Maurice Leclair, about why the name should remain Recreation Canada (Hallett 1981:699). Leclair was convinced by Westland, and the title Recreation Canada remained, but the move to house the directorate under health did take place in 1973. At the same time, the directorate was elevated to Branch status, which meant that it would have its own assistant deputy minister. Lou Lefaive was appointed acting assistant deputy minister, Cor Westland was confirmed as director of Recreation Canada, and Tom Bedecki was appointed as director of Sport Canada. Bedecki brought to the task a professional background and education in physical education and sport, something that had been missing from the position since Lefaive's appointment in 1968.

In the fall of 1973, Robert Giroux, a career public servant, won the competition for the post of assistant deputy minister. This was consistent with the federal government's policy of having career administrators in assistant and deputy-minister posts, rather than persons with expertise in the matters of the specific branch. Giroux soon moved on to other responsibilities, and was replaced in 1974. Lalonde added two new directorates to the newly created Fitness and Amateur Sport Branch, one for planning, research, and evaluation and a second for program operation and administration. These branches were to provide support for both Recreation Canada and Sport Canada.

This structure and these actors remained generally in place until 1976, when a number of important changes took place. In 1976 Iona Campagnolo, a neophyte member of Parliament from Prince Rupert, BC, was appointed as the first minister of state with responsibilities for fitness and amateur sport. It might be argued that political expediency was a major consideration in this appointment. There were few Liberal MPs from western Canada and even fewer in the Cabinet. The appointment of a female to the Cabinet was also in tune with the times. But Campagnolo brought with her a keen sense of the political potential of elite sport and a capacity to capitalize on the publicity inherent in international sport events. This appointment was a landmark for sport in Canada. For the first time, a Cabinet minister was in place with specific responsibilities for sport and fitness. The year 1976 also saw the resignation of Cor Westland; his position as director of Recreation Canada remained unfilled for sixteen months. Hallett (1981:707) states that many "insiders" believe that Recreation Canada never recovered from this resignation, but a more realistic view is that Recreation Canada was never a viable concept because recreation was clearly a provincial responsibility. In 1977, Peter Lesaux became assistant deputy minister. Recreation Canada became Fitness and Recreation Canada in 1977 and John Pickett was appointed director of this division late in that year. These changes were precursors of the eventual formal withdrawal of the federal government from recreation in 1980. (It should be noted that we use recreation here in a sense that does not include national parks and wildlife. In these areas, the federal government continued to maintain its jurisdiction.) This withdrawal from recreation was accomplished in two stages. In 1979, two separate branches, Recreation Canada and Fitness Canada were established, and in 1980, Recreation Canada was dissolved.

Another significant change in actors was the appointment of Roger Jackson in 1976 as director of Sport Canada. Jackson had been an Olympic rowing medal winner for Canada in 1964 and had subsequently gained a PH D in exercise physiology. His keen interest in elite sport and his science background brought a greater emphasis on performance and record in sport. Jackson's tenure, however, was short-lived, as he accepted the position of dean of the Faculty of Physical Education at the University of Calgary in the fall of 1978. Campagnolo then chose Lou Lefaive to head Sport Canada into the 1980s. By this time, work had commenced on the federal government's green paper on sport. The appearance of this document, *Toward a National Policy on Amateur Sport: A Working Paper*, in 1977, marks the third major shift in federal government sport policy and is the subject of the next chapter.

The role of the National Advisory Council on Fitness and Amateur Sport in the 1970s has been described aptly by Westland (1979) as a council in search of a purpose. Its role as an executive arm of the program and as primary adviser to the minister in the 1960s was abruptly closed off by John Munro in 1968. The Advisory Council was relegated to a long-range planning role, ostensibly with a remaining advisory function. It struggled in the 1970s to identify a viable function, finally formalizing a constitution and terms of reference for itself in 1977. But even these efforts were frustrated when Iona Campagnolo objected to several sections of the constitution that she saw as overstepping the council's proper role. With the change of governments in the late 1970s, the council reached the sorry position of having only five of a possible thirty members appointed and in place. There was almost a two-year hiatus in the period of 1979 to 1981 when the council had no meetings. Resources made available to the council for travel, secretarial assistance, and to support research were kept to a minimum. It is not surprising, therefore, that the council's role in influencing federal government sport policy in the 1970s was relatively minimal, and that little or no attention or interest was attracted to its undertakings and pronouncements (Vail 1981). Despite this fact, the federal government attempted to keep the council functioning, largely because the Act required this, and in part because the government could pawn off unwanted philosophical questions and matters of long-range policy on the council. The council did play the role of raising questions about the federal government's role in elite sport vis-à-vis mass participatory programs.

INFLUENCE GROUPS

The Canadian Olympic Association (COA) played an important role in monitoring the direction of federal government sport policy in the 1970s. The COA received scathing criticism in the Task Force Report; it was labelled as being symbolic of all the weaknesses found in almost every sport association in Canada. The Task Force characterized Canadian sport organizations as being dependent on part-time workers, lacking in full-time administrators, concentrating directors and executive members in one area of the country, having no long-range plans, and lacking funds and fund-raising programs. The COA responded immediately to this criticism by commissioning a study of its purposes and operations. The resulting Maxwell Report accepted most of what the Task Force Report had seen as weaknesses of the COA, so the COA set about to rectify these shortcomings. One of its major thrusts was to establish the Olympic Trust in 1970. The concept of the Olympic Trust was to mount a concerted effort to raise funds in the private sector to support the costs of sending Canadian athletes to the Olympic and Pan-American Games. This was one of the most far-sighted steps ever undertaken by the COA. As a consequence, the COA was able to maintain an arm's-length relationship with the federal government, something that other sport governing bodies were unable to do because they gradually became more dependent on the federal government for financing and other resource support.

Another important decision that the COA took which enabled it to maintain some independence from the federal government was to remain in Montreal rather than to move to the National Sport and Recreation Centre in Ottawa. The COA had just moved into Olympic House in Montreal, built with funds donated by the Hudson's Bay Company, and the property had been exempted from tax by the Montreal Harbour Commission. In 1970 there was considerable pressure exerted by the federal government on the COA to move. Although the COA relinquished many of the financial rewards that it would have received from being housed in Ottawa, its decision to stay in Montreal was another factor in maintaining independence from the federal government.

The COA played an important role in the 1970s by promoting Game

Plan '76, which formally got under way in 1973 as a co-operative effort among the COA, the federal government, the national sport governing bodies, and the provincial governments. The precursor to Game Plan was the extensive core program set up by Sport Canada to support Canada's 1972 Olympic athletes. The athlete assistance fund was also instituted in 1973 under similar arrangements to provide direct funds to athletes of international calibre. Both these plans were ultimately taken over by Sport Canada in early 1976 because neither the COA nor the national sport governing bodies had the money or staff to run the program effectively. During the 1970s, the COA also played an important role in providing broken-time payment for athletes not attending universities. The federal government could not pay for time lost from jobs for training and competitions without jeopardizing the amateur status of the athletes. The federal government's university and college scholarship program, however, was considered to be within the limits of the amateur code.

The lack of a unified voice for sport in Canada was a persistent issue in the 1970s and the COA made a number of attempts to rectify this shortcoming. The COA's proposal that it form the nucleus of any new organization to represent amateur sport, however, was simply not realistic. The COA was seen by other sport governing bodies and interested individuals and sport participants as being an elitist body concerned primarily with high-level international sport. With this as its primary objective, it was natural that persons who were more interested in mass sport programs would not want to relinquish their voice in sport to a COA-dominated umbrella organization.

In another sense, the COA played a supportive role in federal government efforts to improve performance levels of Canadian athletes. It gradually applied increasingly strict standards for athletes to qualify for Olympic and Pan-American competitions; in this way, the COA assisted the federal government in putting pressure on sport governing bodies to concentrate on better athletic performance levels. The COA thus served as a buffer between Sport Canada and the sport governing bodies. Frustrations about the refusal to take promising young developing athletes to the Olympic and Pan-Am Games caused the national sport governing bodies to direct their anger towards COA instead of at Sport Canada.

The Sports Federation of Canada (SFC) was another organization that was linked with the rhetoric about a single unified voice for amateur sport in Canada. Indeed, on the surface, the SFC appeared to qualify as just that. The SFC moved to the National Sport and Recreation Centre in Ottawa in 1970 and appointed its first full-time executive director in 1971. By 1973, eighty-one sports and recreation organizations were members. But the SFC never became what it envisaged itself, "the link between sport in Canada and the federal government" (Fawcett 1977:34). Although the SFC played a role in the successful lobby to bring about the federal government fitness and amateur sport legislation in 1961, the primary advisory role it perceived for itself in the 1960s was usurped by the National Advisory Council for Fitness and Amateur Sport. Indeed the SFC, then called the Canadian Sports Advisory Council, was asked to change its name to the Canadian Amateur Sports Federation in 1962 to avoid confusion with the National Advisory Council. The council, because it pre-empted the role of recommending sport policy to the federal government, became the unofficial voice of sport in the 1960s.

When the National Advisory Council lost its place as a direct voice in sport policy making in 1968, the time was ripe for the Canadian Amateur Sports Federation to fill the gap. The federation undertook a review of its role in the 1970s, and subsequently changed its name to Sports Federation of Canada. The SFC undertook some worthwhile projects in the 1970s. It instituted a non-resident administrative service for sports not resident in the National Sport and Recreation Centre (1971); introduced an accident and medical benefit plan for athletes and coaches (1973); a national uniform program (1974); and brought out the first of its yearly sport and recreation directories in 1974. It also lobbied the government successfully for the establishment of a national sport lottery (1975), for exemption from the Combines Act for amateur sport (1975), and import tax relief on sport equipment (1978). It also initiated a Canadian Sports Award Program designed to bring recognition to amateur sport athletes, teams, and volunteer workers.

The SFC, however, never became an effective unified voice for amateur sport. The fact that national sport governing bodies themselves felt they had jeopardized their own autonomy vis-à-vis the federal government by accepting monies, administrative, and other services and technical support made them reluctant to relinquish more autonomy to a single umbrella organization such as the SFC. The national sport organizations preferred for the most part to lobby on an individual basis with the federal government; thus the concern about a single independent voice for Canada continued through the 1970s. The annual meetings of the SFC, however, did provide a discussion forum in the 1970s between representatives of national sport governing bodies and officials from Sport Canada, thus keeping channels of communications open between these two important components of the sport delivery system. The one predominate theme of the SFC from its inception in 1951 to the present has been "the concept that the mandate of a Canadian Sports Federation should be to co-ordinate and administer sport at the national level, supported by – not controlled by – the federal government" (Hallett 1981:453).

SPORT PROGRAM OUTCOMES

Direct Governmental Output

A number of forces and events combined in the early 1970s to bring about a great increase in the federal government's efforts to improve Canada's performance levels in international sport competition. The Task Force Report had provided a justification for such a concentration of efforts; better international performances would not only increase pride and promote national unity, but would provide motivation for more sport participants. The announcement in 1971 that Montreal would host the 1976 Summer Olympic Games provided more fuel for this argument. The 10-Year Master Plan developed by the National Advisory Council on Fitness and Amateur Sport in 1972 emphasized the growing need to consider physical fitness as a preventive health measure, linking motivation and participation with Canada's performance in the Olympics. Both the Master Plan and the 1971 Conference on the 1976 Olympics called for greatly increased federal expenditures on fitness and amateur sport. Although the Master Plan focused on ways and means to improve physical fitness, the acting director of Recreation Canada, Cor Westland, was intent on promoting the wider concept of recreation (T. Bedecki, personal interview, March 1984).

It is not surprising, therefore, that the 1973 Speech from the Throne committed the government to significantly greater funding for fitness and amateur sport and hinted that some $20 million per year would be available by 1975 (FASD Annual Report, 1972–3). Indeed, expenditures did escalate rapidly in the 1970s. The Fitness and Amateur Sport budget grew from approximately $6 to $11 million from the 1971–2 to the 1972–3 budget year. It remained around this level until 1975–6 when it jumped to $17 million. In 1976–7, it rose to approximately $25 million and then jumped again in 1978–9 to almost $35 million. By 1978–9, the Fitness and Amateur Sport budget was allocating about four and one-half dollars to sport for every dollar to recreation and fitness. In 1972–3, this split was approximately three to one. These figures do not include the substantial outlay the federal government made to support the construction of sport facilities for the Canada and Commonwealth Games during this period.

The National Conference on Olympic '76 Development, hosted by the minister for national health and welfare in Ottawa in October 1971, was a major factor in shaping the initiatives that Sport Canada took in the 1970s. The minister's opening speech reiterated the government's official position that a broad-based sport and fitness program and the development of elite athletes were inexorably tied together, and emphasized that the government's role was to *help* Canadians to reach these twin goals. The major aim of the conference, however, was to devise ways and means to improve Canada's performance in international sport events, and particularly in the Olympics. Among the key recommendations that came out of the conference was an appeal to the prime minister for a significant increase in Fitness and Amateur Sport spending in the period, 1971–6, a call for immediate federal aid to athletes and coaches for the 1972 Olympic Games, and a request for government action to provide more opportunities for females in sport programs. One immediate outcome of the Olympic '76 Conference was the "intensive care program." This program was designed to provide additional support to Canadian athletes who had potential to win medals at the 1972 Olympic Games. These athletes were identified by the respective sport governing bodies and Sport Canada provided appropriate support. The intensive-care program, which was too late to have any impact on Canadian performances in the 1972 Olympics, was replaced by Game Plan.

The avowed purpose of Game Plan was to improve Canada's position in Olympic competition from twenty-first in Munich in 1972 to tenth in Montreal in 1976. Game Plan was a more carefully planned and formal program than had been the previous athlete-assistance program. It called for each Olympic sport to develop a plan to ensure the best performances possible in the 1976 Olympics. Under this plan, Canadian athletes in Olympic sports were classified into three categories, A, B, or C, according to their current performance level in world competition; the level of financial and other support was tied to the athlete's classification. Once athletes were accepted in the plan, they committed themselves to a training and competition program set by their respective sport governing bodies.

Game Plan was initiated by the Canadian Olympic Association in conjunction with its fund-raising arm, the Olympic Trust, in 1971. The concept was based on the premise that Canadian athletes, with reasonable support, could compete well and excel in world-class competition, and that this excellence could best be fostered through increased support for sport federations through the existing structures. By February 1972, the idea had been approved by COA member sport federations, as well as the provincial directors of sport and recreation.

The COA commissioned a study by P.S. Ross and Partners and in April 1972, a document entitled "Improving Canada's Olympic

Performance: Challenges and Strategies" provided the foundations for Game Plan '76. Officially announced as a co-operative venture of the COA and the provinces in May 1972, Game Plan '76 was a significant event in Canadian sport. It was the first plan to be accepted in principle by all provinces, and it was felt that with or without federal government support, it was a concept that should be pursued (COA *Minutes*, November 1972). A unique characteristic of Game Plan was the attempt to bring together all the key agencies who sponsor amateur sport to co-ordinate the financing and planning of elite athlete development (Jackson 1977:12). By the end of 1972 the Canadian Intercollegiate Athletics Union, the Coaching Association of Canada, and other multi-sport agencies had expressed their support for Game Plan. The two basic assumptions of Game Plan were 1) responsibility for developing excellence must lie with the individual sport federation; and 2) Game Plan must not impinge upon, or distort, the overall long-range development of the sport but complement and extend it (COA *Minutes*, November 1972). These were certainly pious hopes.

In November 1973, only four months after the federal government made a commitment to Game Plan, D.D. Maxwell Limited, the public-relations firm for the Olympic Trust, warned that the public perceived Game Plan '76 as a government program. There was not enough promotional emphasis on the original shared-sector concept. The report stated that while government support must be recognized, a proper balance must be ensured to create public awareness of private-sector participation.

A 1974 change in International Olympic Committee eligibility regulations made allowances for lost-time income compensation for athletes. In April 1975, the COA received a delegation of athletes representing all sports asking for such direct assistance. The nature of this program precluded Sport Canada from participating. The government could provide student aid such as bursaries but could not risk the precedent of broken-time payments for athletes (COA *Annual General Meeting*, 1976). Such funding was introduced by the COA in April 1975 and subsequently the co-operative funding of Game Plan between Sport Canada and the COA was modified. The COA and Olympic Trust took over the lost-time compensation payments and some other direct aid programs. The federal government assumed financial responsibility for the original Game Plan operations (COA *Quadrennial Report 72-6*, 1977).

The provinces initially committed themselves to Game Plan with much enthusiasm. But with the exception of Ontario and Quebec, these commitments failed to materialize. Although the provinces had been represented at each Game Plan meeting, they opted out when it came time to pay for commitments. This created problems because new sponsors had to be found, resulting in frustrating delays in payments to the national sport governing bodies. Finally, in December 1975, the provinces agreed among themselves not to continue their involvement (Jackson 1977:12).

Game Plan continued under the auspices of Sport Canada following the 1976 Olympiad. The COA meanwhile introduced new direct assistance programs for clubs and for athletes who were not supported by scholarships. As a result, the Game Plan budget increased from $1.8 million in 1974–5 to $3.7 million in 1975–6.

Concern about the "brawn drain" to the United States – that is, young Canadian student athletes accepting athletic scholarships at colleges and universities in the United States – caused the federal government to institute a student athlete grants-in-aid program in 1970. These awards were given to students on the basis of ratings provided by their respective sport governing bodies. There were two categories of support: students of international calibre received $2,000, renewable for four years; and national-calibre student athletes received $1,000 grants that had to be renegotiated each year. From a modest beginning of 18 grants in 1970, the program peaked in 1975–6 with 530 athletes in 56 different sports receiving a total of $643,000 (FAS Annual Report, 1975–6). From this point on, the numbers and funds declined as Sport Canada put greater emphasis on its Game Plan assistance program. Eventually in 1981, the grants-in-aid program was completely meshed with Game Plan. By this time, some provinces were providing financial support to student athletes in their respective jurisdictions.

Arm's-Length Agencies

One of the most important legacies of the Task Force Report and John Munro's tenure as minister with responsibilities for fitness and amateur sport was the creation of a number of arm's-length agencies. These agencies provided the support structure for both government and national sport associations and were central to the sport delivery system in the 1970s. Although these arm's-length organizations all received, at one level or another, funds from the federal government, they were not considered part of the government bureaucracy. Their employees were not public servants and they were responsible in theory to their respective boards of directors.

National Sport and Recreation Centre. One of the barriers to developing elite athletes in Canada that was uncovered in the 1960s was the poor organizational and administrative capacities of most national sport associations. The National Advisory Council recognized this short-coming early, when its grants to these associations did not appear to bear fruit in producing improved performance levels. By 1965, the National Advisory Council was making small administrative grants to national sport associations. But by 1968, only six or seven sport governing bodies had the financial resources to hire full-time administrators (Cliff 1981:1). Most were still operating out of the kitchens of volunteer executive members of the national sport governing bodies (Task Force 1969:58). The Task Force proposed to remedy this shortcoming by separating elite sport entirely from the federal government with the creation of an independent Sport Canada. Sport Canada was to serve as the administrative arm for the national sport associations. But as noted earlier, the concept of an arm's-length Sport Canada was rejected by the federal government. John Munro, however, moved rapidly to create the National Sport and Recreation Centre, based on a model developed by Dan Pugliese, a sport and physical education consultant from the University of Water-loo. Pugliese subsequently became the Centre's first co-ordinator (Cliff 1981:6). The centre commenced operations in Ottawa in temporary quarters in September 1970 and moved to its new location in May 1971. Some sport governing bodies objected to the Ottawa location because they already had some type of national office capacity located elsewhere. But thirty-three national associations were on hand as resident occupants of the new Centre with some thirty-six additional associations receiving financial support as non-resident members of the centre. The initial budget allocation from the federal government was $430,976. By 1978–9, the number of resident associations housed in the centre had grown to fifty-seven and the budget to almost $3 million. The level of support from the federal government had grown to almost $4 million. The centre provided office space and secretarial support. Monies to pay full-time professional staff hired by the national sport governing bodies and to support travel for national executive meetings came directly from the Sport Canada budget. The centre also provided a wide range of support services to the resident and the non-resident members. These included printing, translation, audio-visual, library and com-puting facilities and services, and legal, management, and promo-tional guidance (Westland 1979:74).

The creation of the National Sport and Recreation Centre certainly was a significant event in the development of sport in Canada. It increased greatly the capacity of national sport governing bodies to support the development of their respective activities. The monies provided to hire initially national executive directors and subsequently technical directors created for the first time in most national associations a full-time professional arm to their organizations. The location of these persons in one central site provided an ideal opportunity for improved communications among sport governing bodies. The centre certainly contributed substantially to the present level of sophistication of many national sport and recreation organizations and to the improved level of sport performances by Canadian athletes in international sport events in the 1970s.

The development of sport bureaucracies at the provincial level was less dramatic, but nevertheless has gained momentum since 1970. Increasing budgets and sport personnel and the growth and increasing importance of provincial, regional, and Canada Games, "each at its own level a mini-Olympics," indicate that governments at both levels no longer feel that their involvement in sport must be "hidden behind the skirts of fitness and recreation" (Broom & Baka 1978:70). The creation of the National Sport and Recreation Centre has stimulated the creation of services in the provincial governments "to the point where now all have centralized sports administrative services, thus providing a coherent network across the country" (Westland 1979:74).

But the creation of the centre was not without its problems. The close proximity of the technical and executive directors to the seat of power created tensions between the professional staff of sport governing bodies in Ottawa and their respective volunteer national executives spread across Canada. An increasing reliance on federal government monies put the national sport and recreation bodies more squarely in the pockets of the federal government and, as a result, their capacity to act independently became seriously jeopardized. This issue is raised again in chapter 10. Although conflicts and tensions remain with respect to the perceived loss of autonomy of individual sport governing bodies in relation to the major arm's-length agencies created and supported by Sport Canada and the Fitness and Amateur Sport Branch, the centre has played an essential role in the development of the present sport delivery system in Canada.

Hockey Canada. Hockey was a national concern in Canada throughout the 1960s. Three issues were central to this concern. The first was Canada's declining fortunes in international hockey. The second was the National Hockey League's (NHL) control over amateur hockey, and in particular, the contracts signed by young hockey players with professional hockey teams. The third was the dominance of the NHL by American interests, further aggravated by the expansion of member teams in the United States. The first two issues had been tackled by the National Advisory Council on Fitness and Amateur Sport in 1966. The third became the topic of debate in Parliament and revolved around whether the National Hockey League should come under the purview of the Combines Investigation Act (HC *Debates*, 13 June 1966:6364).

The National Advisory Council's *Report on Amateur Hockey in Canada* (1967) served as the basis of a new agreement between the Canadian Amateur Hockey Association (CAHA) and the NHL. The key clauses in this agreement were that the NHL was to cease sponsoring teams within the CAHA structure, and was to abandon the controversial C player contract clause (which bound adolescent players to a particular club) in favour of a universal player draft when players had reached the age of 21 (Task Force 1969:98–9). Given this preoccupation with hockey, it is not surprising that the Task Force Report focused most of its attention on remedying the ills of Canada's "national" sport. Action on the Task Force Report's central recommendation, the creation of an arm's-length agency to deal with these issues, was taken even before it was formally submitted to John Munro. In December 1968, Munro called a meeting with representatives of amateur and professional hockey, federal government officials, Task Force members, and selected individuals (FASD *Annual Report*, 1968–9:2). Shortly thereafter, Munro announced the creation of Hockey Canada, which, among other responsibilities, would have the sole jurisdiction over operating a national hockey team to represent Canada in international competitions. Subsequent to this announcement, a formal agreement was signed with the CAHA to transfer responsibility for the national hockey team program to Hockey Canada (ibid.).

The major concern of Hockey Canada in the 1970s was to carry out the task of putting together teams for special competitions and to develop a scheme for the development of a national hockey team. Negotiations over player rights with the NHL and the CAHA made this a very delicate and difficult task. Hockey Canada did manage to assemble competitive teams for the 1972 Soviet/Canada hockey series and the 1976 Canada Cup by depending on proven National Hockey League stars. These successes served to assuage the feelings of Canadians that had been stung by previous international hockey defeats. But the problem of developing and fielding a competitive national hockey team for Olympic and World Cup competition was not solved. Canada continued to turn in mediocre performances, using amateurs and fringe professional players against other national teams who ostensibly met the international definition of amateur athletes.

Another attempt to resolve this issue was undertaken in 1977, when a Committee on International Hockey was established with Senator Sidney L. Buchwald as chairman, in response to the negative publicity centred on Team Canada's participation in the 1977 World Hockey Championships. Because these championships took place in the spring during the NHL Stanley Cup playoffs, the Canadian team consisted of only those professional players whose teams had been eliminated, and did not include most of Canada's top players, who were still involved in the playoffs. Following Canada's "humiliating" defeats at the tournament, Iona Campagnolo announced the all-party parliamentary committee, stating that it was time to identify Canadian responsibilities in this regard, as well as to tackle the issues Canadians felt were at stake when competing at the international level. Hearings were held across Canada between June and October 1977. The committee received briefs and analysed the results of a questionnaire sent to some 13,000 Canadians. It became obvious that the roots of the international problem lay in the domestic hockey situation. The overwhelming influence of professional hockey was deemed to be the major issue. Canada needed to develop a national team structure for representation at all levels of international hockey, and alternate development programs were needed for minor hockey players. A committee was subsequently established to study hockey within Canada as a result of this report (FAS *Annual Report*, 1977–8: 3–4). Another issue that remained unresolved was the extent to which the government should become involved in amateur international and Olympic hockey. Perhaps one positive outcome of the report was the fact that Canada returned to Olympic hockey competition in 1980, after a twelve-year absence, with a hastily assembled national team (COA *Minutes*, 1977–8).

The difficulties that young hockey players experienced when they wished to combine higher education with the pursuit of a professional hockey career had been raised in the 1960s and articulated in the Task Force Report. One step that Hockey Canada took in attempting to resolve this dilemma was to take over the hockey scholarship program from the Fitness and Amateur Sport Directorate. Ninety-eight scholarships were made available to young hockey players who wished to attend institutions of higher education and play hockey, either for their university or college teams or in the junior hockey ranks.

Another issue plaguing Hockey Canada was the violence in the game. The spread of professional hockey into the United States brought the game to an audience less attuned to the fine points of the game than fans in Canada. Hockey owners and management in the United States soon learned that their fans were attracted by the physical violence of the game, and in particular the fighting and brawls. Violence in the game was condoned by management in order to attract fans to the newer franchises in the United States. Television conveyed these fights and brawls to young aspiring hockey players across Canada and these acts were emulated in youth hockey. The McMurtry inquiry into violence in amateur hockey in Ontario was one manifestation of the concern (Ontario Ministry of Community and Social Services 1974).

Hockey Canada was one of the most visible of the arm's-length agencies created by the federal government as a result of the Task Force Report. It was created primarily to develop better national hockey teams for competition in the Olympics and World Championships. The potential for conflict with the CAHA on one hand and the NHL on the other has made this task a most difficult one. Indeed, the resentment that the creation of Hockey Canada caused in the CAHA has never subsided. Although the 1972 Soviet/Canada series and the 1976 Canada Cup, in which professional players were used, were considered to be highly successful, Canada has not fared well internationally in either professional or amateur competition in more recent years.

The basic problem of how best to develop young Canadian hockey talent also has never been resolved. Although this was one of Hockey Canada's mandates, it never did take any concerted measures to come to terms with the player-development issue. Canada's "national sport," the primary concern of the Task Force Report, continues to be the source of study and investigation as the Canadian government periodically tries to solve the recurring problems surrounding hockey.

The Hockey Canada saga took place largely outside of the mainstream of federal government involvement in sport. Hockey Canada had considerable prestige because of the stature of the persons appointed to its board of directors and the importance of hockey to Canadians. As such, it was able to maintain more distance from the federal government than was the case with most of the other arm's-length agencies. It is a story that deserves a study in itself.

Sport Participation Canada. There was considerable backlash about the preoccupation of the Task Force Report on elite sport and, in particular, about hockey. Protests by the National Advisory Council on Fitness and Amateur Sport that this report ignored the issue of mass sport and fitness programs prompted Minister John Munro to commission a study of these wider issues. The consultants hired to undertake this study, P.S. Ross and Partners, recommended that a communications agency within the Fitness and Amateur Sport Directorate be established to promote physical activity for the general population (Baka 1975). This matter was referred to the National Advisory Council. The council, however, recommended that this communications agency be set up independent of the existing federal government bureaucracy. It argued that this would allow the agency to operate outside the influence of politics, and thus Canadians would be more receptive to persuasion about the value of exercise. It also, argued the council, would allow the agency to better tap the private sector for communication budgets to promote physical fitness (ibid., 7). This concept was approved by the federal Cabinet and Sport Participation Canada was incorporated in 1971 with Keith McKerracher, a marketing specialist, as the first director general. An impressive board of directors was put together, representing business, the media industry, and various elements of the physical fitness sector. Lester Pearson was the first chairman of the board. "Participaction" was taken as the offical motto of Sport Participation Canada shortly after and soon became synonymous with the work of this arm's-length agency.

The objective of "Participaction" was to motivate Canadians to lead physically active lives, using awareness education and motivation strategies. Mass media and business marketing techniques were to be used, and the media campaign was to be supported in the private sector (Baka 1975:5). Although the operating budget of Participaction has come mainly from the federal government, this hope has largely been realized. In the first year of its operation, it received an estimated $500,000 worth of advertisement sponsorships from the private sector (DNHW 1972:110). In this initial year, operating funds from Fitness and Amateur Sport amounted to some $260,000. By 1978, the federal government operating subsidy was about one-half million dollars, but an estimated $8 million of free advertising was forthcoming from the private sector (*Financial Post Special Report*, 1978).

One of Participaction's best known ventures, the comparison of the 60-year-old Swede with the 30-year-old Canadian was introduced in fifteen-second sport television commercials, sponsored by the Canadian Football League. This simple, direct, and innovative campaign was to become the trademark of Participaction. The effectiveness of the awareness campaign can be seen in a 1978 survey that revealed that 79 percent of Canadians were aware of Participaction and that 72 percent believed the agency was being effective. By 1980, these figures had risen to 87 percent and 85 percent respectively (*Financial Post Supplement*, 1980:22).

The Saskatoon "Participaction" pilot project was initiated in 1973 and became another success story. This Participaction contest between Saskatoon and sister cities in Japan and Sweden in the late 1970s attracted national press coverage. The Saskatoon pilot project was followed up with a similar campaign in Peterborough in 1976. The "ParticipAction" logo became familiar to most Canadians and acquired an international reputation for its unique marketing success. It is the major program funded by Fitness Canada; there is no similar organization for the promotion of amateur sport. The first stage of Participaction's campaign, that of creating an awareness of fitness on the part of Canadians, took some six or seven years to accomplish. Subsequent efforts, built on public awareness, have focused on phases 2 and 3 of the campaign, i.e., education and motivation.

The arm's-length status of Participaction has been one of its most significant features. In the first instance, this independence has meant that the public has been more receptive to the fitness message because it comes from an independent source rather than from government (Mills 1982:7). Second, it has made it much easier for Participaction to tap the private sector for donations in kind for the media campaign. Participaction has successfully resisted attempts by the federal government to change from block to project funding. This has allowed the agency's board of directors, made up largely of prestigious businessmen, to take its own decisions, and to act quickly without interference from government bureaucracy. It has also meant that Participaction has been able to remain free from political interference, something the subsequent, parallel organizations established and funded by provincial governments have not been able to achieve (R. Kisby, personal interview, 2 March 1984).

Participaction certainly has been a most successful venture. Part of this success must be attributed to the dynamism of Russ Kisby, part to the effective tapping of corporation funds by the board of directors, and part to the organization's ability to stay at arm's-length from government. But the timing of Participaction's efforts was fortuitous. These efforts coincided with certain social and economic changes in Canadian society in the 1970s that contributed greatly to the "fitness boom" in the second half of that decade. We discuss these changes in chapter 9. Participaction's role in the promotion of national fitness vis-à-vis those of Recreation Canada and the Department of National Health and Welfare is discussed in chapter 8.

Coaching Association of Canada. Inadequate coaching was one of the barriers to developing elite athletes in Canada that was identified in the early days of the fitness and amateur sport program. Although the federal government allocated monies to national sport governing bodies to stage regional and national coaching clinics, these efforts were sporadic. In addition, there was a large turnover in persons who attended clinics from year to year, and there was little continuity or long-range commitment to the coaching profession. It is not surprising that the Task Force Report recommended that a body be established to provide technical support to sport organizations. Accordingly, in December 1970, a National Coaches' Association was formed that subsequently became the Coaching Association of Canada (CAC). It was housed in the National Sport and Recreation Centre in Ottawa and received its funding from the Fitness and Amateur Sport budget. The CAC saw its mission as being "dedicated to coaching development and the profession of coaching for the purpose of achieving excellence in all amateur sport" (CAC 1983a:2). This was to be accomplished by providing program information, leadership, promotion advice, technical development, resources, and a public image for all levels of coaching. Its major mission, however, was the development of a national coaching certification program. Work on this project commenced in 1972 in co-operation with the Council of Provincial Directors of Sport and Recreation. This group pledged its support to this project and at its May 1973 meeting, endorsed the development of a pilot project in Ontario, which was to be the model for the rest of Canada. Thus the Coaching Association, in co-operation with the Ontario Department of Youth and Recreation, commenced work on the project. To better meet the needs of this growing program, and to ensure a national and co-ordinated effort, the National Coaching Development Council was created and held its first meeting in January 1977. Council members include representatives from the CAC, Sport Canada, and the provincial governments; these groups worked closely with the national and provincial sport governing bodies and used university and other personnel to develop manuals and training programs.

The CAC budget grew from a $15,000 grant from the federal government and an additional $50,000 subsidy from Mutual Life of Canada in 1971 (FASD *Annual Report*, 1971–2:5) to $1,581,554 by 1978–9. The National Coaching Certification Program accounted for 30 percent of this figure. By 1978–9, thirty-six sports had developed level I programs, twenty had reached level II, five had level III, and two sports had completed all programs, including levels IV and V (FAS *Annual Report*, 1978–9). With the exception of Ontario's major contribution to the development of theory I and II, the federal government bore the full cost of the level I to V theory and technical curricula. The provinces' responsibility was to pay the costs associated with conducting the coaching certification program in their jurisdictions (Campagnolo 1977b:14). By the early 1980s, some 100,000 persons, exclusive of the hockey certification program had participated in at least one level of the program (Macintosh 1984).

Once the coaching development scheme was well under way, the Coaching Association turned its attention to another problem, that of providing opportunities for Canadians to develop into top-line international coaches. A number of national sport organizations had deemed it necessary, in preparing for the 1976 Olympics, to bring in foreign coaches to develop Canadian athletes and teams. The rationale was that Canada did not have the necessary internationally experienced, seasoned coaches within its own boundaries. The National Coaching Apprenticeship Program, which commenced in 1977–8, was designed to remedy this deficiency by providing funds whereby aspiring Canadian coaches could work as full-time apprentices under master coaches at selected clubs and institutions across Canada. In many instances, these apprentice coaches were able to work with the persons brought in from abroad to coach athletes for the 1976 Olympics. This was in contrast to experiences in other countries and particularly in Mexico, where imported coaches came and went without passing along any of their expertise to aspiring native coaches (T. Bedecki, personal interview, March 1984).

The CAC also carried out some other important mandates during the 1970s. One of these was the development of the Sport Information Resource Centre (SIRC), which officially opened in August 1973 in the National Sport and Recreation Centre in Ottawa (CAC 1983a:1). The development of a centralized documentation service was proposed in the years preceding the formulation of the Act. Finally, in 1962, the University of Ottawa received a grant of $5,000 from the National Advisory Council on Fitness and Amateur Sport to set up a Canadian sport documentation centre. In 1964, because of financial problems, the centre's operations were taken over by the Department of National Health and Welfare, although the University of Ottawa location remained the same. Doris Plewes, one of the initiators of the whole idea, was appointed full-time director of the centre with a grant of $30,000. In 1968, the centre was relocated in the building housing the new Fitness and Amateur Sport Directorate offices, where it came under the immediate supervision of the directorate (Hallett 1981: 427–32). After the establishment of the National Sport and Recreation Centre in 1970, SIRC was finally incorporated under the auspices of the CAC in 1973. This move coincided with the growing need that coaches had for specific information about the art and science of coaching; as a result, the focus of SIRC narrowed considerably during the 1970s to concentrate on information that could be of specific use to coaches. In 1980, SIRC merged its data base with the sport information centre in Western Germany. A regularly updated *Sport Bibliography* has provided a comprehensive subject index since 1975.

The CAC also took steps to improve sport officiating in Canada by co-operating in the hosting of a national officiating conference in May 1978. Another topic of concern for the Coaching Association was poor communication among coaches across Canada. In order to remedy this problem, the association undertook to produce and distribute information. Among the publications produced by the CAC were *Coaching Review*, a bi-monthly national coaching magazine; *Timeout*, a newsletter for coaches; *Coaching Science Update*; and *Select Sport Book Catalogue*, containing a listing and short review of sport-specific literature and audio-visual materials that are produced or recommended by the various national sport governing bodies (CAC 1983a).

Certainly the Coaching Association of Canada has been a very successful organization. The number of Canadians who have participated is most impressive. The coaching certification model has been emulated in other countries. Indeed, Australia borrowed liberally from Canada in establishing its own coaching certification program in the late 1970s. The theory and technical manuals produced for each level of certification have received praise from many quarters. But there is still controversy about certain aspects of the program. Proponents of elite sport claim it has done little to improve coaching for Canada's international athletes. Certainly, few people ever attain the fifth level of certification. At the grass-roots level, the program is often seen as being too theoretical and not practical enough. Women and people from lower socio-economic backgrounds apparently are underrepresented in the program (Macintosh 1984). The extent to which people who enrol in the program actually coach for any significant period of time is not known. These and other issues caused the CAC to initiate a formal evaluation of the program in the fall of 1985. An effective study is an essential first step in resolving the problems raised here and elsewhere about the coaching certification program.

Canada and Arctic Winter Games. The Canada Games were conceived in the early 1960s; the first of these "Games" was held in Quebec City in

1967 with "Unity through Sport" as the theme. More than 1,500 athletes from every province and both territories participated in the inaugural Games. The first Games were planned largely by federal government public servants. When the decision to continue the Games was made; it was necessary to put some formal organization in place. To this end, the Canada Games Council was established in 1969. The council served as the principal authority for the Games and included representatives from the Fitness and Amateur Sport Directorate, the Sports Federation of Canada (representing the national sport governing bodies), and provincial sport and recreation personnel. It was responsible for determining the philosophy and rules and regulations of the Games. Funding came from all three levels of government, with federal, provincial, and municipal authorities contributing in approximately equal amounts to the capital costs of new and upgraded sport facilities. The federal government provided most of the operating and travel costs, but the host province was responsible for transporting its own teams and support officials to the Games sites.

The official goal of the Canada Games was to "provide a national development competition of high calibre for maximum number of athletes from all provinces and territories" (Canada Games Council 1979:9). This definition was broad enough to leave much room for debate about the relative emphasis on participation versus elite athlete development. At any rate, the Games have provided an avenue for competition for many Canadians. Approximately 16,000 athletes competed at the seven Canada Games that had been held up to February 1979. More than 350,000 were involved in regional and provincial games or in selection processes prior to the final selection of the provincial teams (ibid., 12). Summer Games were held successively in Dartmouth/Halifax, NS (1969), Burnaby, BC (1973), St John's, Nfld (1977) and Thunder Bay, Ont. (1981). Following the first Winter Games in Quebec City in 1967, subsequent Games were held in Saskatoon, Sask. (1971), Lethbridge, Alta (1975), Brandon, Man. (1979), Saguenay-Lac-St-Jean, Que. (1983), and Saint John, NB (1985).

The Canada Games Council claims that the staging of the Games biennially in various communities across the country assists in developing a public awareness of an enthusiasm for amateur sport and serves to familiarize Canadians with major competitions. "Through the pageantry of the opening and closing ceremonies and through the social milieu of a national multi-sport event, the Games help to strengthen mutual understanding among the athletes and encourage national unity through sport" (Canada Games Council

1979:9). This claim for sport receives more attention in our final chapter. Other more tangible outcomes of the Games are discussed in the next section.

Soon after the inception of the Canada Games, the Fitness and Amateur Sport Directorate recognized that native peoples in northern Canada did not have an equal opportunity to compete in this event. The different cultural background of the native peoples meant they were not often exposed to the sports that made up the Canada Games. As such, some native leaders and northern politicians felt that this group was being left out of a national event. As a result, the directorate forwarded a memorandum to the federal Cabinet in 1970, recommending that the government sponsor an event to be known as the Arctic Winter Games. These Games would feature not only some of the more popular sports from the Canada Games, but also native games such as high kick, the whip contest, rope gymnastics, hand tug-of-war, and the Eskimo drum dance. This proposal was received favourably by the Cabinet, in part because Canadian sovereignty in the Arctic was being called into question by the United States and the Soviet Union. The federal government was anxious to establish whatever presence it could in the Arctic (L. Lefaive, personal interview, May 1986). For whatever reason, the Arctic Winter Games became a reality in Yellowknife in 1970. Prime Minister Trudeau was on hand in parka, mukluks, and wolf-head hat to open the week-long competitions. Eight hundred athletes, representing the Northwest Territories, the Yukon, and Alaska competed in these first Arctic Games (Leclair 1970).

Another more radical alternative to the Canada Games also emerged at this time. Some native people perceived that the Arctic Winter Games would also be dominated by "southern-type" sports, and proposed that a truly native games program be organized. This native group received a Northwest Territories Centennial Grant; subsequently, the first Native Games were held in summer 1970 at Inuvik. Because these Native Games have not been sponsored by either federal or territory sport agencies, any further discussion of them here is not appropriate. However, the reader is referred to Paraschak and Scott (1980), not only for an account of the financial and organizational arrangements for these Games, but also for a provocative discussion of the political struggle for recognition and support of the concept of an event that reflects an authentic native culture.

Since 1970, the Arctic Winter Games have been held every second year. Two were held in Alaska, one in 1974 in Anchorage, and another in 1982 in Fairbanks. The federal government's financial contribution to each of these Games has averaged about $250,000 since 1974, except when they were held in Fairbanks. In this case, the federal government only assisted with team transportation costs to Alaska. The present cycle of these Games ends in Alaska in 1988. Fitness and Amateur Sport has had some concerns about the Arctic Games. First, although the Games are international in the sense that athletes from Alaska compete, the branch sees them as a regional sport event. As such, it is the federal government's policy to phase out its involvement in regional events, as it did in the case of the Western Canada Games. Second, the heavy emphasis on social and cultural activities also raises questions as to why it should be sponsored by the Fitness and Amateur Sport Branch. Finally, the branch does not feel that it has received any significant recognition for its contribution to the Arctic Games. All of these concerns put the future of these Games in question. The branch recognizes that it needs to conduct its own evaluation of the Arctic Winter Games before any final decision about its future can be made.

CHANGING RELATIONS, CONFLICTS, AND EMERGING PATTERNS

The cancellation by the federal government in 1970 of the federal/provincial cost-sharing programs, which were an important part of the fitness and amateur sport program in the 1960s, did not bring about an end to the tensions between these two levels of government over matters pertaining to sport and physical recreation. The backlash from the National Advisory Council on Fitness and Amateur Sport to the preoccupation in the Task Force Report on Sport with amateur sport, and particularly hockey, began a chain of events that led to the federal government's decision to establish a Recreation Canada division within the Fitness and Amateur Sport Directorate in 1971.

During the 1970s, there was a constant struggle to identify appropriate ways in which the federal government could be legitimately involved in recreation programs. That this was fought so long was in part because of the tenacity and commitment of Cor Westland, who was director of Recreation Canada from 1971 to 1976. Besides the jurisdictional problems with recreation, this move towards physical fitness programs was consistent with the increasingly rational and instrumental view that government and society were taking towards sport. Physical fitness programs could be justified easily on the instrumental grounds that they contributed to the health of Canadians and, therefore, to an increased productivity and output in the Canadian economy, coupled with a reduction in health-care costs. Physical fitness also was much more readily "measured" than were many recreation programs, which fitted better with the social programs in the welfare domain. This affinity for measuring physical fitness status and programs was consistent with the rational approach that was pervading sport – the preoccupation with objective measures of performance, record keeping, and striving towards and exceeding previous high standards of performance.

The move towards rationalized instrumental physical fitness programs was also enhanced by the presence of Marc Lalonde as minister of national health and welfare for the period 1972–6. Lalonde believed that the promotion of positive health measures could reduce health-care costs significantly. *A New Perspective on the Health of Canadians*, which was brought forth in 1974 during Lalonde's term as minister, argued that Canadians had a choice about their health and that there were a number of positive steps individuals could take that would lead to improvements in their health status. This document was a significant factor in turning Recreation Canada towards fitness. Lifestyle became the operative term in the 1970s; exercise was seen as one of the positive steps Canadians could take to improve their lifestyle and subsequently their health.

But the creation of a Recreation Canada division within the Fitness and Amateur Sport Directorate in 1971 heightened the suspicion with which the provinces viewed federal government activity in recreation. On the one hand, the provinces objected to the limited definition of recreation that the Fitness and Amateur Sport Directorate took, i.e., only those activities that involved a substantial physical aspect. They urged that this definition be broadened in scope to allow greater support to be given to national recreation associations and agencies. On the other hand, the provinces insisted that mass sport participation and physical recreation programs were primarily the prerogative of the provinces and resented federal government sorties into this domain.

Prime Minister Diefenbaker's predilection in striking the word "recreation" from the title of the original Act proved to be right. However, there were a number of factors other than the jurisdictional dispute between the provinces and the federal government that contributed to the replacement of recreation by fitness in the Fitness and Amateur Sport Branch at the end of the decade. One prominent reason was the increased importance of physical fitness to the health of Canadians in the 1970s. There were also other obstacles in the way of effective federal government policy in recreation. One was a belief that recreation meant a free choice by individuals about type of activity, the time for participation, and the place for the activity. This view was antithetical to government initiatives for recreation programs that often stressed economic development and tourism as a justification for expenditures in recreation. Another factor mitigating against effective federal government involvement in recreation was that many agencies and departments in the federal government were in one way or another involved in various aspects of recreation. Although there was token rhetoric about integrating these widely diverse interests and involvement, nothing came of it. The only time that the numerous federal government agencies dealing with sport and recreation ever got together was to plan for major sport events (T. Bedecki, personal interview, March 1984). One reason for this lack of interdepartmental co-operation was that the various agencies often saw the purposes of recreation in different ways.

The inability of the federal government to overcome the obstacles to playing an effective role in recreation became more apparent as the decade wore on. The Fitness and Amateur Sport Branch gradually changed its focus from recreation to physical fitness, changing the name of Recreation Canada to Fitness and Recreation Canada in the fiscal year 1977–8, and creating two separate entities the following year. The 1979 federal government green paper on recreation implied that this area was to be given over to the provinces. When the provinces refused to recognize the legitimacy of the commission established by the federal government to conduct cross-country hearings on the green paper on recreation, no further action was taken on the matter. Recreation ceased to be a mandate of the Fitness and Amateur Sport Branch, and the name Recreation Canada disappeared in 1980.

There were tensions and conflicts between the provinces and the federal government in the realm of sport as well. The provinces complained that monies awarded by the federal government to national sport governing bodies did not filter down to assist sport at the provincial level. Moreover, the provinces complained that they were neither consulted in advance nor kept informed after the fact on initiatives by the federal government and sport governing bodies. The establishment of the National Sport and Recreation Centre brought calls from the provinces for such services to be provided by the federal government at the provincial level. The provinces also pressed the federal government to contribute to sport and recreation facilities across the country. But the federal government restricted its support of facilities to those constructed for the Canada Games and international sport events. The only other contribution made to sport facilities was a limited support program for facilities that met international competitive standards built at post-secondary educational institutions during the period 1977 to 1979 (see Hallett 1981:1068 for details of these expenditures).

The Canada Games was the one bright spot in a rather stormy relationship between the provinces and the federal government in sport and, indeed, in most matters of common concern during the 1970s. After a shaky beginning, the Canada Games Council, with representatives from the provinces, national sport governing bodies, and the Fitness and Amateur Sport Branch was able to bring about effective co-operation in the staging of the Winter and Summer Games in the 1970s. An agreement to focus the attention of these Games on young, potential athletes instead of established, national-calibre athletes helped to win over the provinces. Indeed, these Games were a major factor in bringing about the development of sport divisions within the provincial government bureaucracies. Provincial activities hitherto had focused largely on recreation and fitness. Sport divisions within provincial bureaucracies were followed shortly by provincial sport administration centres in the larger and more prosperous provinces, leading to a commitment by at least one jurisdiction, Ontario, to the construction and support of a provincial sport training centre.

The establishment of two divisions within the Fitness and Amateur Sport Branch, one for sport and a second for recreation, was made ostensibly so that the federal government could serve both these areas with equal effectiveness. In reality, it allowed the branch to move with the tide that was sweeping it towards greater support for elite sport. The mounting pressure for a creditable performance by Canadians at the Montreal Olympics – and the growing acceptance and continued commercialization of sport in Canada – made this direction an attractive one for the federal government. These factors accounted for the growing discrepancy during the 1970s in the budgets allocated to the two divisions respectively. In fact, Recreation Canada was pressed to find ways to expend the monies that it did receive.

This move towards greater support for elite development, however, was not without its problems. The avowed purpose of the creation of the arm's-length support agencies in the early 1970s was to prevent a federal government take-over of amateur sport in Canada (Campagnolo 1977b:5). But two of these key arm's-length organizations (the National Sport and Recreation Centre and the Coaching Association of Canada) were funded largely by the federal government. Thus, the professional staff responsible for their operation, located in Ottawa and paid largely from federal coffers, had at best divided loyalties between the Fitness and Amateur Sport Branch and the sport organizations that it served. As federal government contributions to national sport organizations grew in size and proportion of total budget, these organizations themselves lost their autonomy. More and more, they were tied to contributions whose terms required meeting specific performance conditions in international sport as established by Sport Canada (Kidd 1981). The relegation of the National Advisory Council to a purely advisory and a long-range planning role at the start of the decade eliminated an important independent voice that had strived to maintain a balance between elite sport and mass participation programs.

Marc Lalonde, the minister responsible for fitness and amateur sport, was one strong opponent of this slide towards elite sport in the 1970s. During his tenure, he convinced the federal Cabinet in 1973 to make a three-year commitment of funding to the branch on the basis that he would strive to strike a better balance between expenditures on elite sport and mass participation programs. Even with this strong advocate, the goal was never met (T. Bedecki, personal interview, March 1984).

The growing influence of Sport Canada and of the arm's-length organizations created to support elite sport also had a divisive effect on sport in Canada. In the face of these new influences, the Sports Federation of Canada, a congress of national sport governing bodies, had little or no power and was unable to present a unified, independent voice for amateur sport. This was partly because the individual sport governing bodies were reluctant to give up the little autonomy they had left to the federation, but mainly because of the pervasive influence of Sport Canada and its associated arm's-length sport organizations. The National Sport and Recreation Centre added to this divisiveness because many of its functions duplicated those of Sport Canada and of the individual sport governing bodies.

A lack of a unified voice for sport has often been identified as a shortcoming in Canada. It was alluded to at the Olympic Conference staged by the Canadian Olympic Association and the federal government in 1971. In 1975, at a meeting of the governors of the National Sport and Recreation Centre, a proposal was made for a study of how sport in Canada could become more unified. The ensuing study, headed by York University physical educator Bryce Taylor, contained an elaborate analysis of the problems and proposals for their solution. But the ensuing document, *The Unification of Sport Report*, had little apparent impact. The fears of the national sport governing bodies of further loss of autonomy to a "family of sports governing bodies," as the proposed co-ordination agency was called, were not alleviated. In 1979, the COA presented a proposal to Prime Minister

Clark to establish an "amateur sport trust" that would provide funds to amalgamate, under the aegis of the COA, the two existing national multi-sport organizations in Canada – the COA and the Sports Federation of Canada (SFC). The proposed "sport trust" was an alternate use of Loto Canada funds, the rights for which the Conservative government intended to give up to the provinces. This new umbrella organization was to promote and develop Canadian amateur sport at the national and international levels, and with the assistance of national sport governing bodies, increase greatly private-sector support of sport. This proposal was endorsed by the Clark government in a speech that the prime minister gave at a state reception for athletes, coaches, and officials in October 1979 (COA 1980b:60–2). Subsequently, however, the Conservative government handed the rights for the sport lottery over to the provinces and this put an end to this initiative. The COA and the SFC persisted and, in 1980, the COA executive prepared another proposal entitled the *Consolidation of Amateur Sport*. The report lamented what it saw as the declining commitment of the federal government to sport following the 1976 Olympics and criticized sport governing bodies for resisting government initiatives in their domain. Consolidation of sport was what was needed; sport governing bodies could then become the general partner in development and promotion with government playing the role of a limited partner (ibid., 27).

Central to the federal government's involvement in fitness and amateur sport in the 1970s was the balance between the "twin aims" set out in the 1970 Proposed Sports Policy by John Munro. These two aims, mass participation and the pursuit of excellence, were advanced as being mutually reinforcing and inseparable. The reality of the 1970s, however, was that the federal government was being pulled away from mass sport and recreation programs by two different forces. The staging of the Olympic Games in Montreal in 1976 put increasing pressure on the federal government to provide financial and other support to ensure a creditable showing by Canadian athletes. The federal government committed itself to the Olympic Game Plan as proposed by the Canadian Olympic Association and other sport governing bodies. Once committed, it virtually took over this support program and established and maintained direct contact with elite athletes who were to perform for Canada in 1976. The Olympic Games pushed all other non-Olympic programs to the background in the period 1973 to 1976, and funding for sport increased dramatically during this time (Hallett 1981:641). The relative success that Canada experienced in the 1976 Summer Olympics (overall improvement in unofficial standings from twenty-first in Munich in 1972 to eleventh in Montreal) was attributable in no small manner to federal government efforts to support elite athletes and, according to Iona Campagnolo helped create the climate that allowed her to become the first minister for fitness and amateur sport (cited in ibid., 642).

Perhaps the most significant sport event held in Canada relative to federal government sport policy, however, was the Commonwealth Games held in Edmonton in 1978. It was at these Games that the federal government efforts to improve elite sport performance bore fruit. For the first time in the history of these Games, Canada placed first in the unofficial standings, ahead of the traditional front runners, England and Australia. The excellent television coverage of this sport event provided by the CBC meant that millions of Canadians savoured this international sport triumph. Iona Campagnolo was quick to capitalize on this victory; she was paraded around the track on the shoulders of triumphant Canadian athletes at the closing ceremonies, an event captured on the national television network. This was the culmination and the vindication of the federal government's sport policy direction, established in the *Proposed Sports Policy for Canadians*. These two major international sport events, the Olympics and the Commonwealth Games, combined with the fitness movement to block any effective momentum towards a real federal government commitment to mass sport and recreation by the Fitness and Amateur Sport Branch in the 1970s.

The National Advisory Council remained one of the few advocates of federal government mass promotion of sport and physical recreation programs. Its call in 1975 for the concept of "sport for all" seemed to be out of touch with the direction in which the federal government was moving. The Canadian Association for Health, Physical Education and Recreation and the Canadian Parks and Recreation Association were two additional zealous but largely ineffective advocates of sport and recreation for the masses. The federal government moved inexorably to the position that it took in the green, and subsequently in its white paper on sport, which committed the federal government firmly to elite sport and conceded responsibility for recreation and mass sport program development to the provinces.

CHAPTER SEVEN

Towards a New Sport Policy, 1979

The last chapter provided a number of clues about the intended direction of the federal government in sport. This chapter focuses on the events and forces that brought about a new federal government sport policy in 1979.

THE POLITICAL SCENE

The political scene in Canada in the 1970s was dominated by two themes: federal/provincial relations, and the energy crisis and recession in the Western industrialized nations. The shift in power from the federal government to the provinces that had commenced in the 1960s continued unabated through the 1970s. Central to this shift of power was the provincial constitutional prerogative to manage and direct matters concerning health, welfare, education, and natural resources. As these areas of concern became more prominent and important, provincial expenditures continued to grow faster than those of the federal government. Consequently, provincial bureaucracies grew in size and competence. Partly as a consequence, rivalry between the federal and provincial governments also grew. Stevenson (1982:104) has argued that this emphasis on the centrifugal concept of federalism resulted in "a very imperfect realization of Canadian unity." The federal government, perhaps against its wishes, appeared to define its role less in terms of nation building and more in terms of assisting cultural minority groups and disadvantaged provinces. The Liberal government of Prime Minister Trudeau, which was in power throughout the 1970s except for a short hiatus when the Conservatives formed a minority government in 1979, suffered the consequences of this continued shift of power to the provinces.

A Trudeau minority government between 1972 and 1974 was forced to accommodate the New Democratic Party (NDP) in order to stay in office. As a result, there was pressure to increase federal government spending in support of the welfare role of the central government. Pressures from the NDP and the province of Ontario also brought about the "Made in Canada" oil-pricing policy, designed to protect Canadians from rapidly rising oil prices in the mid 1970s. This circumstance did not, however, resolve the fundamental problems of the energy crisis of the 1970s and − by deferring the reckoning with world oil prices − in some ways made the final reckoning worse. A parallel policy also pursued by the Trudeau minority government was that of economic nationalism, a theme dear to the hearts of some politicians of all parties, but particularly to the NDP.

In 1974, Allan MacEachen, then government House leader, engineered the defeat of his own minority government; this strategy paid off as the ensuing election returned the Liberals to power for five more years, this time with a majority. One of the first major steps taken by this government in the fall of 1975 was the implementation of wage and price controls, a measure Trudeau had opposed when it was advocated by Robert Stanfield, leader of the Conservative party, in his 1974 election campaign.

A major issue facing this new Trudeau majority government of the mid 1970s was austerity. Rapidly rising oil prices and the onset of a world-wide recession resulted in growing federal government deficits. The economic recession caused higher unemployment in Canada. This meant greater federal government expenditures on unemployment insurance and welfare payments at a time of a fall-off in tax revenue. These events caused growing concern over governmental fiscal policies. In December 1975, the federal government announced reductions in over-all spending of about $1.5 billion. Prime Minister Trudeau returned from an economic conference of the major Western democratic governments in Bonn, West Germany, in 1978 with the news that new government austerity programs would be instituted and that all federal government expenditures would be scrutinized much more closely. Further government cost-cutting projects were announced to include the spending plans of some 100 federal projects; the public service was to be subjected to trimming of up to 5,000 jobs; and federal/provincial cost-sharing agreements were to be reviewed with a view to reducing federal expenditures (*Canadian News Facts* 1977−8).

A third important fiscal policy introduced in the 1970s was the concept of a comprehensive auditing system. J.J. Macdonnell was appointed auditor-general in 1973 with two important mandates. First, there was to be close accountability for the expenditures of federal funds, and second, there were to be increased efforts to ensure that there was value accruing from these expenditures. The comprehensive audit was developed to achieve these goals. This was, in part, an extension of the Trudeau "rational policy making" and was another force in a more centralized federal bureaucracy.

These fiscal policies put pressure on the federal budget allocations for sport. To accomplish its goal of even-better performances in the 1980s, Sport Canada had looked forward to ever-expanding budgets. Although the allocation of funds to sport by the federal government did not undergo any significant reductions in the late 1970s and early 1980s, there was no room for the hoped-for expansion of funds. This fiscal dilemma led to increased support for the concept of seeking funds for elite sport from the private sector, which was already involved with several national sport associations. We say more about the consequences of this thrust, which gained even greater momentum in the 1980s, in the last three chapters of the book.

Federal/provincial relations continued to deteriorate in the mid 1970s. The federal government was unable to sort out Canada's energy problems or to achieve agreement on how the enormous economic benefits from oil and gas ought to be shared. As a result, Peter Lougheed, premier of Alberta, became a champion of western Canadian demands for greater provincial rights and powers. The election of the Parti Québécois in 1976 set federal/provincial relations back a further step. The outright advocacy of separatism by the Parti Québécois paralysed relations between Ottawa and Quebec and these remained stymied until the sovereignty-association referendum was defeated in 1980.

The impact of these events and a growing sentiment on the part of Canadians was that Trudeau's concept of rational decision making within a highly centralized government was not effective. There was a feeling that the federal government had lost touch with the public and the clientele of its programs. Business interests felt estranged from the government and perceived that there were few new programs of direct benefit to them.

These events had their impact on sport. There was a corresponding sentiment that the federal government had no significant role in the mass sport and fitness program delivery system. At the same time, it became clear that provincial and municipal input would be necessary if the federal government's elite performance goals were to be met. The federal government and the national sport organizations themselves could not identify and train the young talent necessary to achieve optimum results for the elite performance thrust.

The Trudeau government was defeated in the election in the fall of 1979, and the Clark Conservative party came to power with a minority government. But this was to be a short-lived government. Proposals to move the Canadian embassy in Israel from Tel Aviv to Jerusalem and to "privatize" Petro-Canada alienated many voters. In addition, the Lougheed government remained intransigent about an oil-pricing agreement, even in the atmosphere of a "friendly" federal government. The defeat of the Clark government over the Crosbie budget led to the return of a Liberal majority early in 1980, with the problems of inflation and unemployment, a national energy policy, national unity, and federal/provincial relations unresolved. These rapid turnovers in government had a disruptive effect on the implementation of new federal sport and fitness policies. Iona Campagnolo's proposed new sport policy languished for some time before the pieces were picked up by Gerald Regan in 1981.

One of the few legacies of the Clark government that was to have implications for sport in the 1980s was the fulfilment of a previous commitment of the Conservatives to turn over rights to the sport lottery to the provinces. The federal government had been using these monies to help write off the huge deficit accumulated in financing the 1976 Montreal Olympics. Because of the Clark government's action, the revenues from the sport lottery that the Liberal government had intended to use in part for additional funding for Sport Canada were diverted to the provinces. This decision was to have a greater impact on Sport Canada's budget than the federal government austerity program. It made more urgent the need to find private-sector support for elite sport. These political forces combined with other sport-specific events to shape the federal government's sport policies for the 1980s.

CENTRAL ISSUES IN SPORT

A number of sport-specific issues in Canada in the 1970s played a role in determining the direction and shape of federal government sport policies in the 1980s. Some of these related to federal government sport program initiatives in the 1970s and were outlined in some detail in the previous chapter. A brief overview of these initiatives which were important in determining future federal government sport policy will suffice in this chapter. Foremost among these was the success achieved in improving Canada's performance in international amateur sport events. Despite the fact that the support programs put in place in the early 1970s for the 1976 Olympics were hastily conceived, and in the opinion of many, too late to really have any impact, Canada improved its position from twenty-first in 1972 in

Munich to eleventh in Montreal in 1976. There was also a significant increase in the number of Canadian athletes who were internationally rated during the 1970s. Canada's triumph at the Commonwealth Games in Edmonton in 1978 was a key event in federal government sport involvement. The "ceremony" of Iona Campagnolo's victory parade at Commonwealth Stadium made it clear that sport could not only be used politically to promote national unity, but that it also could further the careers of particular politicians.

The federal government's difficulty in mounting any effective initiatives in recreation also played an important part in determining the directions of federal government sport policies in the 1980s. This topic also received considerable attention in the previous chapter. Briefly, despite the availability of specific resources, the creation of a separate Recreation Canada division, and the personal commitment of Marc Lalonde in the early 1970s to the promotion of personal well-being, the federal government did not gain any significant foothold in recreation. Certainly, the grass-roots nature of mass recreation programs, the nebulous nature of recreation itself, and the continued insistence that recreation was the prerogative of the provinces all contributed to this development. At the same time, there were other factors that pulled the federal government away from recreation and towards physical fitness. This direction was attractive not only because of the growing health and fitness craze of the 1970s, but it represented a more concrete and measurable endeavour than recreation. Improved physical fitness on the part of Canadians was much easier to link with better health, and thus, with lower medical costs, than was increased participation rates in recreation.

The change in the nature and role of sport in society that occurred in the 1960s (documented in some detail in chapter 4) continued unabated in the 1970s. Sport's strong affinity with television became even more prominent, and as the dominant forms of sport became more entertainment oriented, these sport forms became even more attractive as commodities to sell goods and services. Sport heroes themselves were able to command large sums of money to sell goods on television and other communication media. By the late 1970s, it had become acceptable for prominent Canadian amateur athletes to associate their talents with the sale of goods and services, and the monies forthcoming accrued either in special trust funds or to the athletes' respective national sport governing bodies. The propensity to judge sport performances on purely objective measurements continued unabated in the 1970s. The dominant forms of sport were valued by the distance jumped or thrown, the time elapsed, the number of goals and assists and points accumulated, rather than the versatility and aesthetic nature of the performance and the struggle or give and take of the competition. This rationalization of sport fitted nicely with the values that sport bureaucrats had assimilated in the scientifically based undergraduate and graduate programs in which they received their training in the 1960s and 1970s.

The great growth of the amateur-sport bureaucracy in Canada, given its bias towards performance evaluation of sport, in turn, added impetus to the propensity to evaluate amateur sport performance largely on the basis of objective record – and to set goals for respective sport organizations to achieve even better performances and records. The development of "Game Plan" in preparation for the 1976 Olympics gave additional impetus to this rationalization of sport.

Another factor that influenced the direction of federal government sport policies in the 1980s was the creation of a minister of state for fitness and amateur sport. The prominence that sport had gained in the 1970s changed the government's view of its importance and significance. The visibility of the 1976 Olympic Games in Montreal and the successes of the Canada Games during the early 1970s provided support for Prime Minister Trudeau's vision of sport as a unifying factor. As a result, Iona Campagnolo was appointed as the first minister of state for sport in 1976. The increased prominence of sport brought greater attention in the House of Commons to the government's role in sport. There were calls for a policy statement on sport. Initially, Campagnolo did not respond to these pressures, but as is the case with most new ministers, she was anxious to establish policy to guide the actions and directions of her branch. Thus were the seeds of the 1977 green paper on sport sown.

DEVELOPMENT OF A NEW
SPORT POLICY

Events Leading to the Green Paper

One of Iona Campagnolo's most important mandates as the first minister for sport and fitness was to produce a coherent national policy. With her appointment came promises to upgrade the fitness and amateur sport program. The ministry was initially intended to be a temporary one and, therefore, it remained under the Department of National Health and Welfare. The minister had been appointed to formulate a national policy and reorganize the branch, but there had been no intention of establishing a permanent and independent Ministry of Fitness and Amateur Sport.

The Speech from the Throne opening the second session of the thirtieth Parliament on 12 October 1976 stated that: "In the after-math of the highly successful Montreal Olympics, and the gratifying results achieved by Canadian athletes, federal support for selected amateur sport and fitness programs will be further augmented" (HC *Debates*, 12 October 1976:3). Campagnolo's first speech in the House expressed a concern for the larger picture of participation and fitness across Canada. She concentrated, however, on Sport Canada plans. She stressed a need to strengthen the sport governing bodies, to increase the understanding of amateur sport in Canada, and to increase coaching development – all aiming towards the building of the foundation necessary for excellence in both competition and in personal fitness (ibid., 14 October 1976:76–7).

While the opposition parties applauded the appointment of a sport minister (the Conservatives reminding the government that they had recommended such a post three-and-a-half years earlier), they now were impatient to see a national policy for fitness and amateur sport. The issues of concern related to participation opportunities for all Canadians, a nation-wide facilities survey, a study of federal/provincial jurisdictions, as well as a general strategy for sport development from schools through to the Olympics (ibid., 19 October 1976:241–7).

In response to this debate, Campagnolo informed the House that her ministry was preparing a policy and that she intended to meet with provincial education and recreation ministers individually, before calling a joint federal/provincial meeting. These meetings were to commence in December 1976; however, they were delayed until the new year. As a result of these meetings, Campagnolo asserted a need for the various government and private-sector organizations to work together. She reiterated her ministry's commitment to the development of both mass recreation and sport excellence, and dismissed suggestions that there was a conflict between these two aims. She conceded, however, that because her branch had more direct access to high-performance sport, it was likely that it would have a correspondingly greater influence there than in recreation. She concluded by promising that a comprehensive national sport policy and a new sport program were forthcoming (FAS *Annual Report*, 1976–7:1–2).

As economic restraints came to dominate parliamentary concerns during the spring of 1977, Campagnolo was once again questioned in the Commons about her branch policy objectives. She again listed the official priorities:

1 To increase the appreciation for and understanding of fitness, physical recreation and amateur sport.

2 To improve the Canadian delivery systems of fitness, physical recreation and amateur sport.
3 To improve the quality of participation in physical recreation and amateur sport.

(HC *Debates*, 5 April 1977:4647).

Although Campagnolo continued to espouse the mass participation thrust, there appeared to be some disagreement between her plans and Sport Canada. Roger Jackson, the director of Sport Canada expressed concern with the ranking of branch objectives. He conceded that they were all important; however, he pointed out that the federal government had been most successful at the national and international levels, and with the development of arm's-length agencies (cited in Hallett 1981:656).

Within a year of her appointment, Campagnolo stated that the first priority of the minister of state for fitness and amateur sport was high-performance competitive sport. This shift in her public posture has been attributed to the influence of her advisers. Many of these key individuals, such as Roger Jackson and Lou Lefaive, had been closely connected with the fitness and amateur sport program since the time of the Task Force and were strong advocates of intensifying federal government efforts to improve international sport performances.

After numerous queries from the opposition, Campagnolo finally announced her intention to release the green paper during a speech entitled "Sportfuture," her first major speech related to sport, delivered at the Canadian National Exhibition Sports Day on 27 August 1977 (Campagnolo 1977a). Public discussions of the government's proposals were to be held in the months immediately following the release of the document. Such a process, she noted, had never been followed before in the making of federal sport policy (ibid., 39). *Toward a National Policy on Amateur Sport: A Working Paper* (the green paper) was tabled in the House of Commons on 24 October 1977, during the first week of the third session of Parliament (HC *Debates*: 166).

Green Paper on Sport

Following the release of the green paper in October 1977, public hearings were scheduled across Canada from 22 November to mid January 1978. Iona Campagnolo set a tight schedule, designating the month of February for the analysis of the briefs, March for the actual writing of the policy paper, and April 1978 as the target date for the announcement of the new sport policy (FAS *Green Paper Briefing Book*, 1977).

Campagnolo resisted considerable pressure to extend the discussion period; despite sticking to that timetable, the white paper was almost one year late. It did not appear until April 1979, just before the Liberal government fell. The short period set aside for a public forum on the discussion paper was deplored by most of the participants in this process. In particular, the structure and constitutions of sport governing bodies did not allow them to respond effectively within this time frame. Their normal pattern at that time was to hold only annual meetings. Thus the typical response to the white paper was put together hurriedly by professional staff members and whatever voluntary executive members were available.

The most controversial aspect of the green paper from the moment it was tabled was the fact that it dealt exclusively with sport, only part of the mandate of the Fitness and Amateur Sport Branch. Although a second paper was promised on fitness and recreation, this announcement did not satisfy many of the respondents. Campagnolo anticipated this criticism by tempering her remarks in the House of Commons, referring to sport in the contexts of social and health benefits, as well as in the political contexts of national pride and unity. Her remarks on the occasion of the tabling of the green paper, however, made it clear that elite sport was the central theme:

The main theme of the sport policy formation document set before the House and Canada's sport family today is the scale of the federal role in sport – the structure of sport, its administration, its technical development, its promotion and many other programs. The commitment of this government to sport access is complete. That is one immutable factor in the paper tabled in this House today. Everything else, I submit, is once again subject to the people.

(HC *Debates*, 24 October 1977:178)

Stressing the federal government's role at the international level of competition, Campagnolo outlined future programs to augment Canadian performance as follows: an upgraded Game Plan for training and coaching support; coaching schools in co-operation with the universities; a coaching apprenticeship program; and increased international competitive opportunities both at home and abroad. The green paper also set an agenda for upcoming international events. The objectives were to achieve first place at the Commonwealth Games to be held in Edmonton in 1978, second place at the Pan-American Games in 1979, and then on to Moscow in 1980, where, Campagnolo hoped, Canada would exceed her tenth (sic) place finish in Montreal (HC *Debates*, 24 October 1977:179–80). The green paper concluded with the statement that the one emerging theme since the 1960s was to "Do something about the sorry performance of most Canadians in international competitions" (Campagnolo 1977b:3).

Reactions to the Green Paper

Nevertheless, the cross-Canada hearings provided the sport community with a unique opportunity to provide input on federal government sport policy and it responded enthusiastically. But negative reactions and criticisms of the green paper erupted as soon as it was tabled in the House of Commons. The long-awaited national sport policy discussion paper was a disappointment to many. Opposition MPs questioned the minister's logic in expressing the need for increased accessibility, and yet proposing for the most part elitist programs and policies. The fact that the already limited time allotted for the public discussion process was further constrained by the intervening Christmas holidays sparked further criticism in the House and from many sport associations.

The public's perception of the green paper process brought into question the access of non-government viewpoints to the government. The timing, in particular, was seen as an indicator of the lack of government interest, especially because the white paper did not appear until April 1979 (Clarke 1980:14–15, 45). Surprisingly, perhaps, there was little reaction from the non-sporting public. The limited distribution and public access to copies of the green paper may have been responsible in part for this apparent lack of interest or concern.

The frustrations expressed during the public hearings were suggested by a Globe and Mail headline following the final hearing in Ottawa on 15 January 1978. "Give it another try, athletes tell Ottawa" summed up some of the feelings of dissatisfaction with the green paper's contents and general thrust. Non-government sport people wanted less government bureaucracy, less government control, and less emphasis on elite athletes. The same people asked for more money for sport, more concern for mass sport participation, and more consultation with amateur sport officials.

The briefs presented at the public hearings varied in appearance and in length from the response of the Canadian Olympic Association, which was "as flashy looking as the Government's own publication" and nearly twice as long, to simple one- or two-page submissions from concerned individuals (*Globe and Mail*, 16 January 1978). They also ranged from the generally positive Canadian Coaching Association submission to the highly critical paper from sport activists Bruce Kidd and Abby Hoffman. Kidd and Hoffman essentially rewrote the green paper, submitting an alternate: "Toward a REAL National Policy for Sport." Their submission received the endorsement of the City of Toronto. However, there was no real coherent theme or plan for sport development in this brief. The views of current elite athletes were conspicuous by their absence. Sport governing bodies did not have any formal mechanism in place to consult athletes when preparing their briefs. Neither was there any great inclination on their part to do so.

Almost every brief criticized the government for its single-minded promotion of excellence at the expense of mass recreation. Bruce Kidd argued that separating sport from recreation presented the Canadian public with an unfair choice. It was suggested that the outcomes of the hearings and the analysis of the briefs should be presented to the national sport governing bodies before a final policy was made. Campagnolo concluded the discussions at the final hearing in Ottawa by saying that the "exercise had been valuable" but commented on the criticism of the government proposals by saying that "the pros and cons are in the eye of the beholder" (*Globe and Mail*, 16 January 1978).

W.J. Trudeau, Diane Rajotte, and other public servants were assigned the task of analysing the responses to the green paper. They examined over 300 submissions, not including the responses from the provinces (Trudeau 1978). In addition to the criticisms about the hearing process and the absence of a parallel document on fitness and recreation, a number of common themes appeared in the Trudeau analysis of responses. Most sport associations indicated that they wanted much more government funding, but they wished these monies to be free of any strings attached. In other words, they wanted to be free of government and arm's-length agency control. However, no proposals were forthcoming as to how national sport governing bodies could support themselves, despite the demands for greater autonomy. Many respondents saw the current administration of sport as being too costly and top heavy. At the same time, there was support for expanded services to be provided at the National Sport and Recreation Centre. There was strong support for coaching, officiating, and national team training programs; however, some respondents felt that the Coaching Association of Canada should be made accountable to the national sport governing bodies. Briefs from the universities expressed the fear that the proposal to locate national team programs at various universities would upset the philosophy and balance of intercollegiate athletic programs. Although there was a need expressed for an umbrella organization for all sports, there was little agreement on the format. A revitalized Sports Federation of Canada was the most often mentioned body for this role. Criticisms of the failure of the government to incorporate the reactions of the sport community in the writing of the white paper on sport need to be tempered in the light of these contradictory positions taken by the petitioners.

The proposal to establish a promotion agency for amateur sport, which was one of the few concrete suggestions in the green paper, met with general opposition. The national sport governing bodies felt that the promotional role belonged to each specific sport. There was also some dissatisfaction with the way "other programs" had been dealt with. It was felt that programs for those with disabilities, older people, and the native peoples should have been discussed in greater detail.

Respondents were largely indifferent to the proposed domestic structural changes, such as the need for a separate ministry of sport and the issue of regional offices. The major recurring concern was the autonomy of the sport governing bodies in relation to government and arm's-length agencies. There was a feeling that the volunteers on whom all sport relied so heavily were increasingly being alienated by the large and complex bureaucracy.

The subsequent white paper was written by Sidney Wise, a historian at Carleton University. He had been a member of the group that wrote the Task Force Report. Wise had a great interest in sport and was a friend of Doug Fisher, a syndicated news columnist and television personality at that time. Fisher also had been a member of the Task Force Report writing group. He had been an advocate of government intervention in sport in the years preceding the Fitness and Amateur Sport Act. He was then an NDP member of Parliament from the Port Arthur-Fort William federal riding. Fisher's influence on sport policy was considerable in the 1970s. As noted in chapter 5, he had been a confidant of John Munro. He was able subsequently to establish this same relationship with Iona Campagnolo. As such, he had considerable input into the white paper. Besides the previously mentioned roles of Roger Jackson and Lou Lefaive, there were three other sport administrators whose influence can be seen in the white paper: Geoff Gowan, the technical director of the Coaching Association of Canada; Marion Lay, a former Olympic swimmer and at this time, a consultant with Sport Canada; and Dan Pugliese, who was located at the National Sport and Recreation Centre. The predilection of these five sport administrators for a technical and bureaucratic approach to sport influenced greatly the content of the white paper (L. Lefaive, personal interview, May 1986).

There was little apparent regard in the white paper for the concerns expressed in reactions to the green paper. The white paper took what it wanted from these briefs and was able to ignore those suggestions that did not fit with the government's prevailing views. This was possible because of the lack of unity in the sport community. The following comment concerning the priorities of Sport Canada provides, perhaps, the best summary of the overall reactions to the Green Paper: "If Sport Canada is really only interested in gold medals at the Olympics it should say so and give up the pretense of trying to be all things to all people. Whatever its mandate, it should be clearly defined" (Trudeau 1978:11).

Green Paper on Fitness and Recreation

Despite the public outcry over the release of two separate green papers, one on sport and one on fitness and recreation, the government maintained that this was both a practical necessity and a result of existing circumstances. One obvious reason for the separation was the unresolved problem of federal/provincial jurisdiction in recreation. Second, unlike Sport Canada, Recreation Canada had a low profile, lacked key spokespersons, and had experienced high staff turnover. These factors had resulted in internal disarray and the lack of clear policy direction. Thus, while attention was focused on the green paper on sport, Recreation Canada spent the year re-evaluating its own role. In January 1978, a nation-wide fact-finding process was initiated. A committee of selected officials from across Canada compiled information on the country's complex recreation system. Meetings were held in the capital city of each province and territory, and a total of 165 oral and written presentations were received. These views were integrated into a discussion draft, which was circulated widely to interested persons and groups. On 20 March 1979, Iona Campagnolo appointed the Canadian Association of Health, Physical Education, and Recreation (CAHPER) and the Canadian Parks and Recreation Association (CPRA) to conduct hearings on the resultant recreation green paper, *Toward a National Policy on Fitness and Recreation* (FAS *Annual Report*, 1978–9: v, 6).

The green paper was intended to provide national objectives for all levels of recreation services and to clarify terms and jurisdictions. It described the evolution of the federal role from "Recreation Canada" to "Fitness and Recreation Canada" in 1977. This change was intended to "better align the objectives of the Branch to the growing awareness of the need for leadership and guidance in the fitness area, as well as to reaffirm the interest in and primary responsibility for physical recreation" (Campagnolo 1979a:14). The branch's position was further clarified by the prime minister in a June 1978 letter to CPRA. He made it clear that the fitness and amateur sport mandate would not be extended beyond athletic activities and fitness; however, he felt it was necessary to have a co-ordinating mechanism for the multilateral area of recreation services (ibid., 14).

The green paper expressed the branch's commitment to continue to promote the values of fitness and physical recreation with some proposed structural alterations. It advocated that the Fitness and Recreation Canada directorate be split into their two distinct components. The functions of the Recreation Canada directorate would be to provide a federal liaison in physical recreation matters and to provide funds for national recreation-oriented associations in their national endeavours. A part of this directorate would be a Sport Participation Unit, the purpose of which would be to increase participation by Canadians in amateur sport. The rationale provided for this organizational structure was the apparent difficulty in adapting the organizational philosophy aimed at high-performance development to one that would be more favourable to participation development (ibid., 15).

The role of the new Fitness Canada directorate was to provide an awareness and link to traditional health services that had the potential to deliver fitness services, to act as a catalyst and co-ordinator with related groups, and to initiate specific programs with other levels of government and in co-operation with other agencies. A partnership role was advocated, whereby the fitness mandate would be broadened. Meanwhile, recreation was to be concerned simply with national-level programs (ibid., 16).

The Interprovincial Council of Sport and Recreation Directors and Recreation Ministers reacted bitterly. Recreation had long been a controversial and ambiguous issue at the federal level. In response to questions in the House of Commons in 1976, Campagnolo had stated that her clear mandate was in sport and fitness and did not in any way deal directly with recreation. She assured the House that there had not been a change in her mandate, rather just a change in the manner in which it was described! The provinces had requested that the Government of Canada no longer participate in recreation at the provincial level, although it could continue to refer to "physical recreation" but not recreation, per se: "The federal government is merely acquiescing in the request of the provinces to remove itself from this sphere by gradually diminishing services so that the provinces take them up. The provinces are prepared to move into this field as we gradually move out" (HC Debates, 31 May 1978:5913–4).

In spite of the apparent acquiescence to provincial demands for jurisdiction over recreation, the green paper was released. However, because Campagnolo chose to use CAHPER and the CPRA to steer this process without involving the Interprovincial Sport and Recreation Council, the council closed ranks and caused the hearings to collapse (Hallett 1981:723).

Two months after the appointment of the CAHPER/CPRA Joint Committee, the Liberals fell in the May 1979 federal election. In the 1980–1 FAS *Annual Report,* Recreation Canada had disappeared without any notice, leaving the two distinct areas of Sport Canada and Fitness Canada.

WHITE PAPER ON SPORT

The analysis of the green paper on sport continued during the fitness and recreation discussions. Finally, after numerous delays, Campagnolo released the white paper, *Partners in Pursuit of Excellence – A National Policy on Amateur Sport,* on 30 April 1979. The federal election campaign was nearing its end and Parliament was not in session at this time; thus the white paper was never officially tabled in the House of Commons.

The white paper dealt exclusively with sport, although Campagnolo stated in its introduction that "I recognize that the two fields overlap and in practice have a mutually reinforcing relationship. From the public discussion on the sport Green Paper and preliminary drafts of the Fitness-Recreation Discussion Paper, I have concluded that the federal government must accord a higher priority to sport" (Campagnolo 1979b:5). She proceeded to wash her hands of recreation, stating that the primary role in this domain had been taken over by the provinces and the municipalities. Campagnolo maintained, however, that the federal government had a continuing responsibility to ensure appropriate national goals and standards in health and fitness (ibid., 5–6).

The white paper commenced with a definition of terms and government roles. Sport, although defined initially as a diverse area, was placed in the Canadian cultural context, and the national unity theme was incorporated once again. The assumption was made that "Canadians, surely, want to win in international competition. Disagreement arises over the means. Most of us, I believe, want to win by creating an athletic excellence that flows naturally from a broad participatory base" (ibid., 5). The authors of the white paper perceived from the green paper hearings that the major issues were related to the recent government involvement in sport, the degree of

this involvement, the erosion of the autonomy of sport, the indispens-
able role of the volunteer, the profusion of "arm's-length" corporations, and the fact that too much attention was being paid to elite sport
at the expense of the development of a broad participation base. But
at the same time, Campagnolo made it clear that her white paper
focused primarily on a national sport policy that would produce
programs to better Canada's performances. This would be accomplished, she maintained, by the sport governing bodies (ibid., 6).

According to the white paper, a summary of the previous ten years
in Canadian sport development showed "real, substantial and measurable progress" (ibid., 6). This progress was attributed in large part
to the work of full-time sport administrators, technical experts, and
coaches. The federal government took much of the credit for these
new elements in Canadian sport, but admitted that it had caused some
unease within established Canadian sport organizations. Despite a
continued government leadership commitment, a modified federal
presence was recommended for several reasons (ibid., 7).

First, the growth of provincial government programs necessitated
an increase in federal assistance and general co-ordinating functions.
Second, the participation of volunteers and corporate sponsors
needed to be enhanced. Finally, there was a need to modify the role of
government in sport. It was doubtful that the next decade would see
an expansion of the federal role comparable to that of the previous
ten years. Thus, it was argued that there was a need for structural
changes in the administration of sport at the national level, as
opposed to a further enlargement of the federal role in sport (ibid.,
7).

In terms of proposed action, the white paper argued that an
internal reorganization of the Fitness and Amateur Sport Branch
would not be enough. The frustrations resulting from the previous
administration and its financial procedures had generated much of
the criticism of the federal government's role during the green paper
discussions. Although it would be irresponsible for the government to
relinquish the role it had established, it was felt that:

sport depends ultimately upon the willingness of private citizens and business
to assist the athletic and recreational endeavours of their countrymen.
Government has a responsibility to avoid any action, including an over-
solicitous paternalism, that would inhibit the enthusiasm, inventiveness and
dedication of Canadians ... Athletic excellence demands funding and
technical expertise beyond the reach of athletes and most voluntary associations.

(Campagnolo 1979b:8)

Thus, the new national policy advocated a partnership of shared-sector responsibilities.

Among the significant new members of this partnership would be Canadian university resources, business and corporate sponsors, a responsible and efficient sport community, and a new federal amateur sport structure. The federal government proposed to establish an amateur sport council. Those elements now a part of Sport Canada in the Fitness and Amateur Sport Branch of the Department of Health and Welfare were to be transferred to this new umbrella organization.

Campagnolo stopped short of establishing an autonomous Sport Canada, preferring instead to leave the organization within government. The proposed sport council was to have greater flexibility but would remain a Schedule B Crown Corporation under the Financial Administration Act, subject to legal and financial control by the Treasury Board. It was suggested that other agencies "which owe their origins to government initiatives," such as the National Sport and Recreation Centre and the Coaching Association of Canada, would also be included as part of the sport council (Campagnolo 1979b:10). Fitness and mass sport programs would remain with health and welfare. The sport council would permit a greater degree of flexibility in administration and financing. It was hoped also that the Loto Canada share of revenues to sport would continue beyond 1979. In addition, a national sport trust was to be established to ensure a solid base of funds. Ultimately, "the bridge to excellence will stand on the financial support pillars of public sector revenue, Loto Canada revenue and private sector revenue" (ibid., 11).

The white paper also proposed that the government sponsor a national congress of sport. This was an attractive concept for the government because it would provide a single forum and a legitimate link between voluntary sport organizations and government. It was a proposal that was not included in the green paper, nor in the vast majority of briefs.

The second part of the white paper focused on a national plan for sport. An outline was provided of the federal objectives and organization in this regard, projected for the next five to ten years. The plan was based on the structural recommendations put forth in Part 1 of the paper. Based on the fundamental premise that "sport is a continuum" (ibid., 15), the pursuit of excellence and the development of a shared-sector partnership were to serve as both the goal and the means. The federal government was to act as the co-ordinator. The successes of recent years were cited to support the government as the most appropriate organization for this role. It was pointed out that underlying this progress had been an increase in federal spending in sport from $6 million in 1971 to $30 million in 1977 (ibid., 16).

The paper argued that it was time to strive for a whole-hearted effort towards the unification of sport. An integral part of the planning process was to be an evaluation and reassessment of recent experiences. Although every national sport governing body had undergone such an exercise following the 1976 Olympics, these had been carried out in isolation from each other (ibid., 17).

The national goal for sport was to achieve the highest pinnacle of athletic performance in international competition and to improve Canada's 1976 position over the next decade. This goal would require a common agreement and a common commitment – both to the national goals and to developmental thrusts – to maximize sport resources and to rise to the challenge (ibid., 18).

The developmental thrusts proposed in the paper were based on three areas: technical, administration, and promotion and funding. The recommendations were similar to the green paper proposals. The federal government would continue its involvement in each of these three areas, based upon the availability of public funds. It would support those sports dedicated to the pursuit of excellence in national and international competition – "especially those with a broad base and a demonstrable record of competent fiscal and technical adminis-tration and success or high prospects of achieving success" (ibid., 19). Despite the general opposition to a promotion agency for sport, the white paper reiterated a commitment to establishing an agency of this nature.

The successful implementation of the national plan would depend upon three principles: "accountability, clear delineation of roles and partnership" (ibid., 21). The major shareholders of this partnership would be the federal government, the national sport governing bodies, the national service and multi-sport organizations, and the provincial governments. The roles and responsibilities of each were outlined. Their common role was "to reach agreement with all National Plan partners on a plan and on each partner's responsibili-ties designed to achieve the goals of the plan" (ibid., 24).

IMPACT OF NEW POLICIES

The impact of the 1979 white paper on sport was dampened considerably by a number of unfortunate events. First, the program clients, that is, the sport organizations and governing bodies, were never fully convinced that the process had not been somewhat of a sham. The very short time allowed for responses to the green paper, the subsequent long delay in the issuing of the white paper, and the perception that the client input had been largely ignored in producing the white paper led to a great deal of scepticism about the outcome. Second, the white paper was issued after Parliament had been dissolved and shortly before the Liberal government fell in 1979. The uncertainty and political instability of the next eighteen months meant that there was little the Fitness and Amateur Sport officials could do in moving ahead to implement the proposals in the 1979 white paper. By the time the Liberal government returned to office in 1980, Iona Campagnolo was no longer a member of the government; it was necessary for the new minister, Gerald Regan, to be briefed on the issues that faced sport.

The green paper on recreation brought to a head the matter of jurisdiction for mass recreation programs. The federal government abdicated its responsibilities in this area and resolved to concentrate on the more narrow field of physical fitness. The matter of the relationship between Fitness Canada and Participaction, however, was not addressed; this meant that there continued to be an overlap of services between these two organizations and conflicts over areas of responsibility and jurisdiction, particularly in regard to promotional activities.

The matter of co-ordination between federal government efforts in elite sport and those of the corresponding municipal and provincial government levels also was never appropriately addressed. The process certainly did clarify that the federal government was anxious to continue its efforts to promote high-performance sport in Canada. The federal government still perceived sport as a unity symbol and one that could be used politically to good advantage by the Liberal government of the day. The insistence of the government on more objective accountability of federal expenditures was to keep national sport governing bodies under continued pressure to apply for conditional grants; these grants were more and more often tied to specific goals to be achieved in high-performance sport.

Despite concerns from the sport community, the white paper on sport proposed the creation of a government department to co-ordinate, publicize, and promote elite sport in Canada. Some saw this as a parallel agency to Participaction. This recommendation was omitted in the 1981 statement and there would be no apparent efforts to put such a department in place. Little attention was paid to the burgeoning sport bureaucracy. The implications of this bureaucracy for the autonomy of sport governing bodies and the growing tendency to serve and pursue its own ends were not addressed. The rapid turn over in ministers in the 1980s was to create a policy-making vacuum into which senior sport public servants would step. These loose ends lead us to a preliminary discussion of federal government sport policy and programs in the early 1980s.

CHAPTER EIGHT

Policies and Programs
in the 1980s:
A Preliminary View

In chapter 7, we described how pressures that mounted in the mid 1970s for new federal government sport policy making culminated in the 1979 white paper, *Partners in Pursuit of Excellence*. However, in the subsequent political instability arising from the election and the ensuing defeat of the Conservative party, little action was taken to implement the white paper proposals. The Conservative government was defeated in 1980, but it was not until June 1981 that the new minister, Gerald Regan, was in place and was sufficiently informed that a second white paper, *A Challenge to the Nation: Fitness and Amateur Sport in the 80s*, was produced. This document was more in tune with events of the early 1980s. It confirmed that the government was intent on pursuing its own priorities in elite or high-performance sport. It would focus on further improvements by Canadian athletes in international sport events. In this chapter we are concerned mainly with these directions in elite or high-performance sport. Fitness Canada programs are discussed only briefly in order to put in context relative program expenditures and joint efforts between Sport Canada and Fitness Canada.

REGAN WHITE PAPER

The 1979 white paper had addressed the issue of the autonomy of sport in Canada and recommended that a sport council be established. The sport council was to be composed of representatives of the national sport governing bodies, umbrella organizations, and volunteer associations. Those elements of Sport Canada now in the Fitness and Amateur Sport Branch were to be transferred to the sport council, while fitness and recreation activities would remain in the

Department of National Health and Welfare. The primary responsibilities of the sport council were to be in the areas relating to Canadian participation in national and international sport, dedicated to the pursuit of excellence at these levels of competition. The 1981 Regan statement, however, made no mention of this proposal. This left the matter of elite sport policy in the 1980s largely in the hands of the minister and the Sport Canada bureaucracy. Thus, the rhetoric in the white paper about shared government and private-sector responsibilities for elite sport and the desirability of a quasi-independent sport council were once again brushed aside. This left the government free to promote high-performance sport.

The attempt by the federal government to develop a white paper on recreation ended in failure and the federal government was forced to abandon any formal responsibility for recreation. Instead, this new 1981 Regan policy narrowed its focus to physical fitness and made much of the government's commitment to promote and develop programs for special target groups who were known to eschew physical activity. The 1979 white paper on sport had included considerable rhetoric about the government's successes in mass sport and fitness programs. But the 1981 document conceded that more needed to be done to promote physical activity for the poor, for women, and for those with disabilities. This white paper also established specific priorities to ensure the continuation of the Canada Fitness Survey, the funding of practical research projects in recreation, continued support of Participaction, and new initiatives in leadership development in co-operation with the provinces and in employee-fitness projects (FAS *Communique*, 1981:3).

The 1981 Regan paper also made clear the federal government's primary intention to pursue its desire to promote high-performance sport in Canada. A government press release described the policy paper as "confirmation of the federal government's commitment to the pursuit of excellence in amateur sport and to continued efforts to increase the number of Canadians taking part in physical activity" (ibid., 1981:2). The contents of the paper identified "the initiatives the federal government proposes to take to ensure the momentum generated by the 1976 Olympics and the 1978 Commonwealth Games is carried into the 1980s and taken to new heights" (ibid.). Specific notice was given of the courses of action to meet these goals. The most important of these were to be the establishment of national training centres, increased athlete assistance based on performance, and a new hosting policy for major sport events. Priority funding was to be allocated to sports demonstrating a commitment to, and a consistent record of, excellence. National sport technical services were to be augmented to aid in the further development of high-performance athletes (ibid., 3).

The 1981 paper was careful to point out that "the federal government does not manage amateur sport programs ... However, because of the growing complexity of administration, the federal government feels it necessary to work with the national associations in the development of adequate management, accounting, and monitoring processes, without interfering with the autonomy of the national associations" (Regan 1981:7–8). In response to requests from the sport governing bodies, the minister gave the assurance that as these associations demonstrated their competence in administrative and financial matters, the federal government would be prepared to offer a block-funding system, permitting greater flexibility both on a short-term basis and for the purposes of long-term planning. The national sport associations would be required to submit a complete financial audit on an annual basis.

In terms of technical assistance, the federal government renewed its commitment to "focus its energies and resources on the pursuit of excellence in amateur sport" during the 1980s (ibid., 10). This meant that government support would be largely channelled in the direction of international competitions such as the Olympic, Commonwealth, and Pan-American Games. A new emphasis would be placed on the evaluation of programs and outcomes. The promotion of amateur sport would continue to be "professionalized" as the costs and needs of amateur sport escalated. The news in 1981 that Calgary was to be the host city for the 1988 Winter Olympic Games gave additional impetus to this thrust.

CENTRAL ACTORS AND AGENCIES
IN THE EARLY 1980S

The defeat of the Trudeau Liberal government in the spring of 1979 and the subsequent short-lived Clark Conservative government had a disruptive effect on the Fitness and Amateur Sport Branch programs in the late 1970s and early 1980s. Iona Campagnolo was replaced in the Conservative Cabinet by Steven Paproski, veteran MP and former professional football player from Edmonton. There was little time for Paproski to become familiar with the job because the Conservative minority government was defeated early in 1980. Not surprisingly, one of the few statements that Paproski made was to reinforce the proposition that more money would need to be found in the private sector to support high-performance sport in the 1980s. The era of ever-increasing federal government budgets, in Paproski's opinion, was over. As noted in the previous chapter, another legacy of the Conservative term of office was the transfer of the rights to sport lotteries from the federal to the provincial governments. The Liberal government and the sport community had viewed the federal sport lottery as a source of funds that would allow the federal contribution to sport and fitness to grow substantially in the 1980s.

When the Trudeau Liberal government returned to power in 1980, it appointed Gerald Regan, the former premier of Nova Scotia, as minister of state for fitness and amateur sport. Regan was a conscientious and capable minister who took time to become familiar with the issues and problems related to sport and physical fitness. Unfortunately, however, Regan was to be the last Liberal minister of this ilk. In 1982, when Regan was moved to international trade, the Liberal government commenced to use the sport and fitness portfolio in the same manner as other junior posts, to test new Cabinet ministers. There were no fewer than five subsequent appointments to this post during the Liberal's term of office through the first half of the 1980s.

Another disruptive factor was the frequent change of ministry locale for the Fitness and Amateur Sport Branch. In June 1979, it moved from health and welfare to secretary of state. When Regan became minister, he also held the labour portfolio and consequently, the branch moved to Labour Canada. After a brief period back in the office of the secretary of state, the branch was shifted once again to the Department of National Health and Welfare, when Celine Hervieux-Payette took office in 1982.

Roger Jackson resigned in 1978 as director of Sport Canada to take a position as dean of the Faculty of Physical Education at the University of Calgary. Lou Lefaive, who had previously been director of the Fitness and Amateur Sport Directorate and a founding member of Hockey Canada's board of directors, took over the post. Lefaive resigned in December 1979 and was replaced by Richard Knapp. Knapp had been director of finance and administration in the Fitness and Amateur Sport Branch office and he held the interim directorship of Sport Canada until the appointment in 1981 of Abby Hoffman. Hoffman had been one of Canada's most illustrious middle-distance runners in the 1960s and 1970s and was known as a sport activist who had championed the cause of amateur athletes in Canada in the 1970s. Hoffman brought with her to the post a strong bias towards the further development of high-performance athletes in Canada. She set out to realize this objective by tougher negotiations with representative national sport governing bodies in Canada. She also was a champion of equal opportunities for women in sport;

under her leadership, the women's program, which had been languishing for some years, took on a new and revitalized role in the branch. The one point of continuity through this period of changing actors was Peter Lesaux, who was appointed assistant deputy minister in 1977; he continued in this role until 1986.

The National Advisory Council on Fitness and Amateur Sport also suffered from the changes in federal government. When the Liberal government returned to power in 1980, there were no less than twenty-five vacancies in the council and it had not met for a period of eighteen months (J. Barber, personal communication, February 1984). The council was able to revitalize itself somewhat and in 1981, it established subcommittees to study four critical issues in sport and physical fitness, that is, fitness and the aging, sport-funding policies, a review of the original Act, and family recreation. The federal government, however, continued to maintain considerable distance between the council and the branch itself so the council remained relegated to a long-range planning and advisory role. It did not become involved in the development of policies or the day-to-day operations of the branch.

Certain reorganizational steps taken within the branch in the early 1980s reflected changing emphases and priorities. Fitness and recreation were officially amalgamated under Fitness Canada in 1980–1. The federal role in recreation was reduced to that of co-ordinator and overseer of national and federal/provincial activities. A major internal restructuring of Sport Canada occurred in 1982–3. Four new units were established to facilitate the implementation of the "pursuit of excellence" mandate. Thus, Sport Canada was divided into an Association Management Unit, a High Performance Unit, a Planning and Evaluation Unit, and Special Programs.

SPORT CANADA POLICIES AND PROGRAMS

High-Performance Sport Centres

Sport training centres were not a new idea. The concept of a national sport training centre was raised by the National Advisory Council on Fitness and Amateur Sport in the 1960s. By that time, national sport training centres had become a part of the efforts to achieve success in international sport by certain Eastern European countries. But the geographic and political barriers to establishing a single such centre in Canada were too great to overcome and no concrete action was taken. In the 1970s, it became apparent that multi-purpose centres that served the needs of a number of sports were not practical or effective. Alternate models, such as those developed in England in the 1970s, where a number of sport-specific training centres were established in various locations were better suited to the political and geographic idiosyncracies of Canada. It was in this context that the federal government proposed, in its 1979 white paper on sport to establish a number of sport training centres as one of its priorities in the 1980s.

One of Gerald Regan's first moves as minister of state for fitness and amateur sport was to appoint Bob Hayes in the fall of 1980 as a special assistant to the assistant deputy minister to study the feasibility of national sport training centres. Bob Hayes was director of athletics at St Mary's University, and a friend and political supporter of Gerald Regan. Hayes worked for one year on this project and submitted a report to assistant deputy minister Peter Lesaux in July 1981. Hayes's position as an outsider responsible directly to the assistant deputy minister naturally caused resentment inside Sport Canada. Subsequent criticisms of his report as being too general must be evaluated in the light of these sentiments. Hayes departed from this consultant's post in the summer of 1981, but left the government with a number of obligations. Prior to Hayes's arrival, a committee of Sport Canada consultants had been formed to work on the concept of sport-development centres. A two-year pilot project had been initiated under the auspices of the Canadian Track and Field Association at York University. Hayes reviewed this project in his report, and prior to his departure, he recommended the establishment of twelve training centres for five sports, specifying that government contributions be limited to $30,000 per centre.

Upon receiving the Hayes report at a November 1981 federal/provincial meeting, the provincial ministers responsible for sport and recreation established a High Performance Blueprint Committee to review forthcoming centre proposals from a provincial perspective. With Hayes gone, Sport Canada was left with the task of completing the development of the concept of high-performance sport centres. During the latter half of 1981, a small task-force group consisting of Sport Canada and Coaching Association of Canada consultants had conducted studies of Canada's major Games sports. In 1982, the federal government established the High Performance Sport Task Force to study the technical requirements of national sport governing bodies. The Task Force was to make recommendations regarding appropriate funding levels, improved technical planning and the provision of technical services (sports science, coaching, technical planning, and evaluation) to national organizations from both government and non-government sources. The outcome of these studies was a Sport Canada policy for high-performance sport centres. Two separate documents were produced in 1983: *High Performance Sport Centres – A Sport Canada Policy* and *High Performance Sport Centres – General Criteria*. The first outlined the Sport Canada mandate in relation to high-performance sport, and provided a framework for jurisdictional responsibilities in this regard. The second document provided a description of the general criteria to be considered in the establishment of centres. Experts from the sport community, including national coaches, carded athletes, facility administrators, medical and paramedical professionals, technical directors, and sport scientists worked together to develop the general criteria. The criteria designated two major areas of emphasis for proposed centres: the provision of appropriate training facilities for national teams and high performance athletes and coaches; and the use of a sports science facility for assessment, evaluation, and research purposes.

By June 1984, fourteen sports had established one or more centres. Five sports had two or more regional centres while the rest were based on single-location national centres for men, women, and/or specific events, varying from sport to sport. A 1983–4 review of existing centres recommended improvements in the areas of administration, athlete assistance, coaching, sports science and medical support, and facility standards. The federal budget for high-performance sport centres was estimated at $500,000 for the 1984–5 fiscal year and as such, it was a high priority item in the Sport Canada budget.

Negotiations for some twenty-five new centres in the near future soon got under way. Sport Canada committed itself to providing more and improved centres to be linked with the national sport governing bodies. Although the Sport Canada mandate is the pursuit of excellence, the provincial sport governing bodies also make use of the centres to maximize the developmental aspect of their mandate.

Although the establishment of national sport training centres in the 1980s represents a major step forward in the drive for better international sport performances, there remain many unresolved problems. Three brief case studies serve to illustrate some of these. Consider men's basketball. There has never been a national training centre established for this team. The head coach, Jack Donohue, has been content to allow his players to train and compete at United States and Canadian universities, bringing his team together after classes ended in early spring. After a training session in Ottawa, the team typically embarks on an exhibition schedule. Then it is deemed ready for any international events that might be on the books. This approach has been quite successful. Canada finished fourth in both the 1976 and 1984 Olympic Games. In 1983, Canada scored a major triumph by defeating the United States team in the semi-finals of the World Student Games in Edmonton and subsequently won the gold medal by beating Yugoslavia. However, appropriate training and competitive schedules for players once they graduate from university remain a problem. These difficulties have been partly resolved by placing some of Canada's top players in "semi-professional" leagues in Europe over the winter months. Still, some of Canada's national team members lack appropriate training and competitive opportunities once they complete their university-playing eligibility.

The Canadian Amateur Wrestling Association (CAWA) took an opposite tack. When the federal government announced it would help finance national training centes, the CAWA called for bids for such a centre in wrestling. A number came forward, but the bid from the University of Regina was judged to be the best. Plans went forward to establish the centre in Regina. However, problems arose immediately. Many national team wrestlers who relocated could not find appropriate employment or education opportunities in Regina. In addition, the remoteness of the site to top-flight competition added extra travel time to the wrestlers' schedules. The selection of a national coach who was not a Canadian caused resentment and animosity in the coaching ranks across the country (J. Albinson, personal interview, 13 June 1986).

The pool from which national wrestlers are drawn is largely Canadian university wrestling teams. The potential loss of top-flight wrestlers from these teams to the national training site created additional tensions. University coaches did not encourage their best wrestlers to go to Regina. As a result of these problems, only three nationally carded wrestlers turned up at the national training centre in Regina. None of these three was from the Canadian university wrestling program (ibid.).

Thus, the concept of a single national training centre in wrestling collapsed. A temporary national training centre was set up at the University of Western Ontario in order to prepare athletes for the 1984 Summer Olympics. Once these Olympics were over, three primary centres, located in Vancouver, Montreal, and Guelph, were established, with a number of "secondary" centres designated at Toronto, London, St Catharines, and Winnipeg. The position of national coach was changed to national team director, whose prime responsibility was to co-ordinate coaching and training programs across these primary and secondary training sites.

The weaknesses of this decentralized approach are obvious. There simply are not enough top-flight wrestlers in Canada to spread over six or seven training centres. Thus the competitive training environment is not adequate to prepare international-calibre athletes. The difference in style and quality of coaching over a number of centres also detracts from the objective of producing world-class wrestlers. A system whereby wrestlers can move from university programs to regional training centres and then to a national centre still appears to be out of reach.

Track and field has its own unique set of problems. The talent pool for high-performance athletes lies largely in various local clubs, many of which have existed in Canada for some years. There is, however, another pool of athletes who are attending United States and Canadian universities. The first national training centre in track and field was established in 1981 as a pilot project at York University, with the Scarborough Optimist Track and Field Club forming the membership base. It was recognized early that there would need to be a number of centres, each of which focused on a group of related events. Thus, York University was designated as a "sprint" centre. In 1982 a middle distance centre was placed at the University of Victoria. Here there was no strong resident club and the formation of a university high-performance club played a central role in this centre's development. A third centre was established at the University of Saskatchewan at Saskatoon in the same year, focusing on multiple events for women. Successive specialized-event centres were subsequently set up at the University of Toronto and at the University of Manitoba in 1984, and in Montreal in 1985. The University of Toronto was designated as a multiple-event centre for the decathlon and heptathlon. Its development was based on the concept that it would serve all existing clubs in the greater metropolitan Toronto area, thus alleviating the resentment that some clubs felt about the primacy of the Scarborough Optimists at York University (R. Lund, personal interview, 25 May 1986).

But two of these centres have floundered. Government funding was withdrawn from the University of Saskatchewan centre in 1985; it had depended greatly on the personal attraction of Diane Jones-Konihowski, the heptathlon athlete who attracted so much media attention at the Commonwealth Games in Edmonton in 1978. When she left to take a job developing Alberta athletic talent for the 1988 Olympics in Calgary, much of the attraction of this centre disappeared. Federal government support of the centre at the University of Manitoba also was subsequently withdrawn. Neither the Saskatchewan nor the Manitoba centre was deemed by Sport Canada to have satisfied the development criteria established for these track and field events (ibid.).

Of the seventy-eight sport training centres in existence in 1986, the majority (fifty-five) were located at Canadian universities (R. Pugh, personal interview, 23 May 1986). This circumstance has added another dimension to the problems related to national training centres. On the one hand, Canadian university athletic directors and coaches are quick to complain when national training centres are established at "other" universities. They argue, with some justification, that this gives the chosen university a competitive advantage in attracting athletes. If student athletes connected with the centre compete for the university, it disrupts the competitive level of the league conference. The magnitude of this problem can be seen by the fact that of the 769 athletes carded in the Athlete Assistance Program in 1985–6, approximately one-third were enrolled in Canadian universities (ibid.). This often results in other universities downgrading or eliminating that sport from their intercollegiate sport roster. On the other hand, most Canadian universities have been quick to establish national training centres if the opportunity presents itself. The perceived financial advantages and the associated prestige are too attractive for potential recipients to refuse by standing on principle.

Training centres are essential to the further development of Canada's high-performance athletes. The co-operation of federal and provincial governments, site or host institution, national and provincial sport governing bodies, and where appropriate, any local and regional sport clubs is essential for the concept to work. This amount of co-operation is a tall task and has seldom been fully realized. A strong and committed host institution also appears to be an essential ingredient in successful training centres. Individuals, organizations, and institutions with vested interests in either locating training centres at their favoured location or obstructing the development of national training centres elsewhere have made the task even more difficult. Further rethinking and more real co-operation are needed before the potential of training centres in Canada can be realized.

Hosting Policy

The unprecedented number of major international multi-sport events hosted in Canada in the late 1960s and the 1970s gave rise to a very substantial capital outlay for new sport facilities. For example, capital costs for the 1967 Pan-Am Games held in Winnipeg totalled $5.3 million (B. Kidd, personal communication, 22 May 1984); the Montreal Olympics capital expenditures came to $805.5 million (Quebec 1980); while the Commonwealth Games facility costs in

Edmonton in 1978 amounted to some $36 million (Commonwealth Games Foundation 1978). In addition, considerable tax dollars were spent every two years for upgrading existing facilities and construct- ing new ones at the host sites of the Canada Games. Capital costs for these Games from 1967 to 1983 have totalled $32.5 million (DNHW *1983–4 Estimates*, 1983:4–29). These activities and the continuing increasing attraction of professional sport stimulated a demand for massive spectator sport facilities in a number of major centres that had not benefited from this sport facility spending spree. As a result, professional sport interests were able to command public support to build major facilities in Calgary (the Saddledome) and Vancouver (BC Place) and, more recently, to generate provincial and civic support for a covered stadium in Toronto.

It became increasingly clear that major sport facilities constructed for international and, indeed, often for national sport events were not contributing substantially to the development of high-performance athletes, much less assisting in increasing mass sport participation in Canada. The very high maintenance and operational costs of such facilities, geared to meet international sport standards and to house large numbers of spectators, often precluded their use even by high-performance athletes.

In recognition of these problems, Gerald Regan served notice in his 1981 policy statement that Sport Canada would develop a hosting policy for the 1980s. This policy recognized that some major sport events "contribute only minimally, if at all, to the development of high-performance sport in Canada" (FAS *Sport Canada Hosting Policy*, 1983:4). In future, federal government sponsorship of major sport events was to take into account the extent to which such events subsequently would contribute to the development of high-perfor- mance athletes. This new hosting policy established that capital funds would be forthcoming from the federal government only for international multi-sport "games" events. Other international single, multi-sport, and invitational events could expect to receive assistance for operating costs only. Only under exceptional circumstances should sponsors of national multi-sport games events expect federal funds for operating or for capital costs. The hosting policy noted that the Canada Games were governed under a separate federal govern- ment document and that funding for these events would continue to be provided under the existing arrangements. We have more to say about the ramifications of the hosting policy in the last two chapters.

Athlete Assistance Program

The classification of Canadian athletes by means of an A, B, or C card system, depending on performance relative to international stand-ings, was developed by the Canadian Olympic Association (COA) in 1973. This system, however, did not involve any direct funding to individual athletes. The need for direct financial support was increasingly vocalized in the years preceding the 1976 Montreal Olympics. A 1974 change in International Olympic Committee eligibility regulations made allowances for lost-time income compen-sation for athletes. In April 1975, the COA received a delegation of athletes representing all sports asking for such direct assistance. The nature of this program precluded Sport Canada from participating. The government could provide student aid such as bursaries but could not risk the precedent of broken-time payments for athletes (COA, Annual General Meeting, 1976). Such funding was introduced by the COA in April 1975 and subsequently the co-operative funding of Game Plan between Sport Canada and the COA was modified. The COA and the Olympic Trust took over the lost-time compensation payments and some other direct-aid programs. Following the 1976 Olympics, the program was taken over by Sport Canada. A grant-in-aid program also was instituted at this time to assist non-Olympic high-performance athletes with training and education expenses. The two programs were merged in 1979 into what is now known as the Athlete Assistance Program (AAP). As a part of Sport Canada's High Performance Unit, the program maintained contact with all the recognized national sport organizations; however, a distinction remained between Olympic and non-Olympic sports. Criteria for carding in non-Olympic international sports were somewhat more restrictive. In 1984–5, all carded athletes received a basic $450 monthly allowance. An additional high-performance payment of $100 and $200 was made to B and A card Olympic athletes respectively. Only Olympic sports qualified for C card status, that is, prospective international athletes (J. Brooks, personal communica-tion, 24 July 1984). The carding and subsequent support of an athlete was related to criteria established jointly by the representative national body and the administrators of the AAP. There was an effort made to balance the number of carded athletes with actual national team opportunities.

In 1980, a program was developed to assist athletes who were retiring from international competition. Assistance was offered to help these athletes ease into a career or further education. In 1981–2, the program was modified to an "extended athlete assistance pro-gram" with the deletion of the word retirement, which was seen to be a disincentive to athletes considering a return to active competition. Disabled athletes have also been integrated into the program in recent years. They were carded using criteria similar to the other athletes. In 1984, nine wheelchair and five blind athletes received direct funding.

Since the merging of the various components of the Athlete Assistance Program in 1980–1, the number of carded and funded athletes has steadily increased. In 1979–80, a total of $2.6 million was spent in support of 750 individual athletes. Following the Olympic boycott of 1980, there were numerous retirements and the total fell to 540. Since then, the numbers have risen again to 645 in 1981– 2, and 797 in 1982–3. The $4 million program supported over 750 athletes in 1983–4. A new high-performance training allowance for A and B card athletes was introduced in 1982–3 in recognition of special needs at that level of training and competition. As well, 129 student athletes in the Atlantic provinces received special assistance (FAS *Annual Report*, 1982–3:15).

The AAP has been most successful in allowing young athletes to commit a substantial amount of their time to training and competing while they complete their education. In a 1985 evaluation of the program (Macintosh & Albinson), AAP athletes expressed a high level of satisfaction with the program and the level of financial support. These young athletes were content to extend their post-secondary education careers over a considerably longer period of time than normal. However, two weaknesses of the program were uncovered in this study. The AAP athletes were typically quite young. The average age of carded athletes was twenty-two years. There were only differences of a little more than one year between A and B, and B and C, card holders respectively. It is apparent that Canadian athletes are too young to compete with the more seasoned older athletes that are typically found in many events and teams in the Soviet Union and the Eastern-bloc countries. More incentives are needed to keep the best of Canada's young athletes in their sport until they reach a more mature age. In accomplishing such a goal, the economic and social climate in Canada, which makes it unattractive to remain an "amateur" athlete once desired education qualifications are completed, will need to be overcome. The reward system in the Soviet Union and Eastern-bloc countries, where many athletes are recruited to the state sport system once they retire, will be difficult to replicate in Canada. The number of career opportunities in sport are greatly limited and the status of such existing jobs is much lower in Canada than in the Soviet Union and Eastern-bloc countries.

Another serious weakness of the AAP program was the underrepresentation of athletes from working-class families. The majority (55 percent) of AAP athletes had either attended university or had attained a university degree. For the AAP drop-out athletes surveyed in this study, this percentage was 77. The personal interview survey of some 60 AAP athletes confirmed that Canada's pool of high-performance athletes was drawn largely from the middle and upper class; thus a potential source of athletes from working-class backgrounds is essentially lost to the country. This is a serious problem that has its roots in the more general socio-economic disparities in Canadian society and as such, will be most difficult to resolve. Identifying such potential athletes before they drop out of the formal competitive sport structure is the first problem. Keeping them in the high-performance sport delivery system, which is centred largely in a middle-upper class educational milieu is even more problematic.

The Athlete Assistance Program is an essential part of Canada's efforts to make further improvements in her international sport performances, and particularly to ensure a creditable showing at the Calgary Olympics in 1988. Further relaxing of restrictions on the amount of money amateur athletes are allowed to earn will make it even more critical for Sport Canada to provide its corps of "state" athletes with adequate financial compensation to allow them to train year-round. Although Sport Canada plans to invest more heavily in increasing the number of full-time, paid national coaches, and in the further development of high-performance centres, such investment eventually will boost the numbers of A and B card athletes, who in turn will require direct financial assistance. Some of the broader questions about Canada's use of "state" athletes are raised in chapter 10.

"Best Ever '88"

The "Best Ever '88" Winter Olympic Team Program received federal government approval in June 1982. It was established in an effort to "capitalize on the 1988 Calgary Games by setting the objective of having Canada's best performance ever in Winter Olympic competition" (Sport Canada 1984). There is a $25 million budget for the program, bringing the federal government's total athlete support investment in the ten Winter Olympic sports to nearly $50 million in the five years leading to the Calgary Games. This amount was in addition to the $200 million federal commitment to the capital and operating costs of staging the Games.

Each of the sports involved in the program was required to prepare a five-year plan with the assistance of Sport Canada consultants. The plans were aimed at improving and upgrading various developmental facets of each of the sports, including competitions, coaching, facilities, training opportunities, athlete assistance, training centres, and administration. This program differs from the regular athlete-assistance program in that the monies are turned over directly to the appropriate sport governing bodies for distribution according to their particular priorities and requirements.

In August 1984, Jacques LaPierre, the last of the Liberal government's sport ministers announced that the "Best Ever" program was to be extended to the 1988 Summer Olympic Games. The federal government was to commit some $38 million to this program over the four years preceding the 1988 Games. Nine million dollars of these additional funds were to go to bolster the athlete-assistance programs in Summer Games events, $5 million to improve Canadian coaches, $14 million to support Summer Game national teams, $7.5 million to high-performance centres, and $2.5 million to sport science centres.

The "Best Ever '88" program is an essential part of Canadian efforts to "show the flag" in Calgary at the 1988 Winter Olympics. As such, these monies appear to be secure up to that point. But the funds are not part of any Sport Canada base budget. Given the present drive by Otto Jelinek to greatly expand private-sector support of sport, it is questionable whether the federal government will continue this type of support beyond 1988. This matter receives further attention in chapter 10.

JOINT PROGRAMS

Women's Program

Equal opportunities for women in fitness and sport were the subject of much discussion but little apparent action during the early 1970s. In 1974, however, in anticipation of the International Year of Women (1975) and the beginning of the Decade of Women (1975–85), Marion Lay, a Sport Canada consultant, was given financial support to arrange a conference dealing with the issue. The National Conference on Women in Sport, held in Toronto in 1974, made a series of recommendations to enhance the participation of girls and women in sport. Two nation-wide surveys undertaken by the federal government, the 1972 Leisure Survey and the 1976 Fitness and Sport Survey, identified a significant underrepresentation of women in sport and physical recreation. During the 1974–9 period, however, the women's issue was pushed into the background as federal government energy was funnelled into defining a more general mandate and policy for amateur sport in Canada (Lewis 1980).

Neither the green paper nor the 1979 white paper on sport made any mention of a women's program. Women were not designated as a special target group despite previously documented needs. When women's issues were raised, it was in the perspective of high-performance female athletes and not for the need for more women in coaching and administration. Iona Campagnolo appointed women to two senior executive positions on fitness and amateur sport committees during her tenure as minister: "However, these appointments did not emerge from any policy or program, but from the initiative taken by the Minister. Over and above these appointments, the Minister felt that the needs of women in sport could adequately be met through existing Branch policies and programs" (ibid., 62).

Finally, in 1979–80, in recognition of the need for affirmative action, a Women's Program was developed under the auspices of the Fitness and Amateur Sport Branch. This program was unique in that it preceded any official policy statement by some seven years. The aim of the Women's Program was to promote more involvement by women in sport and fitness activities. The program itself was launched in November 1980 with a budget of $250,000. Sue Vail, a Sport Canada consultant, was appointed to oversee it. A major purpose of these funds was to initiate research into women in physical activity. But a Women in Sport Directory and a Leadership Survey also were developed in the first year.

A second national conference, the Female Athlete Conference, was staged in 1980 at Simon Fraser University, sponsored jointly by the Institute for Human Performance at that institution and the federal government. This conference made a series of recommendations. As was the case in the 1975 conference, some of these were implemented and others were not. The 1980 conference was one of the contributing factors to the establishment of the Canadian Association for the Advancement of Women and Sport (CAAWS) in the fall of that year. CAAWS is a national non-profit organization, partly funded by the Secretary of State and the Fitness and Amateur Sport Branch, whose aim it is to "promote, develop, and advocate a feminist perspective on women and sport" (Sport Canada 1986:6).

The research initiated earlier confirmed, among other things, that although women participated in leadership roles at the middle and lower levels of sport organizations, they were seriously underrepresented at the decision-making level. (Some of these studies are cited in the next chapter.) As a result of this research, an internship program for retired female athletes in sport administration at the National Sport and Recreation Centre was developed and implemented. In 1983–4, the internship program was expanded to provide a seven-month on-the-job training program for retired female athletes and women graduates of physical education and recreation programs.

This program has been most successful in increasing the percentage of women who hold "entry level" professional positions at the National Sport and Recreation Centre in Ottawa. A study undertaken by Sport Canada revealed that 62 percent of the positions at the program co-ordinator level in the centre in 1985 were held by women (Fitness and Amateur Sport 1985c). But this same study confirmed that women still made up only a small minority of chief executive officers, technical directors, and those in the national coaching ranks. As a result, the focus of the internship program was expanded to include potential full-time female coaches. The title of the program has been changing correspondingly to the Women in Sport and Fitness Leadership Program (Sport Canada 1986).

A second major initiative undertaken by the women's program was the National Association Contributions Program (NACP), initiated in 1982–3. The NACP was established to provide funds to national sport associations for initiatives to increase female participation in sport and fitness activities. By this time the budget allocation to the total Women's Program had increased to $350,000.

A number of promotional publications and films on women in sport and fitness also were produced during this period. The NACP also provided more than thirty clients with funds to undertake projects that would encourage more women to become involved as leaders and participants (FAS Annual Report, 1982–3:17). Fitness Canada also undertook to interpret the Canada Fitness Survey data specifically for women.

A culmination of more than a decade of effort in the Women's Program was the release in 1986 of a document entitled *Women in Sport: A Sport Canada Policy*. This document set as the official goal of Sport Canada equality of opportunity for women in all levels of the sport system. It also outlined the action-oriented approach that will be taken by the Women's Program and by Sport Canada to achieve this objective.

Given the changes in attitudes towards women in the work place that have occurred in Canada during the last decade and corresponding gains by women in middle-level professional and management positions, it is difficult to assess the effectiveness of the Women's Program. Certainly there is no doubt, however, that the research and programs initiated and the advocacy role adopted by CAAWS have served to bring to light more objectively the inequality of opportunity for women in sport. The women's internship program has obviously been successful in finding more positions for women at the lower echelons in the National Sport and Recreation Centre in Ottawa. But more efforts are required if middle- and upper-administrative positions and technical and coaching positions in sport are to be filled by a greater proportion of women. Ironically, women are still fighting for the equality of opportunity in sport that was supposedly guaranteed in the Canadian Charter of Rights and Freedoms.

Other Joint Programs

Sport Action Travelcade, formerly known as the Sport Demonstration Project, celebrated its tenth anniversary in 1981. The name change during the anniversary year was intended to "better reflect both the focus and the flair that have evolved within the program since its establishment in 1971" (FAS *Annual Report*, 1981–2:17). The travelling exhibition spotlights local athletes and clubs at major public gatherings such as the Canada Games, Edmonton's Klondike Days, and Toronto's Canadian National Exhibition. Now a year-round program, Sport Action reaches more than half a million Canadians annually and demonstrates over twenty-five sport and fitness activities. This has been one area where all levels of government and the private sector across Canada have worked co-operatively to identify major national, provincial, and local events where the program might appear (ibid.).

Another significant joint program in the early 1980s was that for persons with disabilities. Fitness and Amateur Sport provided $200,000 in 1980–1 to assist with preparations for the International Year of the Disabled (IYDP). A special committee was established to review sport, fitness, and recreation proposals for people with disabilities and a co-ordinator was hired for IYDP activities. In 1981–2, the Canadian Federation of Sport Organizations for the Disabled was developed. This umbrella organization encompasses all national sport governing bodies for athletes with disabilities. The 1982 Pan American Wheelchair Games were held in Halifax, Nova Scotia, assisted by a $1.8 million contribution from the federal government.

In 1982–3, the Program for the Disabled was supported by funds from both Fitness Canada and Sport Canada. Contributions totalled $715,000, with $275,000 from Fitness Canada and $440,000 from Sport Canada. A federal/provincial policy review of support to sports for people with disabilities was completed; criteria for Sport Canada's Athlete Assistance Program were adjusted to include athletes with disabilities. As a result, thirteen such athletes obtained carded status during 1982–3 (ibid., 1982–3:18).

FITNESS CANADA POLICIES
AND PROGRAMS

One of the major roles Fitness Canada played in the early 1980s was the support of a national fitness survey. Preparations commenced in 1979–80 for the Canada Fitness Survey, a project designed to measure the fitness level of Canadians and provide data to national health, recreation, and fitness associations for program planning and evaluation (FAS *Annual Report*, 1979–80:7–8). The Standardized Test of Fitness to be used was developed by the Fitness and Amateur Sport Branch in conjunction with the Canadian Public Health Association. A national planning committee was established and Gerry Glassford (University of Alberta) and Claude Bouchard (Laval University) were appointed as co-chairmen. The committee consisted of representatives of the Canadian Association for Health, Physical Education and Recreation, the Canadian Association of Sports Sciences, the Canadian Parks/Recreation Association, the Canadian Public Health Association, the Canadian Medical Association, the provinces, and the Fitness and Amateur Sport Branch.

The project began in February 1980 with the testing of a random sampling of 40,000 Canadians. This served as preparation for the main study, a six-month in-depth survey of Canadians aged 7–65 that provided a data base of the fitness levels and recreation patterns of Canadians (ibid., 1980–1:10). Eighty-two communities across Canada took part "in the most comprehensive survey of physical fitness and lifestyle conducted anywhere in the world" (ibid., 1982–3:8). Fitness Canada contributed more than $1.4 million in 1981–2 to the testing. Preliminary results were released by sport and fitness minister Gerald Regan in June 1982. A $600,000 contribution from Fitness Canada in 1982–3 enabled the release of several major survey reports: *Canada's Fitness: Preliminary Findings; Fitness and Aging; A User's Guide to CFS Findings; Fitness and Lifestyle in Canada;* and *Canadian Youth and Physical Activity.* Reports on women's fitness and other topics are forthcoming.

Another important initiative of Fitness Canada was to promote co-operation with the provinces. A new federal/provincial council was established in 1979–80 to facilitate the co-operative planning of fitness programs with the provinces, and to encourage information exchange (ibid., 1979–80:7). Fitness Canada provided a secretariat. The council was to meet twice a year, with the chairman selected from among the provincial representatives. Meetings have focused on such special areas as programs for those with disabilities, volunteer leadership development, and outdoor recreation programs. In 1982, Fitness Canada co-sponsored a federal/provincial conference on activity among Canadians. At another level, the Health Promotion Unit located in the Health Services and Promotion Branch of Health and Welfare Canada also has responsibilities to promote the health and social well-being of Canadians. There are, however, few links between Fitness Canada and the Health Promotion Unit. Fitness Canada's position between this later unit and Participaction leaves it in a precarious position. The health and sports team of the Neilson task force on government program review recommended that Fitness Canada and the Health Promotion Unit be integrated in an arm's-length corporation, that would "market concepts and programs within the mandates" of these two divisions (Canada 1986:230). This report recognized that, given the high visibility and success of Participaction, any such new arm's-length agency would need to develop formal links with Participaction's board of directors. The Fitness Summit, held in Ottawa in June 1986 and sponsored by Fitness Canada, should also have a significant impact on the future role of Fitness Canada.

ISSUES, CONFLICTS, AND EMERGING PATTERNS

The events of the late 1970s paved the way for the federal government to concentrate its efforts on the development of high-performance athletes and to define its role in physical recreation more narrowly to the promotion of physical fitness at the national level. In 1978, the provincial ministers recognized a federal role in support of national and international sport. When the provincial governments refused to participate in the vetting of the federal government's 1979 green paper on recreation, efforts to produce a federal white paper on this topic collapsed. As a result, the primary roles of the federal government in high-performance sport and the provincial governments in mass sport and recreation programs finally were defined. In 1983, the provincial ministers signed an interprovincial statement defining their role in support of the broad field of recreation.

The outstanding success of Canadian athletes at the 1978 Commonwealth Games whetted the appetite of Canadians for even better performances in future international sport competitions. These expectations paved the way for the federal government to intensify its efforts to use sport as a unity symbol and allowed for increased pressure on national sport governing bodies to rationalize their programs to ensure continuing improved performances by Canadian athletes. Although this drive was to falter when Canadian athletes fell into their customary third-place role in the 1982 Commonwealth Games in Brisbane, Australia, federal government policy was vindicated at the 1984 Summer Olympic Games when Canadians placed fourth in the unofficial medal standings. Even though these Games were boycotted by the Soviet Union, East Germany, and most of the Eastern-bloc countries, Canada finished ahead of most of her traditional rivals, including Australia, Great Britain, the Scandinavian countries, and all the Western European nations. More important, numerous medal performances by Canadian athletes in Los Angeles were viewed on television with great pride and satisfaction by millions of Canadians.

There still, however, were conflicts among the primary actors and agencies. The major sport federations remained central to success in improving high-performance sport. About one-third of the total fitness and amateur sport expenditures of almost $60 million in 1982–3 was in the form of contributions to national sport organizations. The Canadian Ski Association was the biggest benefactor, receiving about $1.7 million. The Canadian Interuniversity Athletic Union and the Canadian Track and Field Association each received approximately $1 million (FAS Annual Report, 1982–3). In addition, the national sport federations were supported further by grants of $2.3 million and $4.5 million to the Coaching Association of Canada and the National Sport and Recreation Centre respectively. The sport federations continued to lobby for unconditional grants, insisting that they knew best how these monies should be spent in their particular sport. Abby Hoffman, the new director of Sport Canada, however, spent much of her time and effort to get these bodies to develop clear and concise plans for improving the performance of elite athletes.

Hoffman achieved a good deal of success in this endeavour, partly because of increasing performance expectations of the Canadian public and many people in the sporting fraternity. The rapid turnover of ministers of state for fitness and amateur sport in the first half of the 1980s, and the continued minor role played by the National Advisory Council allowed the public servants, and particularly Abby Hoffman, a relatively free hand to pursue such objectives. Hoffman introduced the concept of quadrennial planning, whereby national sports organizations were to establish four-year plans in the period between the 1984 and the 1988 Olympics. These plans were to set specific goals for 1988 medal performances tied to corresponding fund requirements. These quadrennial plans have become part of the operational model of almost all national sport governing bodies and are subject to regular review by Sport Canada. The spectre of withdrawal of federal government funding has played not an inconsiderable role in the implementation of this "rationalization" of national sport association goals.

The provincial governments' appetites for involvement in sport had been nurtured with the introduction of the Canada Games and by the continued commercialization and rationalization of sport in the 1970s. This appetite was whetted further by the prospect of the political advantages that could be gained by association with elite sport. Thus, the matter of the respective roles of the federal and provincial governments in the development of high-performance athletes increasingly became an issue in the early 1980s. In an attempt to develop a rationale for the sharing of responsibilities in this area, the federal/provincial council of ministers responsible for sport and recreation commenced work on the development of such a plan. The development of such a blueprint was an important agenda item at the 1982 meeting of this council. Issues to be dealt with included "the development of high performance athletes, refinements concerning the Canada Games and proposed changes to the federal government's hosting policy" (ibid., 1982–3:15). A working document on this matter is still confidential and there is likely to be considerable negotiation and conflict before these jurisdictional matters are resolved.

Another feature of the first half of the 1980 decade was the use made of the post of minister of state for fitness and amateur sport. It became a testing ground for new Cabinet members. A rapid succession of such ministers was anxious to make political capital out of their portfolio, and they tended to seize on controversial issues and make popular pronouncements on sport policy before consulting with appropriate public servants. When drug scandals involving Canadian athletes broke out at the Pan American Games in Venezuela in August 1983, and shortly after, when Canadian athletes returning from meets in Eastern Europe were apprehended with steroids in their possessions, Hervieux-Payette made a spontaneous statement that Canadian sport federations must take immediate steps to stop their athletes from using performance-enhancing drugs or face the prospect of losing government funds. Sport Canada commenced work immediately on the development of a comprehensive plan to ensure that sport governing bodies were taking adequate measures to discourage athlete steroid and drug use. The result was *Drug Use and Doping Control in Sport – A Sport Canada Policy*, issued in 1984, with specific directives to sport governing bodies to follow. Sport Canada committed over $650,000 to drug testing for the 1983–4 season; $20,000 of these monies was allotted for educational materials, $100,000 for research projects, and $250,000 was allocated to the actual testing procedures (Dickie 1984:53).

Jacques Olivier, who followed Hervieux-Payette as minister of state for fitness and amateur sport, pounced on the bilingual issue as his platform for gaining publicity. During an interview at the Sarajevo Winter Olympics, Olivier stated that amateur sport had "stonewalled" bilingualism (*Globe and Mail*, 9 February 1984). Canadian sport governing bodies and, indeed, Sport Canada itself had fallen well behind other national organizations in the development of bilingual services, particularly the provision of French-speaking coaches and translation services at meetings and conferences. Once again, Olivier had no compunction about using the threat of federal government fund removal. He ordered Sport Canada officials to review all its contracts to ensure that the principle of bilingualism was being upheld. In addition, Olivier in April 1984 instructed federal sport public servants to send only one-quarter of the approximately $46 million allocated to more than 100 sport federations. The rest would be withheld until his office had a chance to ensure that some level of bilingual services were being provided. Twenty-two national sport federations were singled out for special attention (ibid., 19 April 1984).

Olivier also criticized the Canadian Olympic Association and especially the organizers of the Calgary Games for their lack of co-operation in bilingualism efforts, particularly in view of the $200 million contribution the federal government had committed to the 1988 Winter Olympics. Reflecting on his role as sport minister, and alluding to the tenuous nature of the position, Olivier remarked that "As minister I do not have the right to intervene directly in the working of federations and the Canadian Olympic Association, but, before signing an agreement with these organizations for the granting of millions of dollars, I can impose certain conditions ... I may not be there [as minister] very long, but the new agreements I am about to sign will be lasting" (*Globe and Mail*, 9 February 1984).

Another issue that came to the fore in the 1980s was the matter of corporate sponsorship of sport federations and of specific sport events. The federal government had proclaimed in the late 1970s and the early 1980s that additional federal government funds would not be forthcoming in the amounts necessary for continued high-performance athlete improvement and, therefore, that sport governing bodies would have to increase their efforts to tap the private sector for these funds. As a result, many sport federations did seek out and attain corporation sponsorship. But in some cases, these sponsors were tobacco, brewery, and liquor companies. The public association of these products with sport federations and athletes who also were sponsored by the government was problematic. The federal government's position regarding the detrimental effects of tobacco on the health of Canadians was compromised. This issue came to a head when the Canadian Ski Association (csa) signed a multi-million dollar contract late in 1983 with Macdonald Export A to sponsor the national championships in alpine, jumping, and nordic-combined events for five years. This agreement was attacked immediately in full-page ads placed in newspapers across Canada by a coalition of health groups. Federal health minister Monique Bégin and sport minister Jacques Olivier joined in with objections and once again threatened to cut off the annual federal government grant of $2.5 million unless the csa agreed to cancel the sponsorship contract. Steve Podborski and Ken Read, two of Canada's most renowned skiers added fuel to the fire by refusing to accept Macdonald trophies when they won Canadian championships early in 1984. While Olivier sent congratulatory telegrams supporting the skiers' position, csa executive director, Greg Hilton, contended that the winners must accept their awards: "We have to get across to our competitors that things are tight these days and it's difficult to get sponsors. Sometimes people just have to swallow their pride ... I certainly hope we can get a policy in place because I think we owe it to our sponsors" (*Globe and Mail*, 7 March 1984).

This conflict was finally resolved in January 1984 when Conservative government sport minister Otto Jelinek announced that the federal Cabinet would cut off financial help to any amateur sport groups that accepted a tobacco company as a sponsor. Existing contracts, however, could be honoured. The issue of corporate sponsorship of sport by breweries and distillers of alcoholic beverages is raised in chapter 10.

Endorsements and sponsorship of individual athletes also has become increasingly a matter of concern. The International Olympic Committee gradually has acquiesced to the respective world sport federations for more liberal definitions of eligibility, and for extending the conditions whereby individual athletes may accept monies for their endeavours. Most sports now allow amateur athletes to accept sponsorship money but typically require these monies to be placed in trust until the athlete's "amateur" career is finished. Variations among world sport federations' regulations in these matters have led to some interesting contradictions. For example, Wayne Gretzky was not eligible to play hockey in the Winter Olympics because of the millions of dollars he has earned from the sport; however, Steve Podborski continued to retain his amateur status despite his estimated $1.2 million earnings from skiing (*Toronto Star*, 14 April 1984). Earnings of the magnitude of Steve Podborski's also raise the issue of federal government sponsorship of athletes who have the potential to become financially well off through their athletic prowess. Should tax monies be used to support persons who then capitalize on their performances as representatives of Canada to earn substantial sums of money?

The performance of Canadian athletes at international sport events clearly has become of great significance to Canadians and their respective levels of government. The federal government's interest in sport can be seen clearly in the rapidly escalating budget allocation to Sport Canada in the early 1980s. This figure almost doubled from $21.7 million in 1979–80 to $40.4 million in 1982–3, in a period where federal government expenditures presumably were under close scrutiny. Provincial governments have not been far behind in realizing the political potential of sport. This use of sport depends upon ever improving performance measures to illustrate success and government involvement in sport has important consequences for the meaning and practice of sport in Canadian society.

CHAPTER NINE

Major Outcomes and Consequences

In the preceding chapters, we traced the story of the federal government's role in sport since the passage of the Fitness and Amateur Sport Act in 1961. We identified the forces and events that caused the government to become involved with sport; those that motivated it to change from an indirect and passive role to a forceful and direct one in the promotion of elite or high-performance sport in 1969; and those that allowed the government to intensify its efforts to identify with the success of Canada's international athletes in the 1970s. In this story, the emphasis has been on the manner in which the government reacted to certain key forces and events. But as it became increasingly involved, the government itself naturally became an intervening force in the manner in which sport was viewed and practised in Canadian society. This chapter identifies the major outcomes and consequences of recent federal government involvement sport, returning to the major themes introduced in chapter 1 that have been woven into this story of federal government and sport in Canada over the past two-and-a-half decades.

CHANGING VIEWS OF SPORT/ RATIONALE FOR FEDERAL GOVERNMENT INVOLVEMENT

The common themes that characterize government activity in sport include the degree of such involvement in terms of political ideology and the extent to which the country has developed economically and technically. The involvement is usually of a pragmatic and utilitarian nature, motivated by a desire to promote nationalism and propagate dominant social and cultural relations (see for instance, Cantelon & Gruneau 1982; Kidd 1978; and Semotiuk 1980).

Consider the case of the National Physical Fitness Act in 1943. This venture was the result of the high rejection rate of Canadian draft inductees, many on the basis of health-related factors. The National Physical Fitness Act was conceived to assist the provinces in developing physical fitness and sport programs designed to improve the physical capacities of young Canadians. In the years between the repeal of the National Physical Fitness Act in 1954 and the passage of Bill C-131 in 1961, the health values of sport and physical fitness programs remained as central themes on the part of the remaining federal government sport and fitness consultant staff. The placement of this residual group in the Department of National Health and Welfare was also a factor in the prominence of health-related goals in federal government circles during this period. Indeed, the impetus for the original Fitness and Amateur Sport Bill has often been ascribed to the Duke of Edinburgh's speech in 1959 to the Canadian Medical Association in which he deplored the low fitness level of adult Canadians. The material for this speech purportedly was supplied by Doris Plewes, a federal government fitness and sport consultant whose role as an advocate of mass fitness programs was well known.

But another development began to make itself felt in Canada at this time. Sport was emerging as an increasingly important aspect of international politics. The period immediately following World War II saw the Soviet Union incorporate elite sport programs into its foreign policy. Many Eastern European socialist states followed suit and the accompanying sport endeavours were soon seen by many Western industrialized nations as efforts to use sport as a vehicle for the promotion of national identity and ideology. Canadians, who had no comparable federal programs, were concerned about their declining place in international hockey and were beginning to become aware of the role of sport in promoting national pride and unity. This concern was reflected in the press and in the House of Commons debates, where almost all references to sport were related to Canada's sagging international sport accomplishments, particularly in reference to hockey. This concern on the part of Canadians was to grow along with the ever-increasing prominence given in the 1960s to world sport championships, the Olympic Games, and related international sporting events such as the Pan American and the Commonwealth Games. The awarding of the 1976 Olympic Games to Montreal in the late 1960s provided a focal point for these intensified nationalistic sport sentiments in Canada.

Concern about Canada's international sport reputation and efforts by some segments of Canadian society to urge the federal government to assist in providing better representation in international sporting events coincided with the increasing demand for welfare-state programs in other spheres of Canadian life. A growing belief that the federal government had a responsibility to increase accessibility to cultural activities in Canada readily accommodated the interests of the growing number of advocates for federal involvement in the development of elite athletes. Such advocates were most often spokespeople for national sport governing bodies and associations who espoused the universal values of sport, but whose real motives more often appeared to be associated with the development of their own sport associations' interests through the promotion of elite athletes.

There were, however, uncertainties and controversies about Canadian federal government involvement in sport. Those who held that sport's prime value is in its contribution to personal development and self-actualization were in agreement with state intervention to promote these goals, but viewed with suspicion and distaste the various other more utilitarian motives of government. In addition, there were those involved in sport and government who were concerned that an influx of federal funds would bring with it government control over the purpose and direction of sport in Canada. Thus, sport would be in danger of losing its supposedly autonomous character as an area of cultural expression and would simply become a vehicle for meeting the political goals of government. This concern had a parallel in the realm of international sport, where many members of international sport governing bodies and organizations viewed with increasing alarm the tendency to use sport to advance particular political ideologies or as a weapon in influencing or changing the political positions of other countries.

Other residual as well as more extreme views about government and sport also were held. Many Canadians, particularly in the 1960s, still held the view that sport was a form of idle play. Physical fitness was more acceptable as a goal than was the development of super sport stars. Fitness at least had utilitarian value in improving productivity in industry and, if necessary, preparing citizens for war. Competitive sport, in contrast, was seen generally as a non-utilitarian activity. Other people saw involvement in sport and mass participation and industrial fitness programs as activities that contributed to a greater acceptance of the conventional values and traditions of Canadian society. For this reason, government involvement could be justified as a further contribution to the educational possibilities that could be offered to all Canadians. It was against this background of values and attitudes that the federal government became involved formally in the promotion of sport in 1961. The federal government's motives become much more utilitarian and instrumental in the years that followed.

CHANGING POLITICAL AND ADMINISTRATIVE STRUCTURE

In the post-war era, the structure of Canadian politics and bureaucratic administration has been characterized by a strong federal executive, a growing and increasingly influential federal public service, and a relatively weak federal Parliament. The Parliament has had little influence on government policy making; policies have been developed at the senior public-service level and vetted by the federal Cabinet. Parliament focused on only a few issues and tended to deal with these in a fragmented and disjointed manner. Because sport was seen as having relatively little importance until recently, policy making in this area seldom reached the Cabinet level. The ministerial and deputy ministerial levels, then, became a focal point for whatever sport policy making transpired. But in the 1960s, sport was of such little importance to the minister of health and welfare, particularly in relation to the rest of his portfolio, that policy matters were left in the hands of the National Advisory Council on Fitness and Amateur Sport.

This "hands-off" policy was to change dramatically at the end of the 1960s when sport assumed a much greater importance and significance in Canadian society. At the same time, the size and competence of the Fitness and Amateur Sport Directorate was growing. Then John Munro was appointed to the health and welfare portfolio in 1968. He had a strong personal interest in sport and saw its potential to further his own political career. These factors all coalesced; the Advisory Council was pushed to the background and sport policy making reverted to the public servants and the minister. The elevation of the directorate to branch status in 1973 and the appointment of Iona Campagnolo as the first minister of state for fitness and amateur sport in 1976 were also significant changes that caused sport to gain a higher profile within the federal government's priorities.

Federal/provincial executivism became increasingly important during the 1960s and 1970s, resulting in an even less influential role for the federal and provincial parliaments. During this period, provincial governments, led by Quebec, Ontario, and then Alberta, became increasingly concerned about federal abrogation of provincial rights. The growth and expansion of provincial bureaucracies in these and other provinces in the late 1960s and 1970s also played a significant role in many governmental jurisdictions. Sport was no exception. The Task Force Report on Sport had criticized amateur sport organizations in 1969 for their "kitchen table" style of operation. National sport governing bodies were characterized by part-time volunteer officers and officials, national executives who were drawn typically from only one or two regions of the country, and a high degree of inefficiency and disorganization. Few of the nation's sport governing bodies had full-time paid officials. But not even the most zealous sport aficionado would have anticipated the size and scope of today's sport bureaucracy. The Fitness and Amateur Sport Branch staff quadrupled in size from 30 in 1970 to 121 in 1984 (DNHW *Estimates*, 1971–2, 1984–5). In the same time period, the professional, technical, and clerical staff that supports the national sport associations housed in Ottawa grew from 65 to 532 (H. Glynn, personal communication, 4 April 1984).

Increased federal government involvement in the 1970s in promoting elite sport and the success of the Canada Games stimulated a parallel growth of sport bureaucracies in most provinces, which hitherto had concentrated most of their efforts on mass recreation and fitness programs. For example, the Ontario Sports Centre, established in 1970, had a full-time staff of 90 by 1984; in addition, there were about 130 full-time administrative and technical personnel attached directly to provincial sport associations (A. Furlani, personal communication, 9 May 1984).

This expansion was in part because of the general provincial bureaucratic growth of the 1970s, and in part a result of the desire of the provinces to develop a provincial presence in high-performance sport. A growing demand by Canadians in the 1970s for sport and recreation services also contributed to this growth. But another factor also played a role. As opportunities in the teaching profession shrank drastically in the 1970s, the sport and physical education profession was anxious to find new jobs for its recent graduates. Thus, the profession itself stimulated and promoted the growth of the government sport bureaucracy.

This formidable sport bureaucracy, along with the Coaching Association of Canada and provincial delivery systems, has provided an administrative and technical competence for Canadian amateur sport to a degree unthought of in the 1960s. This support system is the envy of many Western democratic nations and certainly is a major factor behind Canada's increased stature on the international sport scene. But the sport bureaucracy is not without its problems. Because the salaries of these bureaucrats are paid largely by government funds, the loyalties of the executive, technical, and program directors are divided between representing the views of their respective organizations and respecting the wishes and directions of the government agency that supports them. This fact has contributed substantially to acquiescence to the federal government's penchant for promoting high-performance sport and to the disappearance of an independent voice for amateur sport, an issue addressed in the next chapter.

SHIFTS IN DISTRIBUTION OF POWER

The distribution of power among the various actors in federal government policy making played an important role in establishing the direction of sport policy. Besides the countervailing forces implicit in discussions of the changing structure of political arrangements in the post-war era (i.e., the respective roles of Parliament, the Cabinet, and the public service, as well as the federal/provincial struggle) a number of other groups and individuals were also involved in federal government sport policy making. Among the most significant of these was the National Advisory Council on Fitness and Amateur Sport, established in the 1961 Act. In the early years, the Advisory Council developed policy and made recommendations directly to the minister of health and welfare. The influence of the council was partly due to the inexperience of the Fitness and Amateur Sport Directorate personnel. As the directorate staff grew in strength and experience, the Advisory Council correspondingly became less active and influential. In 1969, it was relegated to a long-range planning role and throughout the 1970s had little influence in sport policy making. Recent attempts by a more confident and mature branch to use the council more extensively as a sounding board and as an avenue for receiving views and opinions about sport from across the country have not been successful.

Government bureaucracy grew along with federal involvement in sport and fitness. The public service contained, in the 1960s, few persons with the knowledge or the interest to serve as effective advocates for sport. A number of well-meaning but politically naive professional physical educators were recruited successively to the role of director of fitness and amateur sport through the 1960s. The appointment in the late 1960s of Lou Lefaive, who was a career public servant, was a departure from this practice. When Lefaive left in the 1970s, Tom Bedecki, a sport administrator, and Roger Jackson, an exercise physiologist, held the post respectively through most of the 1970s. Upon the departure of Roger Jackson in 1978, Lefaive was reappointed on an interim basis. Then Abby Hoffman, a well-known athlete and sport activist working in sport for the province of Ontario, was selected as director in the early 1980s. But none of these sport administrators was able to move to the senior public-servant level. The role of assistant deputy minister and subsequently, deputy minister, overseeing the activities of the directorate, always remained in the hands of professional public servants who possessed at best only a passing interest in sport and physical activity. In addition, during the 1960s and early 1970s, these people moved rather rapidly to other places in the public service. This "mobility" pattern was changed when Peter Lesaux, another career public servant, took this post in 1977 and held it until 1986.

Significant also in the development of federal government sport policy were the national sport governing bodies. When the Fitness and Amateur Sport Act was passed in 1961, care was taken to allay fears that control would pass from sport organizing and governing bodies to the federal government. Through most of the 1960s, the federal government's involvement in sport was limited largely to cost-sharing arrangements with the provinces and awarding grants to national sport governing bodies. These grants had few strings attached and there was little in the way of accountability on the part of the recipients. The National Advisory Council's role in policy making in the 1960s also contributed to the good measure of independence from government that was maintained.

But the failure of these early efforts to improve Canada's performances in international amateur sport events, coupled with other broader political and social events outlined earlier in this book, caused the federal government to become more directly involved in the development of high-performance athletes. First, the role of the Advisory Council was reduced and program direction and policy advice to the minister was placed firmly in the hands of the public servants in the Fitness and Amateur Sport Directorate. Second, the federal government established a number of arm's-length agencies designed to provide more effective administrative and technical assistance to sport. The National Sport and Recreation Centre in Ottawa was the arm's-length agency that had the greatest impact on national sport associations. The associations found themselves in a position where their rent and services and most of the salaries of their full-time administrative and technical staff were being paid for by the government. In addition, the monies they received became increasingly tied to meeting specific conditions regarding elite development and performance. By the late 1970s, it was estimated that 75 percent of these monies were awarded under such specific conditions (Kidd 1981).

As more importance was placed on Canada's efforts in international sporting events and particularly on the Olympic Games, it was natural that the Canadian Olympic Association (COA) would become more powerful and influential. The role of the Sports Federation of Canada became more ambiguous with the growth of individual sport governing bodies and the importance of the COA and the Canadian Commonwealth Games Federation. Attempts were made throughout the 1970s to form a strong umbrella organization to represent all sport governing bodies more effectively; however, such efforts never came to fruition (see Macintosh 1986 for a detailed account of these efforts).

The distribution of power between the federal government and the national sport governing bodies and among the various associations is only one aspect of power relationships that affect the practice of sport in Canada. Another important series of such relationships is always at play within each of the sport governing bodies (for instance, gender and class relations). These have only indirect relevance to our study of federal government involvement in sport, but one such struggle deserves brief attention here. Reference was made in chapter 8 to efforts by Sport Canada and Fitness Canada to increase female participation rates in sport and physical activity. Although these efforts are commendable, they have made only a modest dent on gender imbalance in high-performance sport participation roles. There is still a substantial gap between male and female elite sport participation rates in Canada. The following figures reflect this imbalance: Canada's 1984 Olympic Team – 22 percent female; athletes competing at Ontario universities – one-third female and in secondary-school athletics in Ontario – 40 percent female (Sopinka 1984); and athletes competing for national Canadian university championships – 30 percent female (Vickers 1984). This participation imbalance becomes even more problematic when the composition of the executives of sport organizations in Canada is examined. A number of studies (Bratton 1971; Hollands and Gruneau 1979; Slack 1981; and Theberge 1980) have shown that females are underrepresented on the executives of national and provincial sport associations, even when taking into account the percentage of female participants in the association. This bias is reflected in the makeup of the executive and technical directors in the sport bureaucracy at the National Sport and Recreation Administration Centre in Ottawa. Some 83 percent of all these positions were held by males in the early 1980s (Fitness and Amateur Sport 1982a). (As noted in chapter 8, the female sport administration apprenticeship program sponsored by Fitness and Amateur Sport Branch has resulted in a considerable increase in the percentage of females in "entry level" positions at the National Sport and Recreation Centre.) Their past record indicates that sport association executive and administrative ranks dominated by males will not likely make any vigorous or effective efforts to redress gender imbalances in sport participation rates. This issue is complicated by the existence of other barriers to sport participation by females, particularly the restrictions that marriage and children put on many young adult women. The extent to which women have the resources to overcome these barriers has a significant effect on their sport and physical activity participation rates.

Besides assuming a larger role in determining sport policy, the federal government commenced using sport more directly as a political instrument. In 1976, Prime Minister Trudeau would not issue visas to the Olympic team from Taiwan unless they agreed not to display their flag nor play their national anthem, despite Taiwan having been granted permission to participate by the International Olympic Committee. When the federal government, following the United States example, imposed an economic and cultural boycott on the USSR because of its military intervention in Afghanistan, the Canadian Olympic Association acceded to pressure from the federal government to extend this boycott to the 1980 Summer Olympics – despite the fact that its executive committee a month earlier had voted overwhelmingly in favour of going to Moscow for the Games. The pressure to boycott the Olympics was exacerbated by threats from the Olympic Trust of Canada to withdraw its financial support of the 1980 Summer Olympics. The membership list of the trust included some of Canada's most prestigious business leaders (*Globe and Mail*, 3 April 1980). This left the COA without either government or corporate support to finance the Canadian contingent to Moscow. Overt pressure that the federal government has put on athletes and sport events organizers to support its boycott of South Africa is another example of federal government control over sport.

The creation of a minister of state for fitness and amateur sport in 1976 also contributed to greater government control of organized sport. Previously, this responsibility was part of the portfolio of health and welfare, and sport was only a small part of a large and important ministry. Iona Campagnolo, the first minister of sport, was able to use this portfolio to maintain a high profile in the news media. Her triumphant victory parade on the shoulders of Canadian athletes at the conclusion of the 1978 Commonwealth Games in Edmonton was symbolic of the federal government's predominance in high-performance sport.

WIDER GOALS OF THE FEDERAL
GOVERNMENT

A number of the wider goals of the federal government have influenced its sport policy. During the 1950s, government policy began to reflect a number of social-democratic ideals. More specifically, the federal government began to respond to a growing belief by Canadians that government had a responsibility to ensure that all citizens had an opportunity to develop to their fullest potential, regardless of differences and in the face of regional disparities. This view led the federal government to excursions into the domain of health and welfare, culture, and education with the result that the matter of sport and physical fitness gradually came under the purview of federal government policy making. Although the federal government actively cultivated the development of a national cultural policy, sport and physical activity were never formally seen as a part of this effort. As sport assumed more importance in society, it was not surprising that it became associated with "popular" culture rather than the "high" culture championed by the elite and promoted by the Canada Council. The reader is referred to Franks and Macintosh (1984) for an elaboration of this development and for a wider discussion of the post-World War II parallel evolution of sport and culture vis-à-vis the federal government.

The Quiet Revolution in Quebec and the accompanying biculturalism/bilingualism issue led to the federal government's national-unity drive in the 1960s. The flag debate and Expo '67 were highly visible events in this endeavour; but sport was also seen as an ideological vehicle for national unity, a fact that did not go unnoticed in Quebec. The new federal sport bureaucracy was soon followed by the creation and rapid growth of a Quebec sport bureaucracy. Substantial funds and efforts were expended to ensure a francophone presence on the 1976 Canadian Olympic team and to increase the francophone representation in Quebec's teams at Canada Winter and Summer Games. It is not surprising that both the federal and the Quebec governments opted to emphasize high-performance sport because it is ideally suited to the implementation of such nationalistic objectives. Elite athletes receive considerable media attention and symbolize the "success" of the sponsoring governing body in a highly engaging and dramatic way. Federal government attempts to promote mass sport and fitness programs in the 1960s had been frustrated by federal/provincial jurisdictional disputes and by the magnitude of this task relative to the resources available. Success in high-performance sport, however, could be attained by focusing federal funds more narrowly on fewer people and could be easily verified in quantitative terms. Because of its high visibility, high-performance sport also had the potential for a much more attractive political pay-off than did mass sport and fitness programs. But for sport to be an effective unity symbol, greatly improved performances by Canadian athletes in international events were necessary.

Federal government efforts in improving performance levels of Canadian athletes bore fruit in the late 1970s and early 1980s. Canada's athletes performed in a creditable fashion at the 1976 Olympics in Montreal, improving substantially in the unofficial points standings compared to the Munich Games four years earlier. The extensive television coverage of these Olympics fanned greater interest and higher expectations. These expectations were realized in the 1978 Commonwealth Games in Edmonton when Canada staged a spectacular sport triumph by finishing first ahead of the traditional leaders, England and Australia. These Games were skilfully covered by the CBC and Canadian successes were watched with satisfaction and pride by millions of Canadians. These and more recent Canadian successes in international sport events alluded to in chapter 1 served to vindicate federal government sport policy because they served to promote, at least among many segments of the Canadian population, a sense of national unity and pride.

The expansionist stance of the federal government after World War II also resulted in its playing a major role in ensuring that all Canadians had access to appropriate health care. But rising health costs in the 1960s and 1970s became of increasing concern. A general concern about physical fitness and its relationship to national preparedness and health was a legacy of the National Fitness Act, repealed in 1954. Health and welfare minister Marc Lalonde, however, took a much more utilitarian and aggressive approach in his assault on lifestyle elements of Canadians that were contributing to burgeoning national-health costs. In *A New Perspective on the Health of Canadians*, brought forth in 1974, Lalonde argued that Canadians had a choice about their health. Lifestyle became the operative word in the late 1970s; exercise was seen as one of a number of positive steps that Canadians could take to improve their health. This thrust coincided with the growing success of Participaction, an arm's-length agency established by the federal government in the early 1970s to promote physical activity for the general public.

At the same time, Recreation Canada, which was established as a division of the Fitness and Amateur Sport Branch in the early 1970s, gradually changed its focus to concentrate more on physical fitness. Recreation held much less attraction to the federal government than did physical fitness because it was far more nebulous and held little utilitarian value; in addition, by its very nature, recreation is antithetical to governmental structure and organization. Recreation Canada began to play a co-ordinating and promotional role in physical fitness, serving as a sponsor for the development of Canadian fitness tests and norms and promoting industrial and corporate fitness programs and fitness programs for disadvantaged populations. Significantly, Recreation Canada became Fitness and Recreation Canada in 1977; by 1980, the term "recreation" disappeared and the division became known as Fitness Canada.

The fitness movement was part of, and stimulated by, other changes in Canadian society. The large population "bulge" caused by the post-World War II baby boom had passed through the school system and had reached young adulthood by the 1970s. Its affluent members congregated in large metropolitan areas where they became special targets for market strategies to sell goods and services. They were very mobile, changing jobs and housing location frequently. As such, they did not have time to make ties with traditional community organizations. Thus, this new generation came to depend more upon the private sector and less on community and family for its recreation and entertainment outlets. Some writers have suggested that this group was also characterized by a fetish for "self" and an emphasis on personal appearance and physique (Lasch 1979).

These developments did not escape the attention of the private sector. Many companies and entrepreneurs capitalized on the economic potential of fitness and sport, marketing equipment and attire as well as exercise, dance, and weight-lifting programs – and books, records, and videos. This combination of events and forces has brought about an unprecedented physical fitness and body cult movement in North America in the 1980s. There are many positive outcomes associated with the greatly increased numbers of physically active adult Canadians. Thousands of Canadians are enjoying the psychological, social, and physical benefits of exercise. The fitness movement also has been linked to the declining incidence of cardiovascular disease in North America. Some of its negative outcomes are discussed in the next chapter.

MAJOR SOCIO-ECONOMIC FACTORS

The manner in which the fitness movement in the 1970s served the interests of both the federal government and the private sector illustrates how socio-economic factors have influenced federal government sport policy making and program implementation. The changes in the allocation of available leisure time and in disposable income in Canada during the 1960s (outlined in chapter 2) created a larger middle class and meant that more attention had to be given by government to the issue of worthwhile leisure activity. Differences in the amount and type of physical activity patterns between the middle and working classes, however, persisted throughout the 1970s, despite the declared intentions of all levels of government to democratize sport and physical activity opportunities. The 1970s also brought a realization that many health problems in Canada were associated with factors over which individuals could exercise control, and that physical exercise could play a role in the reduction of disease in the country. The fact that increased fitness was believed to improve productivity helped the government promote employee fitness programs in the private sector.

These factors combined with others to contribute to an increase in interest and participation in formal sport and physical activity by adult Canadians in the 1970s. This increase in interest occurred in a climate of corresponding growth in commercial activity, and of increasing use of sport as an advertising vehicle for the promotion of all types of goods and services. In the early years of sport participation expansion in the post-war era, this commercial activity was largely independent of any government policies. In more recent years, however, much commercial activity has been focused on stimulating and directing sport participation patterns in a way that interrelates more directly with government policy. Advertising and publishing businesses that are related to the physical fitness boom have also experienced rapid growth. The private sector, therefore, has developed a vested interest in furthering government activity in sport because it is perceived as stimulating interest in activities that require substantial outlays for equipment, facilities, and services.

This interrelationship between government and the private sector in the construction of sport facilities deserves special attention. The monies governments have allocated to build sport facilities quite clearly support the private sector. Some of these expenditures were documented in chapter 8. They are very substantial in comparison to program spending. For instance, the federal government spent some $100 million on sports programs in the decade 1970–9 (FAS *Annual Reports*). But over $800 million was spent to build the sport facilities for the Montreal Olympics (Quebec 1980), and $36 million at the 1978 Commonwealth Games in Edmonton (Commonwealth Games Foundation 1978). Many such sport facilities, constructed with public tax monies, have been of most direct benefit to professional sport organizations. The most conspicuous of these are the Olympic Stadium in Montreal, which serves as the home site for both the Montreal Expos and the Montreal Alouettes; the Commonwealth Stadium in Edmonton, which houses the Edmonton Eskimo football team; the Saddledome in Calgary, which provides home ice for the Calgary Flames; and BC Place in Vancouver, the site for British Columbia Lions home football games. The operational expenses of such facilities usually prohibit their use by elite amateur sport groups and more recreationally oriented community-based organizations.

The 1983 hosting policy by Sport Canada called for a closer scrutiny of the "benefits" of hosting international sport events in the future (FAS 1983). This policy recognized that federal funds spent on major facility construction might be better used in other ways to develop high-performance sport. Ironically, the federal Cabinet shortly thereafter approved expenditures of up to $50 million to support a Canadian bid for the World Football Cup (B. Kidd, personal communication, 2 March 1984). This bid was not successful, but the growing momentum for a Toronto bid for the 1996 Summer Olympics will likely mean another test of the federal Cabinet's "will" about massive capital expenditures for yet another set of "international" calibre sport facilties in Canada.

More recently, Otto Jelinek, the new Conservative government minister of state for fitness and amateur sport, announced a moratorium on operating funds for major sport events. Jelinek said that in view of the financial restraint facing the government, "federal funds are simply not available for major multi-sport events which require funding prior to 1990." The federal government, according to Jelinek, will channel its limited financial resources towards the country's own high-performance athletes (FAS *Communique*, 1985a).

The use of coin sales and lotteries to help finance the 1976 Olympic Games in Montreal drew the attention of all levels of government to the potential use of sport to produce revenue. This lottery was extended when the magnitude of the debt for the Montreal Olympics became known. But Loto Canada fell victim to the federal/provincial jurisdictional disputes that were a feature of Canadian politics in the 1970s. The short-lived Conservative government fulfilled one of its election promises by turning over responsibilities for lotteries to the provincial governments late in 1979. The provinces not only used lottery revenues to support sport, but also to provide assistance to health and culture. The new Liberal government revived the lottery concept to finance the construction of facilities for the 1988 Winter Olympics in Calgary by instituting "SportsSelect," a baseball betting pool. But this lottery did not catch on with Canadians and soon ran into financial difficulties. One of the first steps the new Conservative government took in the fall of 1984 was to discontinue SportsSelect and return lottery rights to the provinces. This was subject to a mutually acceptable agreement to return a portion of provincial lottery revenues to the federal government to help finance the Calgary Olympics. This accord was reached and Bill C-2, an Act to wind up the Canadian Sports Pool Corporation and Loto Canada Inc., was passed in the House in June 1985 (HC *Debates*, 14 June 1985).

The growth of professional sport in Canada in the 1960s and 1970s also exerted a profound influence on certain aspects of the federal government's changing approach to sport. For most of the history of professional sport in Canada, the government has pursued a conscious policy of non-intervention in league operations and league accumulation of capital. During the 1960s, however, this policy began to change. There were repeated attempts, for example, to review the National Hockey League under the terms of the Combines Investigation Act and there was a growing concern, expressed in the Davey commission hearings, about sports' ties to the concentration of ownership in the media.

More notable was the emphasis placed in the first part of the 1969 *Task Force Report on Sports for Canadians* on the relationship between professional and amateur hockey as it affected the youthful participant and Canada's participation in international hockey events. The establishment of Hockey Canada was an attempt by the federal government to intervene in the struggle between professional and amateur hockey regarding control of participants and international representation. Matters relating to other professional sport endeavours, and particularly with proposals for United States intervention in Canadian professional football and with the "Canadian content" of this league, also came to concern the federal government in the 1970s. On occasions when American interests have attempted to bring National or American Football League franchises to Canada, the federal government has threatened to protect the Canadian Football League by introducing appropriate legislation.

But hockey remains the central concern of government and the public. In 1979, the franchises in the World Hockey Association that remained financially viable merged with the National Hockey League (NHL), ending almost a decade of competition for players and spectators between the two leagues. As a result, the NHL was able to stabilize its operation, strengthening some of its weak franchises in the United States and shifting others to more attractive venues. The Atlanta Flames were moved to Calgary and Canadians found themselves with seven healthy NHL franchises. The league, however, was still dominated by an American presence with fourteen teams in United States cities. When attempts were made by Canadian interests to move the faltering St Louis Blues franchise to Saskatoon in the early 1980s, the NHL blocked this transfer. In the view of United States franchise owners, Saskatoon had far too small a population base for a successful franchise and held little or no appeal for the U.S. television audience. Canadians reacted angrily against this domination of its "national" game by foreigners. During the ensuing debate, it became apparent that the NHL was not willing to consider any further franchise expansion in Canada, preferring (as it had in 1967) to seek more lucrative markets in the growing metropolitan centres in the south and southwest of the United States. This development seems to fly in the face of the fact that hockey has been unable to gain any significant national television audience in the United States. In contrast, the Canadian television market has prospered and provided a lucrative return to Canadian clubs.

Because televised sport draws heavily on the 18–45-year-old male audience, it is particularly suited to sponsors whose goods and services are attractive to this segment of the population. It is not surprising, therefore, that breweries and automobile manufacturers are among the foremost sponsors of professional sport telecasts. In order to ensure a stable and sympathetic environment for such sponsorship, breweries have made inroads as owners of professional sport franchises in Canada. The Toronto Blue Jays are 45 percent owned by Labatt's Breweries and the Montreal Canadiens hockey franchise is controlled by Molson Breweries. Carling-O'Keefe purchased the Toronto Argonauts football team and the Quebec Nordiques hockey team and also became major sponsors of the Montreal Expos. Two of these giants of the brewery business in Canada became entangled in a hockey television battle in 1984. Molson Breweries, along with the Canadian Broadcasting Company (CBC), had held rights to professional hockey in Canada. But Carling-O'Keefe signed a contract with the Quebec Nordiques, the only Canadian franchise not included in the Molson/ CBC contract, and the fourteen United States-based NHL hockey teams to telecast games played in the United States on the CBC's rival network, the CTV. The Molson/CBC consortium went to court, claiming it had exclusive rights through a contract called the Trans-Border agreement, which was supposed to define television rights for all NHL clubs in Canada (*Globe and Mail*, 27 September 1984). The courts ruled in favour of Carling-O'Keefe, and the CBC monopoly on all games not originating in Quebec City was broken in time for the 1985 Stanley Cup playoffs.

Football was the only major professional sport in Canada to resist the continentalization thrust of the 1970s and 1980s. Despite a number of threats to establish American-owned teams in Canada, the Canadian Football League (CFL) maintained its exclusivity. Lucrative television contracts were the major factor in the CFL's prosperity. The launching of the new United States Football League in 1983, however, brought about another episode of player tampering and salary escalation in professional football in North America.

It is not surprising that the potential to raise money for sport from the private sector should come to the attention of those responsible for improving Canada's international sport performances. The first major thrust in this direction was made by the Canadian Olympic Association when it established the Olympic Trust Foundation in the early 1970s. The purpose of this trust was to formalize the COA's efforts to raise funds from the private sector. An impressive board of directors was put together and a full-time staff was hired to co-ordinate and initiate fund-raising efforts. These efforts were moderately successful. It is expected that the Olympic Trust will raise some $12–13 million in the 1985–9 period (R. Jackson, personal interview, 14 May 1985). The funds from the Olympic Trust, besides assisting Canadian Olympic athletes, have also allowed the COA to maintain some independence from the federal government, which is its other major source of funds.

Iona Campagnolo's white paper on sport contained the first formal statement on the desirability of private-sector support for high-performance sport in Canada. This has been reiterated by a number of subsequent ministers of state for sport and fitness and appears to be a major platform of the current minister, Otto Jelinek. To a certain extent, such efforts have been successful. Most notable was the Labatt's Sport Foundation Trust, which was put together to hire top-flight coaches for Canadian athletes and to pay certain training expenses for athletes, and the Royal Bank of Canada Junior Olympic program, which has stimulated interest in the Olympics on the part of young Canadians. But corporate sponsorship has not been without its problems. The sponsorship of amateur sport by tobacco companies (see chapter 8), has been one such major problem. Although tobacco sponsorship was rejected by Otto Jelinek, the matter of alcohol and brewery sponsorship remains an issue.

Since the 1984 Summer Olympic Games, there appears to have been a trend for corporate sponsors to withdraw their support for Canadian amateur sport. Perhaps this is a cyclical trend that will reverse itself with the approach of the 1988 Winter Olympics in Calgary. Certainly the Calgary organizing committee is confident that it can follow the lead of the Los Angeles Olympics; it hopes to raise some $60–80 million from corporate sponsors and advertising. But there is a growing concern that "good" corporate sponsors, i.e., those who are willing to let their product take a low profile in sponsorship programs, are becoming more reluctant to sponsor amateur sport, presumably because the advertisement pay-off is not great enough. Corporate sponsorship also has had an uneven effect on amateur sport. Sports with high profiles such as skiing, swimming, and track and field have attracted a disproportionate amount of corporate dollars, and thus athletes in these sports have benefited the most from financial support for travel, competitions, and coaching.

A final issue remains to be discussed. The ranks of elite amateur athletes in Canada have been shown to be underrepresented by persons from blue-collar and working-class backgrounds (see Macintosh 1982 for citations of some of these studies). A study of the Sport Canada Athlete Assistance Program by Macintosh and Albinson (1985) revealed that carded athletes typically had additional financial backing from family or other sources. They also possessed the cultural and achievement paraphernalia that enabled them to attend university. This provides additional evidence that persons who come from disadvantaged family backgrounds are much less likely to become high-performance athletes than those from the middle and upper classes.

As is the case for gender inequalities, this socio-economic imbalance also exists in the composition of the executives of sport associations (Bratton 1971; Fitness and Amateur Sport 1982d; Hollands and Gruneau 1979; and Slack 1981). The extent to which sport executives (dominated by persons from professional and managerial backgrounds) are interested in redressing socio-economic inequalities in participation rates is problematic. In contrast to gender discrimination, however, the federal government has shown little interest in providing more access to competitive sport for persons from lower socio-economic backgrounds.

The major outcomes and consequences discussed in this chapter suggest rather strongly that the federal government has strayed a considerable distance from some of the original intents of Bill C-131, An Act to Encourage Fitness and Amateur Sport. This is not an unexpected nor necessarily an undesirable development. But after twenty-five years, it is time to examine some of the issues that arise from this federal government involvement in sport, and to suggest some modifications to the present system that would be of benefit to both sport participants and to all Canadians. For instance, one of the central reasons for federal government involvement in sport in 1961 was to provide sport and physical activity participation opportunities for all Canadians. This objective, however, has all but been ignored in the rush to develop a corps of elite "state" athletes.

CHAPTER TEN

Issues

The outcomes of recent involvement by the federal government in sport are formidable. The expectations of even the most optimistic sport and fitness advocates of the 1960s have been exceeded. The federal government has put together a cadre of "state" athletes capable of competing successfully at the international level in a number of sports. It has also put into place a substantial sport bureaucracy in Ottawa and its actions have contributed to the growth of similar bureaucracies at the provincial level. The creation of the Canada Games and the hosting of a number of major international sport events in the last ten years have resulted in a substantial government outlay of funds for sport facilities. Furthermore, it has become widely accepted that federal government efforts have paid dividends in promoting national unity by fostering a sense of pride and satisfaction on the part of Canadians in the exploits of their athletes at international sport events, both at home and abroad.

The government's role in changing mass physical activity and sport patterns has not been anywhere near as central as in high-performance sport; however, the benefits for many Canadians are nonetheless noteworthy. Physical activity levels of Canadians have increased substantially. Adult participation in sport increased 23 percent from 54 percent in 1976 to 77 percent in 1981 (FAS 1982c:3). Exercise and sport have become part of a desired lifestyle image by middle- and upper-class Canadians. This is evident in the manner in which the physically active lifestyle has become prominent in advertisements promoting products that have a particular appeal for young, affluent adults. Attractive and physically fit young adults, engaged in some glamorous sport activity along with the inevitable thirst-quenching ceremony, is the trademark of brewery television commercials in Canada.

These and other outcomes, however, raise issues about the federal government's involvement in sport. For instance, has sport actually contributed to a better sense of national unity and identity? To what degree has sport been overly politicized in Canada, and what impact has this had on the practice of sport across the country? To what extent has the recent major sport facility construction binge been beneficial to all Canadians? What has been the impact on the practice of sport in Canada of the large sport bureacracy created by government? What are the implications of all these developments on the values and outcomes of sport? And finally, what is the proper role of government in setting policy for sport in Canada? These are the issues which are examined in this chapter.

NATIONAL UNITY AND IDENTITY

The use of sport to promote a sense of national unity has been viewed by some with scepticism. Critics of Canadian government sport policy argue that concern and pride about the fortunes of Canada's athletes serve little more than a sop to the public, masking more pressing issues such as unemployment and underlying economic and social inequalities in the country. But in Canada, when differing regional loyalties and affiliations threaten to pull the country apart, institutions and concepts that have appeal across these disparate factions are critical to the nation's continued existence. Certainly, community and regional loyalties form an essential basis for a wider sense of national cohesion. Endeavours such as sport, which have the potential to transcend language, cultural, and geographic differences, can serve to tie regional loyalties in a common sense of nationhood. Sport has a unique quality of fostering local and regional rivalries, but subsequently unifying these rival factions around a common national sport endeavour (Dunning and Sheard 1979).

There is little doubt that recent Canadian successes in international sport events have served to unify the anglophone majority across the different regions of Canada. Whether they have been able to transcend the anglo-francophone rift in Canadian society is a more contentious point. The quip "Quebec 2, Canada 0," attributed to Quebec premier René Lévesque when Gaetan Boucher won his two gold medals at Sarajevo, perhaps best illustrates this point. The extent to which sport has been a unifying factor in bridging this most critical divisive force in Canada is a subject that deserves further study.

Many nations, most notably the Soviet Union, its Eastern-bloc allies, and the United States, have used sport as an "export" item whereby the success of a country's athletes serves notice of a superiority of its particular ideological and political bent. Sport has also been used more directly in foreign-policy initiatives to court political alliances with third-world countries. The Soviet Union, for instance, has emphasized friendship and camaraderie in its sport exchanges with such countries, playing down any competitive edge and avoiding overmatching of teams that would cause embarrassment to the third-world countries. The Soviets also have championed the introduction of emerging nations to the Olympic movement. Canada's penchant to use the performance of her international athletes to promote national unity has not led to the jingoistic sentiments that contribute to international tension and belligerence. This jingoism is characteristic of the "sport" warfare between the Soviet Union and the United States of America. Admittedly, Canada's status in world politics as a second-rank nation makes this easier to avoid.

The federal government's efforts to promote high-performance sport have also served to maintain and develop a Canadian sport identity. The attractiveness of sport on television and the use of sport to sell commodities and services has resulted in a North American professional sport image dominated by American telecasts, business, and sport enterprises. The expansion of the National Hockey League across the United States and the introduction of major-league baseball in Montreal and Toronto gave additional impetus to this trend. Improved performance by "made in Canada" athletes in international competitions provides Canadians with sport heroes who are not part of the North American "professional" sport package. It is our view that this has played a role in countering the threat to Canadian identity of the pervasive mass culture of the United States.

POLITICIZATION OF SPORT

The new and important role for sport in Canada has inevitably resulted in a greater politicization of sport. The growing penchant of politicians to use sport heroes to further their own political careers and to legitimize the government of the day is one manifestation of this trend. Shortly after Canada's Los Angeles triumphs, federal government sport minister Jacques LaPierre announced that the 1988 Winter Games "Best Ever" program would be extended to Summer Games athletes. His government would commit some $38 million in addition to its regular athlete assistance program to ensure Canada's continued success in 1988 in Seoul, South Korea. Provincial premiers were quick to make political capital of Canada's sport successes. At receptions held for Los Angeles Olympic medal winners from Ontario and Quebec respectively, the premiers of these provinces both took the occasion to pledge funds for the support of high-performance athletes in their provinces. One Toronto newspaper labelled the premier of Ontario as a "medal exploiter." These announcements brought into sharper focus the growing interest of provincial governments in sharing the political pay-offs in high-performance sport; in contrast, there is little political capital in mass sport and fitness programs.

Reference was made in the previous chapter to the federal Cabinet's decision to support a Canadian bid to host the World Football Cup in 1988, despite an earlier Sport Canada policy calling for a moratorium on capital expenditures for sport facilities. The political pay-off of hosting the World Football Cup in Canada was too great for the Cabinet to resist. This event holds an immense appeal for the European, Latin, and South American ethnic communities in Canada. The support of these ethnic populations is critical to Liberal federal party election success in ridings in large metropolitan centres in Canada. This is but another example of sport as an attractive instrument in the Canadian political process.

The new status of Canadian "amateur" athletes, paid by the state to represent their country in international sport competitions, also has raised new issues. Certainly it is clear today that the traditional concept of amateurism has all but disappeared, given the lost-time payments, living allowances, training and competition expenses, and trust funds that these athletes are now allowed to receive. By the time the 1988 Olympics are staged, it is most likely that any restrictions about professional athletes competing will have completely disappeared. But the creation of the "state" athlete has led to an employee/employer relationship between the athletes and the national sport associations and government respectively. The "contracts" that Canadian athletes who receive financial support from the Athlete Assistance Program are asked to sign with their sport governing bodies have brought the question of athletes' rights to the forefront. Decisions made by sport governing bodies and national coaches regarding athlete carding status, the composition of national teams, and training and competition requirements are increasingly viewed as being arbitrary and unfair. Demands by athletes and their representatives that fairer and more equitable procedures be instituted to protect athletes' rights appear to be leading to legal contracts between "state" athletes and their respective sport associations, much along the line of those entered into by employers and employees in the labour force at large. Whether athletes can indeed be protected from arbitrary and unfair practices by coaches and sport associations and, indeed, government remains to be seen. Certainly the national sport associations and the federal government need to move quickly to develop formal grievance procedures to review appeals by athletes. The reader is referred to Kidd and Eberts (1982) as a starting point for an examination of the issue of rights of high-performance athletes in Canada.

The use of young Canadians as state athletes to further the wider goals of government and to assuage the egos of Canadians also raises questions about the ethics of such a practice. These young athletes devote a number of years and countless hours to training and competing for their country. This commitment usually results in delaying their educational and occupational careers and is carried out at considerable personal and financial sacrifice (see Macintosh and Albinson 1985). In the Soviet Union and Eastern European-bloc countries, the state undertakes a commitment to prepare these athletes for future careers, usually related to sport and physical activity, and upon retirement, to place them in a suitable position within the state bureaucracy. No such commitment has been undertaken by the Canadian government, although the Canadian Olympic Association has recently established a career-counselling service for Olympic athletes. The disillusionment many Canadian athletes feel upon retirement about being used and then discarded by the state raises serious questions concerning the ethics of our current high-performance sport program. Sport Canada and the national sport organizations need to humanize and democratize the relationships with current athletes in the Athlete Assistance Program (AAP) and to further develop plans to provide personal and career assistance and counselling to these athletes once their careers are completed. Sport Canada's extended assistance plan, which provides financial help for athletes who retire from the AAP and wish to continue with their education, is a starting point for such undertakings. The Canadian Olympic Association also has established a counselling and job-placement service for retired Olympic athletes.

Paradoxically, a major reason for the federal government's withdrawal from mass sport and recreation programs at the end of the 1960s was the provincial governments' insistence on exercising their respective prerogatives in these domains. The growing preoccupation by provincial governments with high-performance sport has placed more onus on local governments and agencies to promote mass programs. This comes at a time when financial constraint is the order of the day and when local government is under increasing pressure from taxpayers to pass on the costs of sport, recreation, and leisure activities to participants. Probably the promotion of mass sport and fitness programs is best carried out at the local level. It is at this level that participants can work with local government officials and politicians on a personal level with concrete programs as the basis for planning and decision making. But the penchant of more-senior levels of government to capitalize on high-performance sport and to build sport edifices makes this task more difficult than ever.

A "national" plan for sport and physical fitness in Canada is urgently needed. This concept was bandied about at the time of Iona Campagnolo's green and white papers on sport, but nothing came of it at the time. Certainly, the interprovincial sport and recreation ministers' council provides some degree of information sharing and co-ordination. But the specific roles and objectives of the respective levels of government – federal, provincial, and municipal – in developing and promoting both elite sport and mass sport and fitness programs need to be defined clearly to eliminate the gaps, overlap, and competition for political kudos that exist today. Of primary concern is the preoccupation of federal and provincial governments with elite sport and the need to focus on broadening participation opportunities for all Canadians. But even within the high-performance program, there are serious gaps in the "delivery system." Provincial governments and sport associations in most provinces have created programs to help athletes develop their sport potential within the respective provinces. There are, however, problems regarding co-ordination and movement of athletes from provincial to federal high performance programs that impede further improvement in Canada's international sport performances.

SPORT EDIFICES

Another outcome of the potential political pay-off from sport has been the penchant of governments in Canada to build sport edifices across the country for the hosting of major international sport events. The most conspicuous of these were detailed in the previous two chapters. For the most part, these facilities are subsequently used largely by professional sport and other entertainment enterprises and remain unused most of the rest of the time. The use of public funds to build sport facilities that have little future value as recreation and sport centres for most Canadians puts the use of such funds on behalf of the public in question.

The attractiveness to government of funding these massive spectator sport facilities lies in the appeal of such projects to both the private and public sectors. Involvement in such popular projects serves to legitimize state involvement in sport, regardless of the party in power. The construction of such facilities generates profits in the private sector and creates temporary regional employment. This use of government funds to stimulate the private sector coincided with the new wave of "Reaganomics," which argued a trickle-down theory of economics. Some critics claim that this lends credence to arguments to reduce social-welfare spending and helps legitimize the movement to privatize sectors of public social-welfare programs (see Gruneau 1985).

The profusion of these massive sport facilities has also raised expectations in every major urban centre in Canada; thus, proposals for new facilities raise support wherever they are advanced. Despite attempts by political activists to point out the anomaly of large public expenditures on a domed stadium in Toronto when social-service and welfare budgets were being reduced, this proposal has received wide support from government, industry, and the public at large. Proposed expenditures of approximately $325 million for facilities for the 1988 Winter Olympics in Calgary indicate that the propensity to build massive sport facilities has not receded, despite the recent economic downturn in Canada and, in particular, in Alberta. In addition to the Saddledome, new facilities for bobsleigh and luge, indoor speed skating, and alpine skiing will be unsuited for subsequent use by any substantial number of local sport participants. Large capital expenditures for luge and bobsleigh facilities in Calgary are particularly questionable because there are virtually no participants in these sports in Canada. The considerable capital outlay needed for equipment in these sports precludes the possibility of any significant participant expansion after the 1988 Winter Olympics. Despite these objections, the ability of Otto Jelinek to make his moratorium on federal support for new multi-sport events stick until 1990 in the face of the attractive political pay-off for such projects is problematic.

Paradoxically, it is these massive sport facilities that have allowed sport to be used so effectively as a national-unity symbol. This dilemma could be resolved by using the sport facilities built recently in Canada for future international competitions. The massive costs of constructing completely new facilities for the 1972 Munich and 1976 Montreal Olympics and the financial debacle in the wake of the Montreal Games had a sobering effect on the Olympic movement. With the onset of the economic downturn in the Western industrialized world in the late 1970s, a new approach to Olympic facilities emerged. Both Moscow and Los Angeles used many recycled facilities to host the 1980 and 1984 Olympics respectively. In fact, the Los Angeles Coliseum built for the 1932 Games was the site for the 1984 track and field events. The Los Angeles Olympics were staged without any direct tax contributions from government; the Games were able to turn a profit of some $150 million. Of course, these figures do not take into account indirect costs, which were considerable in Los Angeles. For instance, the anti-terrorist measures taken by the Federal Bureau of Investigation have been estimated by some analysts to cost the taxpayers over $80 million (R. Gruneau, personal communication, June 1986).

Bids for upcoming Olympic and other major international multi-sport events now typically include extensive use of existing facilities. Brisbane proposes to use many of the facilities built for the 1982 Commonwealth Games in its bid for the 1992 Olympics. The 1986 Commonwealth Games were hosted in Edinburgh, which was the site of the 1970 Games. Meadowbank Stadium, the major event site in 1970, was the centre for many 1986 events. The Royal Commonwealth Pool, which was constructed for the 1970 Games, was also used in 1986, despite protests from Canadian competitors about the inadequacy of this facility for modern-day swimming and diving competitions.

The sport construction spree of the 1970s and the facilities being built for the 1988 Winter Olympics in Calgary leave Canada with excellent facilities for future international sport-event bids. The federal government should insist that future bids capitalize on existing facilities. But a major motive for making such bids lies in the attractiveness of getting federal and provincial tax monies for the construction of new sport facilities. This probably was a major reason for Hamilton's bid for the 1991 Pan American Games. The disappointment and anger expressed by Hamilton officials and politicians over the federal government's refusal to support the bid reflects the expectations of those cities that did not benefit from the government sport facilities construction spree of the 1970s.

One new positive aspect of the Calgary Olympics is that the Canadian Olympic Association, spearheaded by its president, Roger Jackson, has insisted that the federal and provincial governments set up trusts that will provide funds to operate new facilities once the Olympics are over. The federal government will put $30 million of its $200 million commitment to the Calgary Olympics into a trust fund. The interest from this trust will be used to defray the operating deficits of Canadian Olympic Park and the new speed-skating oval at the University of Calgary. The Calgary Olympic Organizing Committee (OCO) will also turn over $30 million from its operating budget at the conclusion of the Games to the Calgary Olympic Development Association. This group, which has been established to operate the Calgary Olympic facilities after the Games, will use these monies to operate the other Olympic sites and to support high-performance sport at all of the new facilities in Calgary (R. Jackson, personal communication, 9 May 1986). The extent to which these very costly and specialized facilities will be used, other than by the Calgary Flames in the case of the Saddledome, and by high-performance athletes in the case of the other winter-sport facilities, however, still remains a question.

SPORT BUREAUCRACY

The massive sport bureaucracy that has grown up in Canada in the last decade and a half, and which is the envy of most other governments in the Western industrialized nations who strive for international sport supremacy, also poses problems for promoting more sport opportunities for all Canadians. Many of these bureaucrats initially tended to be former volunteer sport association executive members and/or former athletes. The propensity of these bureaucrats has been to sell sport in the same manner as goods are sold in the private sector. Intrinsic outcomes and reward of sport are ignored in the rush to promote objectifiable outcomes and external rewards. Perhaps the most odious example of these practices was the document prepared by the Council of Executive Directors at the National Sport and Recreation Centre in Ottawa (1983). This document defended the practice of associating high-performance sport programs with the sale of tobacco and alcohol. It was prepared in the face of growing concern by the National Department of Health and Welfare about such promotions and the subsequent ban on tobacco sponsorship of amateur sport.

Not surprisingly, brewing and distilling companies are now being promoted in Ottawa as major sponsors of Canadian sport, despite a document produced by Health and Welfare Canada (1985) that decries the link made on television and in other media advertisement between young, healthy athletes and the consumption of alcohol.

More recently, sport bureaucrats have been recruited more often from the ranks of university graduates in business and/or sport studies. The need for more specified managerial and technical skills in the pursuit of better sport performances has also created new career opportunities in the sport and physical education profession. The "scientific" education these people have received coincides with government and national sport association efforts to promote performance and record in sport. Thus, it is not surprising that the new sport bureaucracy has not been, for the most part, in the forefront of any movement to champion a sport-for-all philosophy.

Executives and officials of national sport associations have also played their part in the preoccupation with high-performance sport. Outstanding performances by athletes have the same impact in a single sport as they do on a global scale. They promote a sense of pride within the association and elevate the esteem and status of the voluntary executive members and paid coaches and bureaucrats. The elite nature of national executives also mitigates against concern for mass sport programs. A democratization of national sport associations will likely only occur after such movements take place at the provincial and local levels. Such a movement probably will come from the grass roots of sport associations, where there is some evidence of concern over the practices and objectives of today's dominant form of sport.

VALUES AND OUTCOMES OF SPORT

The new dominant form of sport in Canada raises a number of other important issues. On the one hand, government has used sport as a national-unity symbol; on the other, the private sector has used it as a vehicle to sell goods and services. "State" sport has developed a high profile in Canada and as such, has become highly rationalized. Its focus has been on objective measures of performance and record; increasingly efficient athletes are essential if sport is to fulfil its role as a unity symbol and to legitimatize the government of the day. At the same time, professional sport has contributed greatly to the reshaping of sport. In an effort to increase the appeal of sport for television audiences, promoters strive to create a sport myth that focuses on virtuosity and superhuman performances by star athletes and teams. This mystique provides the stuff with which viewers can live out their individual sport fantasies. The "show biz" atmosphere of this new dominant form of sport has trivialized the traditional values of sport that were held in Canada until recently. Comparisons with other performers outweigh intrinsic values of self-expression, self-actualization, feelings of well-being, and the joy and spontaneity of contest.

The federal and provincial governments' penchant for promoting high-performance sport has coalesced with the private sector's use of sport as a commodity to sell goods and services, contributing to a growing view that other forms of sport have less value. Some Canadians do not share such competitive and goal-oriented outcomes and thus are uncomfortable in this new rationalized sport and physical activity environment. The commercialization and rationalization of the fitness movement, particularly as it pertains to women's aerobic and dance programs, has exacerbated this dilemma. The preoccupation of such programs with the ideal female body image and accompanying attire is turning away women whose body proportions and dress do not match these standards. In addition, the exploitation of the female body in televised fitness programs and advertisements is distasteful to some Canadians.

If we are to ensure that sport holds attractions for all potential participants, we need to search for ways to promote and maintain alternative values and outcomes that differ from the present dominant, rationalized view. A more clearly defined role for the various levels of government in the promotion of mass sport and fitness programs is a necessary step in this direction. There is a growing awareness by parents of young athletes and by adult sport and fitness participants of the shortcomings of today's dominant form of sport. More responsibility and accompanying financial resources for local authorities from provincial and federal governments for the development of mass fitness and sport programs offer the best hope for maintaining a better balance between traditional and contemporary values of sport. National publicity and promotion campaigns carried out by Participaction Canada need to focus less on the glamour and objective health outcomes of fitness and more on intrinsic outcomes, as well as to promote more often physical activity for disadvantaged sectors of the Canadian population.

SPORT AUTONOMY AND POLICY-MAKING

A final issue arising from recent federal government involvement in sport is the extent to which government has come to dominate policy making. When the Fitness and Amateur Sport Act came into existence in 1961, the federal government took considerable pains not to intrude on the autonomy of national sport organizations. Policy making pertaining to government involvement in sport and physical fitness was left primarily to the National Advisory Council during the 1960s. This group was reasonably representative of the diverse interests of advocates of elite sport, physical fitness devotees, and those who championed mass sport and physical activity programs. The sport and fitness community in these earlier years, however, clamoured for more government financial support and for more emphasis on elite sport, ignoring the consequences of the loss of financial independence. So when the time was ripe for more direct government involvement in elite sport in 1970, there was little concern in the sporting community about the prospect of the loss of independent decision making. The federal government relegated the National Advisory Council to its prescribed role of an advisory body and took a firm grip on the direction of sport at the national and international level. As the size of federal government grants to national sport associations grew dramatically during the 1970s, so did the independence of these bodies decrease. By the early 1980s, federal ministers for sport and fitness were making sport policy pronouncements that were to be ignored by national sport governing bodies only at the risk of losing financial support from the federal government. Some of the most sensational of these pronouncements were outlined in chapter 8. We raised these matters not to question the validity of the position taken by respective ministers, but rather to illustrate that by the early 1980s, the federal government was so confident in its primary role in the development of high-performance athletes that it could blatantly threaten the bodies who ostensibly were responsible for the programs. That there were no public protests or outcries over this federal government coercion indicated that the matter of autonomy of sport was a dead issue.

At present, then, the federal government, through its control of funds to national sport associations, its indirect control of the two key national arm's-length sport agencies (the Coaching Association of Canada and the National Sport and Recreation Centre), and its grip on the sport bureaucrats who staff these arm's-length agencies and the national sport associations in Ottawa, dominates sport policy making in Canada. The government focuses these policies towards the further development of its corps of state athletes at the expense of expanding sport opportunities for all Canadians, and of redressing existing inequalities in sport participation attributable to gender, socio-economic status, and physical and other handicaps. That this has happened with so little opposition is another indication of the connivance of the national sport associations in these goals.

A number of different solutions have been advanced to alter the present imbalance in sport policy making in Canada. There are those who advocate that sport become financially independent of government and depend instead on the private sector for support. This appears to be the direction that the new Conservative government sport minister, Otto Jelinek, is taking. In fact, a 1985 statement from Jelinek called for national sport organizations to obtain 50 percent of their budget requirements from the private sector by 1988 (Ministry of State, Fitness and Amateur Sport 1985:7). To help sport organizations meet this goal, Jelinek established a Sport Marketing Council with the indefatigable Lou Lefaive as its president. Its purposes, according to Lefaive (personal interview, May 1986), were twofold: first, to assist sport associations to better market their "products" (i.e., sport); and second, to educate and sensitize the private sector to the advantages of amateur sport as a marketing vehicle.

Proposals to privatize amateur sport ignore the fact that one master of sport simply would be replacing another. Instead of serving the interests of government, sport would be dominated by efforts to sell goods and services. Should this occur, the commercialization of sport, which already has dominated professional and much of amateur sport, would be complete. This would further diminish other outcomes of sport that we argued earlier were essential if participation in sport is to continue to appeal to a broad spectrum of Canadians.

This "privatization" of sport also runs counter to the original intent of Bill C-131, which was to provide sport and fitness opportunities for all Canadians, regardless of regional or economic differences. Depending on the private sector for support will, as was pointed out in chapter 9, cause substantial inequalities in the ability of different sports to achieve sufficient funding for their endeavours. It will also lead to more dependence by aspiring athletes on the ability of their families and others to support their training and competitive needs. This fact will only accentuate the current socio-economic inequalities that exist in opportunities to participate in high-performance sport. It is a direction that is in tune with the efforts of Margaret Thatcher's government in Great Britain to "privatize" recreation in that county by encouraging the private sector to provide sport and recreational facilities and programs. It runs counter to the social-welfare values that have become part of the fabric of Canadian life since World War II. Privatization should be resisted by all those who see sport and recreation opportunities as a right, and not a privilege, of Canadians.

A second line of argument suggests that all could be put right if the national sport governing bodies regained their independence from government, receiving federal funds, presumably without any strings attached, and were left free to decide how best to allocate these funds to develop their respective sports. The shortcoming of this line of argument lies in the composition of the executives and, indeed, the membership, of most national sport governing bodies. They have traditionally represented vested class, gender, and regional interests that are at odds with providing sport programs for all Canadians. The sport community has also shown itself to be excessively diversive and ineffective at arriving at any consensus on a unified sport policy for Canada.

We believe a third approach offers the best hope for some reasonable balance of power in determining the direction of sport policy in Canada. The first step towards this goal is to mediate the government's role by the establishment of a strong, independent, widely representative national sport council. This concept was a naive expectation of the sport community when the Fitness and Amateur Sport Act came into being in 1961. At that time, some politicians favoured a structure for sport similar to that established for culture earlier in the 1950s. The Canada Council, an arm's-length body with its own executive arm and power to distribute monies to the arts community as it saw fit, however, had already raised the ire of the government of the day. As a compromise, the National Advisory Council was created. An independent Sport Canada was proposed by the Task Force in 1969. A quasi-independent sport council was advocated in the 1979 white paper on sport.

A second major step towards a more equitable sharing in national sport policy making would be to incorporate Sport Canada as the administrative arm of a new sport council. This was a recommendation in the 1969 Task Force Report on Sport. Such a structure would be funded in the same manner as the Canada Council, by parliamentary appropriations (see Franks and Macintosh 1984 for details of government funding of culture in Canada). It is significant that Australia established a quasi-independent Sport Commission in 1984. This body has its own executive and professional arm and holds the power to distribute government funds as it sees fit to national sport and fitness associations and umbrella federations. It also has been given authority to raise monies from the private sector to disperse in the development and promotion of sport (Australia 1984).

A model proposed by Tom Bedecki (1978) would add two additional elements to this structure. One of these elements would be a national sport congress, which would assemble every three or four years. This would be a large gathering, with representatives from all national single-sport and umbrella sport organizations and associations. This congress would have a number of functions. First, it would nominate half the membership of the national sport council. The other half, and the chairman, would be appointed on recommendation of the minister of state for fitness and amateur sport. Second, the congress would have input into national sport policy directions by developing and forwarding to the council its proposals in this regard. Third, the congress would monitor the activities of the national sport council, reviewing policies and programs of the immediate past few years and providing an evaluation of their effectiveness.

The second of these additional elements as proposed by Bedecki would be a parliamentary committee on sport. Sport has traditionally been a non-partisan issue in Canada; as such, a parliamentary sport committee with proportional party representation could provide for an effective public forum for sport. This committee would also review the activities of the national sport council and evaluate outcomes and recommend future directions.

Few would argue that the model we have advocated would resolve all the issues that we have raised. The structure of Canadian society and the disproportionate influence of the elite mitigates against such a radical change. But a sport council such as we have proposed would bring about wide geographic representation and a variety of views on what direction sport policy should take. This kind of representation on the original National Advisory Council in the 1960s did mean that there was some balance between the demands of advocates of high-performance sport and those who championed mass sport and fitness programs for all. The structure we have proposed would also help alleviate the present situation whereby the federal government threatens to withdraw its funding whenever national sport organizations act in a manner not in accordance with current government wishes.

Government has a legitimate and essential role to play in sport. Promoting sport and physical activity for all Canadians is one such role. Providing equality of opportunity to high-performance sport is another. Sport also has an important role to play in any government efforts to promote unity and a unique Canadian identity. Government support of sport for these purposes is justified to the same extent as these functions are widely accepted in other areas of cultural policy. But it is just for these reasons that sport needs to be protected from the political whims of the day and to escape from the narrow definition of outcomes that currently prevail. A federal sport structure such as the one we have proposed would maintain a much-needed government presence, but would temper the disproportionately strong role the federal government at present plays in determining national sport policy.

References

Anderson, D. 1974. "A Synthesis of Canadian Federal Government Policies in Amateur Sports, Fitness and Recreation Since 1961." PH D diss., University of Northern Colorado.

Australia. 13 September 1984. Joint Statement by Prime Minister P. Hawke and Hon. J.J. Brown, Minister of Sport, Recreation and Tourism. Canberra.

Baka, R. 1975. "Participaction: An Examination of Its Role in Promoting Physical Fitness in Canada." MA thesis, University of Western Ontario.

Barnouw, E. 1975. *Tube of Plenty*. New York: Oxford University Press.

Bass, H. 1971. *International Encyclopaedia of Winter Sports*. London: Pelham Books.

Bedecki, T. 1978. "Toward a National Policy on Amateur Sport." Personal response to the federal Green Paper on Amateur Sport. Ottawa.

Bird, R. 1979. *Financing Canadian Government: A Quantitative Overview*. Toronto: Canadian Tax Foundation Publications.

Bliss, J., ed. 1966. *Canadian History in Documents, 1763–1966*. Toronto: McGraw Hill.

Boileau, R.; F. Landry; and Y. Trempe. 1976. "Les Canadiens Français et les Grands Jeux Internationaux." In *Canadian Sport: Sociological Perspectives*, edited by R. Gruneau and J. Albinson. Don Mills: Addison-Wesley.

Boyd, M., and K. Mozersky. 1975. "Cities: The Issue of Urbanization." In *Issues in Canadian Society*, edited by D. Forcese and S. Richer. Scarborough: Prentice-Hall.

Bratton, R. 1971. "Demographic Characteristics of Executive Members of Two Canadian Sports Associations." *Journal of the Canadian Association of Health, Physical Education, and Recreation* 37:26–8.

Brohm, J.M. 1978. *Sport – A Prison of Measured Time*. London: Ink Links.

Broom, E., and R. Baka. 1978. *Canadian Governments and Sport*. Ottawa: CAHPER Sociology of Sport Monograph Series.

Brown, L. 1971. *Television: The Business Behind the Box.* New York: Harcourt Brace Jovanovich.

Campagnolo, I. 1977a. "Sportfuture." *Journal of the Canadian Association of Health, Physical Education, and Recreation* 44, No. 1: 3–5, 37–40.

– 1977b. *Toward a National Policy on Amateur Sport: A Working Paper.* Ottawa: Ministry of State, Fitness and Amateur Sport.

– 1979a. *Toward a National Policy on Fitness and Recreation.* Ottawa: Ministry of State, Fitness and Amateur Sport.

– 1979b. *Partners in Pursuit of Excellence: A National Policy on Amateur Sport.* Ottawa: Ministry of State, Fitness and Amateur Sport.

Campbell, C. 1982. "The Canadian Olympic Association." Student paper, University of Western Ontario.

Canada. 1961. *An Act to Encourage Fitness and Amateur Sport.* Ottawa.

– 1986. "Improved Program Delivery: Health and Sports." A study team report to the Task Force on Program Review. Ottawa.

Canada Games Council. 1979. Canada Games Handbook: An Outline of Policies and Organizational Procedures. Ottawa.

Canadian Broadcasting Corporation (CBC). 1960–1 to 1970–1. *CBC Annual Reports.*

– 1962. *Broadcasting in Canada: History and Development of the National System.* CBC Information Services.

Canadian News Facts. 1973–4, 1975–8. Toronto: Marpep Publishing.

Canadian Olympic Association (COA). 1968–72, 1972–6, 1976–80. *Quadrennial Reports.* Montreal: Olympic House.

– 1970–80. *Minutes of Meetings.* Montreal: Olympic House.

– 1978. "Toward a National Policy on Amateur Sport: Response of the Canadian Olympic Association to the Federal Green Paper on Amateur Sport." Montreal: Olympic House. January.

– 1980a. *Canada and Olympism.* Montreal: Olympic House.

– 1980b. *Consolidation of Amateur Sport.* A report of the Executive Committee of the Canadian Olympic Association. Montreal. 5 March.

Canadian Olympic Association and Coaching Association of Canada. 1977. *1976 Post-Olympic Games Symposium Proceedings.* Ottawa.

Cantelon, H., and R. Gruneau, eds. 1982. *Sport, Culture and the Modern State.* Toronto: University of Toronto Press.

Chester, D. 1971. *The Olympic Games Handbook.* New York: Charles Scribner's Sons.

Clarke, J. 1980. "Canadian Sports Policy." Student paper, Queen's University.

Cliff, H.G. 1981. "The National Sport and Recreation Centre." Student paper, University of Ottawa.

Coaching Association of Canada. January 1978. "A Response to the Federal Government's 1977 Green Paper on Amateur Sport." Ottawa.

– 1980–1. Annual Report. Ottawa.

– 1981. "Timeout." Ottawa. October.

– 1983(?)a. "... Commitment to Excellence." Ottawa.

– 1983b. "Timeout." Ottawa. October.

Commonwealth Games Foundation. 1978. *The Friendly Games: XI Commonwealth Games*. Edmonton.

Cook, R. 1971. *The Maple Leaf Forever: Essays on Nationalism and Politics in Canada*. Toronto: Macmillan of Canada.

Department of National Health and Welfare. 1971. *Proceedings of the National Conference on Olympic '76 Development*. Ottawa. Cited as DNHW.

– 1971–2 to 1984–5. *Estimates*. Ottawa: Fitness and Amateur Sport.

– 1972. *Proceedings of the National Conference on Fitness and Health*. Ottawa.

– 1973. "Notes for an Address by the Honourable Marc Lalonde." BC Conference on Health and Physical Activity. Vancouver. November.

Dickie, D. May 1984. "Doping Crackdown." *Champion*. Ottawa.

Dinning, M. 1974. "The Role of the Government of Canada and the Province of Ontario in the Implementation of the Fitness and Amateur Sport Act 1961–1974." MA thesis, University of Western Ontario.

Dunning, E., and K. Shread. 1979. *Barbarians, Gentlemen, and Players*. Canberra: Australian National University Press.

Elliott, C. 1984. "The Effectiveness of Federal and Provincial Government Publications on Fitness: A Case Study of Fitness Instructors in Kingston." MA thesis, Queen's University.

Elmore, R. 1978. "Organizational Models of Social Program Implementation." *Public Policy* 26:185–228.

Espy, R. 1979. *The Politics of the Olympic Games*. London: University of California Press.

Fawcett, M.J., ed. 1977. *The Corpus Almanac's Canadian Sports Annual*. Toronto: Corpus Publishers.

Federal-Provincial Directors of Sport and Recreation. 1970–6. *Minutes of Meetings*.

Financial Post/Participaction Supplement. 1980. "Fitness Goes to Work."

Financial Post (Special Report). May 1978. "Participaction Packs a Punch." Special Report on the Big Business of Sports and Fitness.

Fitness and Amateur Sport (FAS). 1977. *Green Paper Briefing Book*. Ottawa: Ministry of State, Fitness and Amateur Sport.

– 1981. "Fitness and Amateur Sport Policy Paper Issued." *Communique*. Ottawa. 23 June.

– 1982a. "Women in Sport Leadership: Summary of National Survey." Ottawa: Fitness and Amateur Sport Women's Program.

– 1982b. "We're Catching Up." *Communique*. Ottawa. 21 June.

– 1982c. *Canada's Fitness*. Preliminary Findings in the 1981 Survey. Ottawa.

– 1983. *Sport Canada Hosting Policy*. Ottawa.

– 1984. *Drug Use and Doping Control in Sport – A Sport Canada Policy*. Ottawa.
– 1985a. "Moratorium on Federal Support to Major Sports Events." *Communique*. Ottawa. 5 June.
– 1985b. "Jelinek Signs Lottery Agreement with Provinces." *Communique*. Ottawa. 11 June.
– 1985c. "Women in Sport and Fitness Leadership: Summary of National Survey." Ottawa: Fitness and Amateur Sport Women's Program.
Fitness and Amateur Sport (Directorate). 1961–2 to 1982–3. *Annual Reports of the Fitness and Amateur Sport Program*. Ottawa: Department of National Health and Welfare. Cited as FAS *Annual Report*.
Fitness and Amateur Sport Directorate. 1950–68. *Fitness and Amateur Sport Directorate Files*. Ottawa: Department of National Health and Welfare. For files located in the Public Archives of Canada, the citation used is FASD Files, PAC.
– 1969. *The Proceedings of the Montmorency Conference on Leisure*. Ottawa: Department of National Health and Welfare.
Forcese, D. 1980. *The Canadian Class Structure*. Toronto: McGraw-Hill Ryerson.
Franks, C.E.S., and D. Macintosh. 1984. "The Evolution of Federal Government and Policies Toward Sport and Culture in Canada: A Comparison." In *Sport and the Sociological Imagination*, edited by N. Theberge and P. Donnelly, 193–209. Fort Worth: Texas Christian University Press.
French, R.D. 1980. *How Ottawa Decides: Planning and Industrial Policy-Making, 1968–1980*. Toronto: James Lorimer and Company.
Gilbert, S. 1975. "Differentiation and Stratification: The Issue of Inequality." In *Issues in Canadian Society*, edited by D. Forcese and S. Richer. Scarborough: Prentice-Hall.
Globe and Mail. 16 January 1978. "Give It Another Try, Athletes Tell Ottawa." Toronto.
– 3 April 1980. "COA Retreats from Moscow Stance." Toronto.
– 9 February 1984. "Olivier: Amateur Sports Stonewall Bilingualism." Toronto.
– 7 March 1984. "Winners Must Accept Awards, Ski Group Says – Podborski Denounces Proposed Regulation." Toronto.
– 19 April 1984. "Show Bilingualism, Sports Groups Told." Toronto.
– 27 September 1984. "NHL Governors at TV Impasse." Toronto.
Grant, G. 1965. *Lament for a Nation: The Defeat of Canadian Nationalism*. Toronto: McClelland and Stewart.
Green, T. 1972. *The Universal Eye: The World of Television*. New York: Stein and Day.
Gruneau, R. 1976. "Class or Mass: Notes on the Democratization of Canadian Amateur Sport." In *Canadian Sport: Sociological Perspectives*, edited by R. Gruneau and J. Albinson. Don Mills: Addison-Wesley.

– 1982. "Sport and the Debate on the State." In *Sport, Culture and the Modern State*, edited by H. Cantelon and R. Gruneau. Toronto: University of Toronto Press.

– 1983. *Class, Sports and Social Development.* Amherst: University of Massachusetts Press.

– 1985. "Leisure, the State and Freedom." In *Leisure, Politics, Planning and People*, edited by A. Tomlinson. Sussex: British Leisure Studies Association.

Gruneau, R., and R. Hollands. 1979. *Demographic and Socio-Economic Characteristics of Canadian National Sports Executives.* Report submitted to the National Administrative Centre for Sport and Recreation. Ottawa.

Gruneau, R., and H. Cantelon. 1986. "Capitalism, Commercialism and the Olympics." In *The Olympics in Transition*, edited by J. Seagrove. Urbana: Human Kinetics Press. (In press.)

Hall, M.A. 1976. "Sport and Physical Activity in the Lives of Canadian Women." In *Canadian Sport: Sociological Perspectives*, edited by R. Gruneau and J. Albinson. Don Mills: Addison-Wesley.

Hallett, W. 1981. "A History of Federal Government Involvement in the Development of Sport in Canada: 1943–1979." PH D diss., University of Alberta.

Health and Welfare Canada. 1985. "A Brief to the Canadian Radio-Television and Telecommunications Commission (CRTC) on Alcohol Advertising on Television and Radio." Ottawa.

Heinila, K. 1973. "Sport and Professionalization." In *Sport in the Modern World – Chances and Problems*, edited by O. Grupe, D. Kurz, and J. Teipel, 351–7. New York: Springer-Verlag Berlin.

Helmes, R.C. 1981. "Ideology and Social Control in Canadian Sport: A Theoretical Review." In Sport in the Sociocultural Process, edited by M. Hart and S. Birrell, 207–32. 3rd ed. Dubuque: Wm.C. Brown Company.

Hoch, P. 1976. "Who Owns Sports?" In *Sport Sociology: Contemporary Themes*, edited by A. Yiannakis et al. Dubuque: Kendall Hall.

Hockin, T. 1975. *Government in Canada.* London: Weidenfeld and Nicolson.

Hoffman, A., and B. Kidd. January 1978. "A Brief in Response to the Green Paper on Sport: Toward a National Policy on Amateur Sport." Toronto.

Hollands, R., and R. Gruneau. 1979. "Social Class and Voluntary Action in the Administration of Canadian Amateur Sport." *Working Papers in the Sociological Study of Sport and Leisure* 2, No. 3. Kingston: Queen's University.

House of Commons (HC). 1936–85. *Debates.* Ottawa.

Jackson, R. 1977. "The 1976 Olympic Games: Effects on Canadian Sport, and the Future." *1976 Post Olympic Games Symposium Proceedings.* Ottawa.

Johnson, L. 1974. "The Development of Class in Canada in the Twentieth Century." In *Studies in Canadian Social History*, edited by M. Horn and R. Sabourin. Toronto: McClelland and Stewart.

Johnson, W. 1973. "TV Made It All a New Game." In *Sport and Society: An Anthology*, edited by J. Talamini and C. Page, 454–72. Toronto: Little, Brown and Company.

Jokl, E., et al. 1956. *Sports in the Cultural Pattern of the World: A Study of the 1952 Olympic Games in Helsinki*. Helsinki: Institute of Occupational Health.

Kidd, B. 1965. "A History of Government in Recreation." Manuscript. Toronto.

– 1978. *The Political Economy of Sport*. Ottawa: CAHPER Sociology of Sport Monograph Series.

– 1981. "The Canadian State and Sport: The Dilemma of Intervention." *Annual Conference Proceedings of the National Association for Physical Education in Higher Education*, 239–50. Brainerd: Human Kinetics Publishers.

– 1982. "Sport Dependency and the Canadian State." In *Sport, Culture and the Modern State*, edited by H. Cantelon and R. Gruneau. Toronto: University of Toronto Press.

Kidd, B., and J. Macfarlane. 1972. *The Death of Hockey*. Toronto: New Press.

Kidd, B., and M. Eberts. 1982. *Athletes' Rights in Canada*. Toronto: Government of Ontario.

Kisby, R. November 1982. "Notes on Participaction – The Canadian Movement for Personal Fitness." Toronto.

Lalonde, M. 1974. *A New Perspective on the Health of Canadians – A Working Document*. Ottawa: Department of National Health and Welfare.

Lasch, C. 1979. *The Culture of Narcissism*. New York: W.W. Norton and Company.

Leclair, H. 1970. *First Arctic Winter Games*. Ottawa: Fitness and Amateur Sport Directorate Information Services.

Levitt, B. October 1983. "Summer Competition Review." *Champion*. Ottawa.

Lewis, P. 1980. "Fitness and Amateur Sport Branch Policies as They Pertain to Women in Sport in Canada from 1974 to 1979." MA thesis, University of Western Ontario.

Macintosh, D. 1982. "Socio-Economic, Educational, and Status Characteristics of Ontario Interschool Athletes." *Canadian Journal of Applied Sport Sciences* 7, No. 4:272–83.

– 1984. "The Interface between School Sports and the National Coaching Certification Program in Canada." *Proceedings of the VII Commonwealth and International Conference on Sport, Physical Education, Recreation and Dance*. Brisbane: University of Queensland.

– 1986. "The Federal Government and Voluntary Sport Associations." In *Sociology of Sport in Canada*, edited by H. Cantelon and J. Harvey. Ottawa: University of Ottawa Press. (In press.)

Macintosh, D., and C.E.S. Franks. August 1982. "Evolution of Federal Government Sport Policy in Canada, 1961–1968." Presented at the World Congress of Sociology. Mexico City.

Macintosh, D., and J.B. Albinson. 1985. *An Evaluation of the Athlete Assistance Program*. A report submitted to Sport Canada. Kingston: Queen's University.

McLaughlin, P., and D. McDonald. 1978. *Jeux Canada Games: The First Decade*. Ottawa: Fitness and Amateur Sport.

McMurtry, J.A. 1976. "A Case for Killing the Olympics." In *Sport Sociology: Contemporary Themes*, edited by A. Yiannakis et al. Dubuque: Kendall Hall.

Metcalfe, A. 1976. "Organized Sport and Social Stratification in Montreal: 1840–1901." In *Canadian Sport: Sociological Perspective*, edited by R. Gruneau and J. Albinson. Don Mills: Addison-Wesley.

Miller, D.M., and K.R.E. Russell. 1971. *Sport: A Contemporary View*. Philadelphia: Lea and Febiger.

Mills, C. 1982. "Participaction: Crusade for Canadian Physical Fitness." Student paper, Queen's University.

Ministry of State, Fitness and Amateur Sport. 1977. *Highlights of the 1976 Fitness and Sport Survey*. Ottawa.

– 1985. *Sport Canada Contributions Program 1986–1987*. Ottawa.

Munro, J. 1968. "Canadian Sports Potential." *Journal of the Canadian Association of Health, Physical Education, and Recreation* 35, No.2:5–11.

– 1970. *A Proposed Sports Policy for Canadians*. Ottawa: Department of National Health and Welfare.

– 1971. *Sport Canada/Recreation Canada*. Report presented to the National Advisory Council for Fitness and Amateur Sport. Ottawa: Department of National Health and Welfare. 7 May.

National Advisory Council on Fitness and Amateur Sport (NAC). 1962–70. *Minutes of the National Advisory Council Meetings*. Ottawa: Department of National Health and Welfare.

– 1967a. *Report on Amateur Hockey in Canada*. Ottawa.

– 1967b. *Summary of Policy Statements and Decisions of the National Advisory Council*. Ottawa: Department of National Health and Welfare.

– 1972. *Master Plan for Federal Action in Physical Recreation and Sports Excellence*. Ottawa: Department of National Health and Welfare.

National Coaching Certification Program. Undated pamphlet. *Yea Coach*. Ottawa.

National Sport and Recreation Centre. 1983. "Corporate Sponsors and Amateur Sport: An Unbeatable Team." A brief by the Council of Executive Directors, National Sport and Recreation Centre. Ottawa.

Nigro, F., and L. Nigro. 1980. *Modern Public Administration*. New York: Harper and Row.

Ontario Ministry of Community and Social Services. 1974. "Investigation and Inquiry into Violence in Amateur Hockey" (McMurtry Report). Toronto: Queen's Park.

Ostry, B. 1978. *The Cultural Connection*. Toronto: McClelland and Stewart.

Paraschak, V. 1978. "Selected Factors Associated with the Enactment of the 1961 Fitness and Amateur Sport Act." MA thesis, University of Windsor.

Paraschak, V., and H. Scott. June 1980. "Games Northerners Play – The Arctic Winter Games and the Northern Games: Reflections of One North or Several?" Presented to the North American Society for Sport History. Banff.

Porter, J. 1965. *The Vertical Mosaic*. Toronto: University of Toronto Press.

Pugliese, D. 1970. "Paper Concerning Sport Coordination in Canada." Unpublished paper.

Quebec. 1980. *Report of the Commission of Inquiry into the Cost of the 21st Olympiad*. Vol. 2. Quebec City.

Regan, G. 1981. *A Challenge to the Nation: Fitness and Amateur Sport in the 80s*. Ottawa: Ministry of State, Fitness and Amateur Sport.

Regenstreif, P. 1965. *The Diefenbaker Interlude*. Don Mills: Longmans.

Resnick, P. 1977. *The Land of Cain: Class and Nationalism in English Canada 1945–1975*. Vancouver: New Star Books.

Rice, J. 1979. "Social Policy, Economic Management and Redistribution." In *Public Policy in Canada*, edited by G. Doern and P. Aucoin. Toronto: Macmillan.

Ross, P.S., and Partners. 1969. *A Report on Physical Recreation, Fitness and Amateur Sport in Canada*. Ottawa: Department of National Health and Welfare.

– 1972. "Improving Canada's Olympic Performance: Challenges and Strategies." A study prepared for the Olympic Trust of Canada. April.

Schwartz, M. 1967. *Public Opinion and Canadian Identity*. Los Angeles: University of California Press.

Semotiuk, D. 1980. "Motives for National Government Involvement in Sport." *Proceedings of the Comparative and International Education Society Conference*, 23–8. Vancouver.

Shea, A. 1980. *Broadcasting the Canadian Way*. Montreal: Harvest House.

Simeon, R. 1972. *Federal-Provincial Diplomacy: The Making of Recent Policy in Canada*. Toronto: University of Toronto Press.

Slack, T. May 1981. "Volunteers in Amateur Sport Organizations: Biographic and Demographic Characteristics and Patterns of Involvement." Paper presented at the First Regional Symposium, International Committee for the Sociology of Sport. Vancouver.

Smiley, D.V. 1967. *The Canadian Political Nationality*. Toronto: Methuen.

– 1972. *Canada in Question: Federalism in the Seventies*. Toronto: McGraw-Hill Ryerson.

Snyder, E., and E. Spreitzer. 1978. *Social Aspects of Sport*. Englewood Cliffs: Prentice-Hall.

Sopinka, J. 1984. "Can I Play." *The Report of the Task Force on Equal Opportunity in Athletics*. Vol. 2. Ontario: Ministry of Labour.

Sport Canada. 1983a. *High Performance Sport Centres – A Sport Canada Policy*. Ottawa: Fitness and Amateur Sport.

– 1983b. *High Performance Sport Centres – General Criteria*. Ottawa: Fitness and Amateur Sport.

– 1984. "Scorecard." Ottawa: Fitness and Amateur Sport. July.

– 1986. "Women in Sport: A Sport Canada Policy." (Draft copy.) Ottawa.

Sports Federation of Canada (SFC). 1982. *Sports Directory 1983*. Ottawa.

Stevenson, G. 1982. *Unfulfilled Union: Canadian Federalism and National Unity*. Revised ed. Toronto: Gage.

Stidwell, H.F. 1981. "The History of the Canadian Olympic Association." MA thesis, University of Ottawa.

Task Force Report. 1969. *Report of the Task Force on Sports for Canadians*. Ottawa: Department of National Health and Welfare.

Taylor, B.M. 1976. *Unification of Sport Report*. Ottawa: National Sport and Recreation Centre.

Theberge, N. 1980. "A Comparison of Men and Women in Leadership Roles in Ontario Amateur Sport." A report submitted to the Ontario Ministry of Culture and Recreation.

Toronto Star. 14 April 1984. "The Lucrative World of Ski Racing."

Trudeau, W. 1978. "Analysis of Public Briefs, Green Paper on Amateur Sport." Ottawa.

United Nations Educational, Scientific and Cultural Organization (UNESCO). 1953. *Television: A World Survey*. Paris: Imprimerie Strasbourgeoise.

Vail, S. 1981. "The National Advisory Council on Fitness and Amateur Sport: A Policy Analysis." Student paper, University of Ottawa.

Vickers, J. 1984. "Relative Opportunities for Women in the CIAU: 1978– 1981." A comparative study prepared by a CIAU Women's Comittee.

West, J. 1973. *Fitness, Sport and the Canadian Government*. Ottawa: Fitness and Amateur Sport Branch.

Westland, C. 1979. *Fitness and Amateur Sport in Canada*. Ottawa: Canadian Parks and Recreation Association.

Whannel, G. 1984. "The Television Spectacular." In *Five Ring Circus*, edited by A. Tomlinson and G. Whannel, 30–43. London: Pluto Press.

White, W.; R. Wagenberg; and R. Nelson. 1972. *Introduction to Canadian Politics and Government*. Toronto: Holt, Rinehart and Winston.

Wise, S. 1974. "Sport and Class Values in Old Ontario and Quebec." In *His Own Man: Essays in Honour of Arthur Reginald Marsden Lower*, edited by W. Heick and R. Graham. Montreal: McGill-Queen's University Press.

Index